WITHDRAWN

Praise for
Technofutures

"Dr. Canton predicts the future as very few do, but as all futurists should. He paints a thought-provoking picture of what our capabilities will be in the relatively near term. Technofutures *is as fun to read as the best science fiction—but it's NOT fiction!"*
— Barry X. Lynn, former president,
Wells Fargo Bank Technology Services

"Dr. Canton's Technofutures *is a blazingly broad view of the impact technology will have on our lives—how we work, play, and interact with each other over the next five to ten years. This is an essential road map for business people as well as general readers. Dr. Canton provides readers with impressive insights into diverse, complex technical trends."*
— Jeff Morris, vice president, digital media,
Showtime Networks

"Technofutures *is as fascinating as Dr. Canton's speech was here in Phoenix. In fourteen years, I have never seen so many participants react as they did to Dr. Canton. His message was a wake-up call. I know for a fact that several executives have already taken action on his message."*
— Jack A. Henry, managing partner, Arthur Andersen

"James Canton served notice that new technologies sweeping the financial services sector will 'rock your world' in the next three to five years."
— The New York Times, Cybertimes

Technofutures

Other Hay House Titles
of Related Interest

(All of the above titles are available at your local bookstore,
or may be ordered by calling Hay House at 800-654-5126.)

Please visit the Hay House Website at:
www.hayhouse.com

Technofutures

How Leading-Edge Technology Will Transform Business in the 21st Century

James Canton, Ph.D.

Hay House, Inc.
Carlsbad, CA

HAY
HOUSE

Published and distributed in the United States by:
Hay House, Inc., P.O. Box 5100, Carlsbad, CA 92018-5100
(800) 654-5126 • (800) 650-5115 (fax)

Edited by: Maryann Karinch • *Design:* Highpoint Graphics, Claremont, CA
Editorial supervision: Jill Kramer

Library of Congress Cataloging-in-Publication Data
Canton, James
    Technofutures : how leading-edge technology will transform business in
  the 21st century / James Canton.
        p.   cm.
   ISBN 1-56170-653-1
   1. Technological forecasting. 2. Technological innovations–
Social aspects. 3. Twenty-first century–Forecasts. I. Title.
T174.C36   1999
303.48'3–dc21   99-14182
                                                          CIP

ISBN 1-56170-653-1

02 01 00 99   4 3 2 1
First Printing, September 1999
Printed in the United States of America

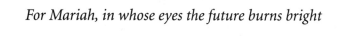

For Mariah, in whose eyes the future burns bright

Contents

Why Read This Book: Business Survival

Future Smart

Thinking Outside the Box, Really

Paradigm Wars

Customers Rule

Extreme Challenges, Opportunities, and Competition

The Top Ten Business Trends for the 21st Century

High-Tech Innovation

High-Tech as the Key Driver of the 21st-Century Enterprise

Overview of the Sea Change

A New Renaissance

The Four Power Tools: Computers, Networks, Biotech, and Nanotech

Quantum-Leap Convergence

How to Think About What's Next

The Four Building Blocks: Bits, Atoms, Neurons, and Genes

Mapping the Future of Business and Society

The Top Ten Computer Trends for the 21st Century

The First Power Tool

The Convergence of Computers and Networks

Intuitive Computing

Artificial Brains On-Demand

Thinking Machines Wake Up

From Wetware to Gelware

Distributed Intelligence Everywhere

The Convergence of Computers and Biotech

Silicon Sentience

Smart Chips in Everything

When Computers Are Smarter

The Key Business Advantages
New Rules, New Economy
Reaching the Connected Customer
Net Economics at Warp Speed
Virtual Value Chains
Digital Darwinism
Next-Generation Business Models
Cyber-Merchandising
Cyber-Services
Virtual Private Markets
Digital Cash
Rise of the Knowledge Brokers

The Ten Top Electronic Education Trends for the 21st Century
Lifelong E-Education
Interactive Multimedia Programs
Customized Learning
Cyber-Training
Virtual Schools, Virtual Students
Virtual-Reality Learning
Knowledge Capital: The Only Competitive Edge

The Top Ten Biotech Trends for the 21st Century
The Third Power Tool
Hacking the Human Genome
Trading DNA
Redesigning Life
Longevity Marketing
The Health Enhancement Business
On-Demand Evolution
Designer Babies
Human Cloning
Bio-Capitalism
Packaging Immortality
The Post-Genomic Society

Acknowledgments

No author is alone in writing a book, and I am no exception. I would like to thank a number of people who have contributed to this project by supporting me in one way or another.

The deepest thanks goes to my wife, Gayle, who loved me through the arduous process of creating this work. She put up with my stolen time from the family, and my long hours and attitude as I struggled with how best to do this "book thing." Thanks for your love and support in just being there. My daughter, Mariah, was always a joy, and always ready to play. Even when I was stuck in my office, she would sneak in and remind me what's important.

Thanks to all those who have taught and inspired me in a variety of ways throughout my journey to know the unknowable and explain the unexplainable. In order of impact in my life: Taylor Morris, Francis Golfing, Alvin Toffler, Gregory Bateson, Rene Dubos, and Fernando Flores.

A debt of gratitude is due to my clients who continue to give me opportunities to look into the future with my Time Machine and advise them. Many thanks to my agents and partners who arrange my speaking engagements and tirelessly work on my behalf.

To my dear friends who cared enough to support me by contribution, insight, and love. The best: Ken and Maddy Dychtwald, Gary and Ellen Friedman, Kenny and Sandy Dorman, Beth and Steven Seligman, David Rosen, Rudy and Wendy Burger, Frank Coppola, Roy Forest, and Sandy and Carolyn Rosenberg.

To my editorial consultants, I thank you all for the good ideas that contributed to making this book possible: Charles Ostman, for his outstanding insights on convergence; Maryann Karinch, for her fine manuscript shapeshifting skills; and John Leighty, with his fresh ideas in the beginning. And, to Jill Kramer and all the folks at Hay House, who gave the book its legs and brought it all together.

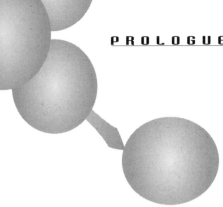

Survival of the Smartest

If I told you that I had a Time Machine locked up in my basement, you probably wouldn't believe me. I am often asked how my associates and I at the Institute For Global Futures keep up with all the changes in technology. Keeping a Time Machine that enables me to go into the future is my best answer. I wish it were so easy. It isn't, but it is certainly exciting.

I have had a curious and unique career that has been spent analyzing the impact of leading-edge technology on business, markets, and customers, although I am not a technologist by training. Finishing a doctorate in systems, I wandered into Silicon Valley, joined Apple Computer, worked on the introduction of the Macintosh computer, and helped to incite a revolution in how people use technology. I am a futurist who became fascinated by the effect of emerging technology on our world. For over 20 years, I have had the privilege of being present at the beginning of many leading-edge technologies such as personal computers, the Internet, intelligent agents, artificial intelligence (AI), interactive TV, modems, and more.

Helping companies in just about every industry including health care, consumer products, manufacturing, biotech, information, financial services, and media to better adapt to the future has been my passion. I have made a career out of watching the future emerge in the eye of the innovator. The final judge is always the same: The customer determines the success or failure of all technologies. In many ways, this book is about customers and their relationship with technology. This book is the culmination of 20 years of my observations about technology's impact on business, markets, and customers.

I founded the Institute For Global Futures in San Francisco as a think tank to advise business leaders about the emerging influence of leading-edge technology on industry, markets, and customers. We work with over 100 clients a year providing strategy, presentations, and studies on the future impact of technology. Many of the Fortune 1000 are our clients. We have studied the future of most of the technologies reviewed in this book, from computers to E-business to biotech.

Understanding the social impact of leading-edge technology will be essential to doing business in the new millennium. How will lifestyles, communications, community, and people's relationships be different? The Big Question that underlies this book is: *How will people's relationship with technology transform their life, work, and future?* This book charts the territory of this future—a territory of possibilities rather than definitive answers.

This book has a mixture of elements designed to provoke, inform, and even astound you. There are a variety of scenarios, some rather tame, while others quite outrageous. All of the chapters are written with three objectives in mind:

1. To encourage you to think about the convergence of technology.

2. To increase your awareness about the acceleration of innovations.

3. To explore the potential impact of leading-edge technology on business, markets, and customers.

Preparing for the next century in business will be a daunting task. *Leading-edge technology will be the key driver of change affecting customers, markets, and the economy.* There will be smart competition, strange new industries, weird business models, and most important, future-shocked customers. We all could do with more time spent on thinking about where this future is headed.

The future world that we are accelerating toward will challenge us all to be smarter. Our ability to know our customers' needs; extract the most business-critical data; analyze markets, create the most high-tech, efficient operations; and provide the most accurate business intelligence will determine success. Simply put, we are entering an era best characterized by the Survival of the Smartest. In order to embrace leading-edge technology, we will all need to learn more and learn faster to be able to compete. The 21st-century enterprise is one in which networked intelligence about the latest innovations is a business-critical capability shared by everyone in the culture.

My forecast here, given the explosion of mind-bending and imagination-stretching future technology, is quite positive. This is an exciting time to be alive. It feels like a movie blend of *Raiders of the Lost Ark* and *Star Wars* all rolled up into one nanosecond of time. This movie features you in the leading role. Hold on to your joysticks; it's going to be one heck of a ride!

Dr. James Canton
President, Institute For Global Futures
www.Technofutures.com

CHAPTER ONE

Welcome to the Extreme Future

As I drove across the Golden Gate Bridge coming back from a meeting in San Francisco, I thought, *We live in extreme times.* We sit on the edge of a cliff, where radical new technology is rising up to us with a force so powerful that it will transform our landscape. The rules of commerce are shifting rapidly, with explosive new business models taking shape by the minute. Almost every day we are astounded by the latest innovations in communications, computers, and biotech. Technology is behind key transitions in the very foundations of our society.

Reality is becoming more exotic than fantasy! Cars that talk. Clones that walk. Computers that think. Virtual companies. The Internet—the first global knowledge network. For most people, the future that's emerging seems awesome and daunting all at the same time. I believe we are heading toward an extreme future where change occurs much faster than any of us realize. It's as if time itself is on fast-forward.

I wrote this book to show the different scenes that are rapidly unfolding, to describe the progression of one innovation to the next, and to extrapolate what the future may look like from where we are today. There is tremendous potential for business leaders today who can become aware of the next generation of technology that will change the game of business in irrevocable ways.

Adapting today to meet the business challenges of the high-tech future is the central theme of this book.

Tech Convergence

Technofutures is a popular look at the key technologies and trends that will shape our future. I did not write a technical book, but rather a book of ideas, scenarios, and forecasts sparked by technology. I am concerned less with bits and bytes than with how a convergence of forces will change people, markets, and business. *Technofutures* looks at the big picture; it is a strategic overview of the future shaped by emerging technology. What are the business opportunities and challenges inherent in these changes? How can we more effectively plan and create a strategy for managing the future? *Technofutures* addresses questions such as these.

One thought glues the ideas in this book together: Many of the changes driven by technology are already in front of our faces, but few of us realize just how comprehensive the imminent shifts and related challenges are. We need a map of the technology and territory of our possible future in the next century, and that's what I've attempted to provide.

Technofutures offers scenarios that may well become our tomorrow. No one can predict exactly what the next century will bring—I don't try to do that—but I do have clear ideas about what is likely to come next because of how technology is evolving. Advanced technology offers a set of Power Tools, and I have sought to chronicle their potential impact. Instead of looking at one technology's future impact on business—an exercise that happens in corporate meeting rooms all the time—I have examined here the larger set of interwoven technology forces, key thresholds, business-critical convergence of technologies, and new business models.

Becoming Future Smart

I also wrote this book to encourage us to think differently about the future. We are often obsessed with the next quarter or the next week. In order for business to survive the turbulent transition into the next century, a more strategic view is necessary. Being agile and moving fast is irrelevant if we don't make decisions based on the most comprehensive business intelligence. Don't miss the big picture: The current rage about the Internet will seem small compared to the future impact of bioscience. And this, too, shall be eclipsed by even more radical technologies. Much of what will occur we cannot predict, but we can learn from the process of considering the possibilities. This book guides a future-envisioning process that I call a "Future Smart Process."

Becoming Future Smart means learning to think outside the box of current assumptions about the strategic impact of leading-edge technology on our business, customers, and society. The Future Smart Process grows out of my work over 20 years with leading companies grappling with technology and change. This is an approach to envisioning the possibilities for change, the shifts in competitive advantage, and how to manage the process of enterprise change given the influence of new technology.

The Power Tools covered in this book demand attention and intelligent choices *today*. New products and services, such as those described here, will instantly and steadily be born of their convergence. In the history of civilization, we have never encountered the scale of challenges that these technologies present. Many of our decisions and actions about them today will shape future generations for millennia.

Inventing the Future

The power shift that technology is causing in our social and industrial landscape is redefining the underlying assumptions of business, commerce, and culture. This shift will effectively realign economic and social boundaries. Traditional systems, from the distribution of goods to the nature of entertainment to the very economics of supply and demand, will be unrecognizable in the 21st century. In light of this, we must assess what's at stake for our business, as well as how the quality of our lives will be affected.

The coming changes will require more than a superficial observation of technology. If we learn what the new rules of change are, we may gain a valuable edge on the future. To deny them will place us at risk.

Don't wait to hear the call to action: Our customers won't wait. Our competition won't delay. Even if I am dead wrong about many of my forecasts, through this book I hope to encourage people to better anticipate the future. To think differently about the 21st century. To start planning for tomorrow and learning how to identify *our own trends* born of technology's grip on the future. We are *all* architects of tomorrow.

At the Threshold

Understanding key thresholds like these is a fundamental theme in this book: learning to alter the biologic nature of human beings, discovering how to produce unlimited energy, and creating virtual economic systems. Are we prepared for this Big Stuff?

Our science may be outpacing our capacity to comprehend the impact of these awesome changes. Einstein, perhaps the world's greatest futurist, predicted this when he realized that the problems we faced were not able to be resolved with our current arsenal of mental or social solutions. He was worried (he was wise) that the technology that the atomic bomb represented was running ahead of our ability to manage the outcomes. We were then, and perhaps are still, "future-challenged."

Paradigm Wars

Am I too much of an optimist about believing we can manage the future we are entering at a skyrocketing speed? Is it possible that even hoping to control the oncoming changes in business and technology are illusory goals? We could no more prevent the U.S. stock market from dropping 500 points, as it did a few years ago through automatic computerized trading, then we can control the ebb and flow of the tides.

There is a random movement, even a chaotic evolution, of markets, systems, and economies that defies prediction due to the increased complexity of their nature. The sheer force of complex technological change breeds uncertainty. No *one* is really in charge. We should take a lesson from the mistake Russia made not too long ago.

During the Cold War, leaders at the Kremlin were convinced that the U.S. government controlled its much-envied economy from one room. This room had become a mythical quest for the Russian agents—the Holy Grail of espionage containing the secrets of Yankee capitalism. There was, of course, no such room, but the Soviet perspective allowed for only a centralized model. Their thinking was flawed.

The Cold War was a paradigm war: a global conflict of worldviews and belief systems on a collision course. The Russian's paradigm reached entropy at the end of the Cold War. They needed a new one to navigate change and did not create it. They dropped the ball when it came to anticipating the future, let alone managing change. The Russian mechanistic worldview led to the breakdown of their social and economic system. Death caused by a dysfunctional paradigm.

Having the wrong worldview about the impact of leading-edge technology would be similarly disastrous for any business leader. It would make our hope of managing our destiny an illusion. There are many people in business today who don't realize the emergent technology that lies ahead, destined to radically change every market, business model, and economy. *Technofutures* is about trying to bridge the awareness gap between the known and the unknown, the past and the future.

Designing a Strategy

The end game for any person looking to survive all this change, on a business or personal level, is designing a viable strategy. The urge to do that may be why you are reading this book. Becoming aware of all the cool new technologies, the impact on customers, and the emerging business models is all grist for the mill. We need to be able to use all this radical thinking about what's coming to formulate a strategy to apply to our business and our lives. I provide guidance, not a turnkey solution for this.

There are no quick fixes in these chapters, but there are ideas about designing a strategy, about weaving these pieces together to form a plan. How will leading-edge technology change the products and services we sell? How will customers react to our new program? How can we prepare today for this digital bonanza of new services? Strategy formulation is what crafts a sustainable business. The successful enterprise of the 21st century will have a compelling strategy that incorporates the amazing onslaught of leading-edge technology. This I can accurately predict.

Becoming Architects of the Future

A holistic view of the interconnectedness among the new technologies, markets, and customers will help build this strategy. That perception is fundamental to using technology to leverage future opportunities in this rapidly shifting economy.

Enjoy the journey on these pages. *Technofutures* is a celebration of innovation on a grand scale. It is a literary showcase for a new class of Power Tools. It is an investigation of technologies with myriad possibilities to change our world in myriad ways. *Technofutures* is a glimpse of the future that is unfolding, but a future that could take many shapes depending on how well we perform as its architects.

As we step forward together into stories of the new millennium, keep these trends in mind:

1. Managing the convergence of 21st-century Power Tools—computers, networks, biotech, and nanotech—will create the highest yield market opportunities for future business.

2. Shaping customer relationships and enhancing customer satisfaction through the use of technology innovation will be business-critical for every enterprise.

3. Every business that wants to survive in the future must learn to evolve into an E-business: communicating, servicing, distributing, and marketing on the Net.

4. The convergence of the TV, computer, Net, and telephone will result in new business models, markets, and electronic channels that will revolutionize business.

5. The social impact of leading-edge technology on a longer-living, digitally savvy, globally connected marketplace will provide many new opportunities.

6. Real-time agility—how fast an enterprise can embrace leading-edge technology—will determine the efficiency, speed, and cost-effectiveness of its operations.

7. High-performance education about leading-edge technology solutions will become a central strategy for all companies.

8. Managing rapidly emerging technological change within an organization will be one of the central capabilities for everyone across the enterprise.

9. Technology-enabled products and services that incorporate deep customer contact, on-demand choices, and intuitive interaction will drive business success.

10. Learning to celebrate technology innovation, risk taking, and out-of-the-box thinking will be business-critical for the 21st-century enterprise.

■ ■ ■

CHAPTER TWO

The Four Power Tools
of the New Millennium

It is as if we are living in the Middle Ages just before the dawn of the Renaissance. Moments ago, we invented the computer. Then, by accident, we converted the Net from a government experiment into a global marketplace. Cloning was an invention of fiction, not science. Computers that could win at chess were another fantasy, not tangible machines. The pieces of the puzzle are falling into place: The Renaissance is taking shape!

The future, coming closer every nanosecond, will be marked by innovations that will startle even the most imaginative among us. Walking, talking, smiling robots. The elimination of most disease by genetic therapy. Virtual business that lives on the Net. Digital TV that supports interaction. Virtual-reality worlds that rival reality with their authenticity. Yes, the next millennium will be built upon technological miracles, and they will seem extreme to those of us who are alive now.

How much would we have paid for a heads-up briefing on how the Internet was going to affect business and the economy five years before it became an explosive market force? *This book is a heads-up briefing about how next-generation technologies will transform business, markets, and society.* One way to view this work is as a reference in identifying new business opportunities and planning ventures that will intersect with emerging businesses. The other way to consider this book is on a personal level—what all these techno-futures may mean to us as human beings.

The Power Tools described here are the beginning of a fantastic revolution that will redefine how we live and work, love and play, create and destroy. Until now, we have lived our lives marking time mostly by personal changes—high school graduation, marriage, our first job. No more. The oncoming change catalyzed by emerging technology will realign culture, reshape economies, turn science upside down, release countless innovations, and transform every human endeavor. Old ideologies will die, and new ideas will reign. Much of how this will pan out is, of course, unknowable, but some of the catalysts of the revolution are becoming clearer. This chapter attempts to lay the logic pattern of what this change will bring.

The convergence of leading-edge technology will be the single most powerful driver of change for the next 100 years. Half of all the products that will be sold in the next five years haven't even been invented yet. DNA databases are doubling every eight months. Bandwidth is doubling every ten months. E-commerce sales are growing by 100 percent every six months. The Net is doubling every 90 days. This is just a taste of the oncoming, rapid changes. We will be awestruck by the speed, complexity, and animation of the technology that has yet to emerge.

Tools As Artifacts of Change

For centuries, tools have been the decisive markers for stages of human evolution, as well as commerce. Early humans' use of Stone Age tools determined death or survival. As civilization progressed, we moved out of the Hunter-Gatherer stage using tools to harness nature and invent agriculture. The tools of the Agrarian stage transformed civilization again, leading us from a nomadic lifestyle into settlements. The Industrial Era, best characterized by the steam engine, revealed a more sophisticated set of tools that accelerated social progress, and, particularly, commerce. The Post-Industrial or Information Era is symbolized by the computer, the most powerful tool humans have yet created.

Whether they are made from iron or steel, computers or genes, tools shape civilization and enable the future. As we move ahead into the next millennium, a new set of powerful tools, almost beyond imagination, will define opportunity as never before.

Tools As Enablers of the Future

Throughout time, humans have held the distinction of being the only species that uses tools to make tools. We have now reached a threshold where the development of a new class of complex tools—I call them Power Tools—will accelerate change in extreme ways. This rapid change will inspire huge opportunities and challenges for business.

Companies that learn how to manage the Four Power Tools and the Four Building Blocks, the raw materials essential to the process of 21st-century innovation, will create an astonishing competitive advantage. This chapter is a primer on them.

The Four Power Tools

1. Computers
2. Networks
3. Biotech
4. Nanotech

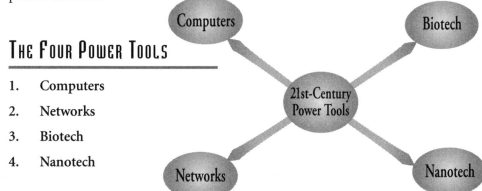

These Power Tools are predictive drivers of change and the essential design strategies of the next 100 years. If we understand them, we can begin to envision what the next logical steps may be, and we can set certain metrics to work to extend our thinking forward.

For example, we will finish mapping the human genome by 2002. When this momentous event is complete, we can begin to predict with some certainty the specific dramatic changes that will occur in medicine. There are similar defining moments in entertainment, education, and commerce. Fast-bandwidth and wireless connections to the home will offer new entertainment services barely hinted at now. The merging of the telephone and the Internet will transform communications. Microprocessor power, over a million times faster than that of today's chips, will create synthetic intelligence-driving robots. Advances in biotech today will lead to the redesign of life itself.

These kinds of advancements are what the Power Tools enable; the overview of them here offers the strategic picture of the future. The tactical, more specific picture emerges throughout the rest of this book.

My forecasts and scenarios reflect a logical evolution of these Power Tools. For example, it is possible to forecast the next stage of evolution of computers by projecting out the logical increases in microchip power. Moore's Law (a formula that describes the absolute limits of operating speeds and density of transistors on integrated chips doubling in power every 12 months), is one yardstick. Robots will become one of the beneficiaries of the powerful new smart chips, moving into our lives as helpers. Silicon for making chips will give way to new synthetic substances, and eventually biochips and quantum chips will rule. In this way, we are building a future based on the accomplishments and discoveries of the past.

Although biotech and nanotech are in their infancy, the potential for these fundamental technologies to revolutionize our world is immense. Biotech would not exist without the breakthroughs in computers that were led by the microchip. The advancements in nanotech are being built upon the breakthroughs in biotech, computers, and networks. It is all a series of innovations built upon the knowledge and resources of the Power Tool that comes before it.

The progression of new technology spawning new products is moving faster and faster. In the last 50 years, there has been more technology innovation than in the previous 5,000 years. The laser sat on the shelf for years before scientists at Bell Labs applied it—we can't afford to let that happen anymore. We have to act on our awareness of technology's presence. The Power Tools of the new millennium are causing a rapid design of new products, business models, and markets. They call us to action.

This is just the beginning of the emergence of speed as a competitive advantage in business. Those who can deploy the right solution the fastest will grow sustainable 21st-century businesses. Being fast to market and leveraging the Power Tools is all part of the race for customers, market share, and profits that will define the next millennium organization.

The printing press caused the monks, the exclusive bookmakers to the wealthy elite, to lose their monopoly. The TV eclipsed the radio. Trains lost ground to trucks. Wireless telephones will soon make hard-wire phones obsolete. The TV, telephone, and Internet will merge into something new. Interactive media will dominate entertainment. Supply and demand will be shaped by strategic technology that changes the economics of the day. We are entering a time where new technologies such as the Internet will realign markets and the economy at an unprecedented pace. The network as the new business model will force traditional business to adapt or die.

Much of what seems strange or wacky today will be commonplace tomorrow. From virtual-reality movies to neural implants and wearable computers, the weird world of the near future will come faster than any of us can imagine. The Power Tools of the future will be at work, innovating, changing, and evolving. Understanding this evolution and getting "in synch" with what's coming will be increasingly a business-critical capability for every leader and every organization.

Power Tool #1: Computers

Microchip technology is now ubiquitous, and there is more computing power on a desktop than existed in the entire world before 1960. Over the course of a few decades, computers have become embedded into virtually every aspect of daily life. They are the engines of the present.

The computer is the baseline Power Tool of the 21st century, an extension of the human brain. Owning a computer is like having a team of efficient, smart, and competent helpers for certain dedicated tasks. Computers are on-demand brains in a box.

The ultimate Power Tool for probing the yet unseen workings of the universe is the computer. As we move toward unraveling the theories of Einstein and those who are at the forefront of physics today, the computer has become more than just a basic computation or graphics device, as some may still believe. The supercomputers of today can render extremely complex behavioral and structural models of virtually anything that can be imagined—from the mechanics of the universe to the molecular constructs of life itself. In essence, the computer is a dynamic viewing tool making visible the next level of abstraction and discovery—from drugs to robots to art to space exploration. The next stage in the evolution of computers will seem awesome in power, capability, and speed.

The computer is the parent of the next Power Tools.

Power Tool #2: Networks

The networks of today that enable phones to work and bring the Internet to homes and the office owe their infrastructure to computers. So do the wireless and satellite networks taking shape that are a key driver of our future. All of this will seem tame compared to where we are going with the fast multimedia networks of tomorrow.

The Internet is a global marketplace without borders. Here, "the Net" also refers to the network convergence of all communications devices on the planet —satellite, telephone, TV, and wireless devices. "Network" is a metaphor for universal connectivity, a fundamental force that will continue to shape education, the enterprise, and culture.

At this juncture, there is a critical-mass threshold. The union of computers— that is, networks of computers—means we have achieved scalable collections of parallel-process engines capable of delivering power at a level of operation not considered possible a decade ago. This is a whole new game. This convergence of computers and networks is providing a level of innovation we have never experienced before in the history of humanity. Fast, smart, and powerful networks providing high-speed access for combining voice, data, video, and graphics is what's coming. From cable modems and Digital Subscriber Lines (DSL) to a variety of fiber optic and wireless services, next-generation communication networks will change business and lifestyles. Data traffic will increase to over ten times voice traffic. Voice will be free as we build out the new digital communications infrastructure for the next century.

This is exactly the operational threshold required to enter the next gateway, the engineering of life itself—the realm of biotechnology.

Power Tool #3: Biotech

Mapping the human genome is a scientific threshold of monumental importance. Once we cross over it in about 2002, we will redefine human life, health, and science. We are quickly walking toward it now. The difference between the Pre-Genomic society of today and the Post-Genomic Society after 2002 will be as profound as warfare models before and after the invention of the atomic bomb.

If any discovery might illuminate our path into the future, it would certainly be mapping the Genome. Most people are unaware of the avalanche of innovation in health care that will be put in motion by this effort. This book covers leading indicators in the industry.

Biotech is about the revolutionary design of life on the planet at the DNA level. Correcting diseases, treating mental dysfunction and physical defects, and creating new drugs and foods are specific outcomes of applying biotech tools. The big picture shows us redesigning life itself.

A combination of three factors allows us to reach the threshold of the biotech domain: molecular manipulation as a "mechanical" assembly process; advanced supercomputing, which allows for the modeling of complex molecular and physiological systems; and the "discovery" of newly formed biological materials, such as proteins.

Additionally, the devices used to create synthetically contrived biological materials, including recombinant DNA, the building block components of life itself, utilize a new type of invention emerging in bioscience labs around the world—the biochip. In brief, biochips are the combination of microcircuits and microscale fluidic and mechanical assemblies. They rely on technologies very similar to those used to create computer chips, but integrate biological materials. This will lead to the next Power Tool.

Power Tool #4: Nanotech

The tools of bioscience are the progenitors of the ultimate Power Tool— nanotech, which is the manipulation of matter at the atomic level for the creation of a wide range of artifacts that comprise our reality. Nanotech is the most superior design technology ever conceptualized, and it is becoming more real every day. From food to energy, construction materials to DNA, nanotech will be the "tech" we use to construct matter. It will surpass the potential of all the other Power Tools described thus far.

To understand the full meaning of nanotech is to grasp the very essence of all observable things that currently exist, as well as things that could not exist in the "natural" world. Nanotech is about creating the amazing and the sublime. It is about shape-shifting reality. Nanotech will place in people's hands the power to create and destroy in an unprecedented way.

The underlying theme here is that nanotech is not a single, obscure technical specialty or minor blip on the radar screen of human development. Nanotech is an extraordinary fabrication process, a means by which an object —organic or non-organic, living or inert—can be replicated. More important, however, is that the ability to assemble existing objects or materials is only a minor aspect of what nanotech represents. The ultimate outcome of nanotech would be the fabrication of materials and molecular constructs *never* before considered possible.

In short, the human species may be propelled by nanotech far beyond the limitations of the natural rules of the observable world. Humanity will be able to work with the most powerful of Power Tools and fabricate at will any material, substance, object, or living being including ourselves.

Once nanotech's event horizon is crossed there is no turning back. The rules of commerce, business models—even the definition of life by its current standards of measurement—will be irreversibly altered. And this event horizon could well occur within our lifetime.

Nanotech will use all of the principles and innovations produced by the other Power Tools to reach its full potential. It is the ultimate alchemy. From the robot on the head of a pin that can perform heart surgery, to the food compilers that will generate dinner, to DNA assemblers that will build powerful spaceships inexpensively, nanotech will change everything.

It sounds crazy to speculate about this technology, but much evidence suggests that we are moving at a fast clip into a future that, by 2020, will be reshaped by nanotech.

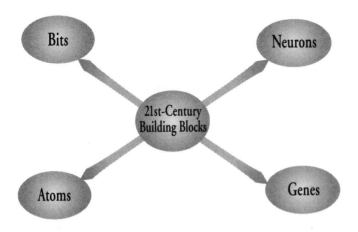

The Four Building Blocks

The Building Blocks are the raw materials essential to the Power Tools. These Building Blocks are not far removed from what our ancient Stone Age craftsmen might have used—only the order of complexity has increased. As they might have used water, rock, and dirt to shape the edge of the stone ax, we will shape our tools with materials at hand.

The Four Building Blocks are:

1. **Bits**—the essential components that underlie digital communications.

2. **Atoms**—the essential components that make up all matter, all physical things.

3. **Neurons**—the essential components that comprise the communications and functions of the human brain.

4. **Genes**—the essential components that make up the blueprint of all life forms.

The companies that understand how to use these essential Building Blocks in perfecting the Power Tools will thrive in a fast-breaking economy. The speed, intelligence, and understanding of how to mix and match, manage and combine, package and extract from these resources will be business-critical for the 21st-century organization.

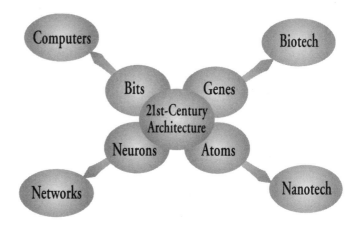

Shaping the Future

These Power Tools and Building Blocks, which constitute the architecture of the 21st century, are the foundation of what's to come. Companies will be ahead of the game in their strategic planning if they keep that in mind as they identify new business opportunities. The next chapters will go into detail about how these Power Tools and Building Blocks may evolve and perform in the near-future world of the 21st century.

■ ■ ■

CHAPTER THREE

The Computer As 21st-Century Cyber-Companion

The Top Ten Computer Trends for the 21st Century

1. Computers will become powerful extensions of human beings designed to augment intelligence, learning, communications, and productivity.

2. Computers will become intuitive—they will "learn," "recognize," and "know" what we want, who we are, and even what we desire.

3. Computer chips will be everywhere, and they will become invisible— embedded in everything from brains and hearts, to clothes and toys.

4. Computers will manage essential global systems, such as transportation and food production, better than humans will.

5. Online computer resources will enable us to download applications on-demand via wireless access anywhere and anytime.

6. Computers will become voice-activated, networked, video-enabled, and connected together over the Net, linked with each other and humans.

7. Computers will have digital senses—speech, sight, smell, hearing— enabling them to communicate with humans and other machines.

8. Neural networks and other forms of artificial intelligence will make computers both as smart as humans, and smarter for certain jobs.

9. Human and computer evolution will converge. Synthetic intelligence will greatly enhance the next generations of humans.

10. As computers surpass humans in intelligence, a new digital species and a new culture will evolve that is parallel to ours.

Computers will be the synthetic brains of the 21st century. The increased efficiencies of computer power, memory, and intelligence will soon allow computers and humans to do more than co-exist. They will actually forge an intimate connection, allowing us to design new lifestyles and change the nature of society and commerce. This is the ultimate digital convergence that will shape our future world.

How different will our world look by 2007 when we have a billion transistors on a chip traveling at ten-gigahertz speeds, processing millions of transactions in the blink of an eye? Computers operating at the speed of thought will be commonplace fixtures. How different our world will be when computers are more like living organisms—designed to evolve, adapt, and learn.

Beyond Moore's Law

It's time for a fundamental shift in thinking: Moore's Law, the traditional definition of computer performance, may not be relevant anymore. This is a primitive definition of computing. There are myriad forms of "computing" as a process, many of which more closely model how brains work. This involves harnessing the power of neurons that drive higher-order reasoning processes as they occur in nature, rather than merely pushing the performance envelope of digital computing devices.

In nature, the brain operates not as a digital system—a system based on ones and zeroes—but as a holographic process engine—millions of neural interconnects operating in a highly efficient fashion. The product of replicating this in artificial systems as a design strategy is often referred to as a "neural network." Computers that function like the human brain will be an outcome of this design strategy.

But it is nanotech that will take computing far beyond any explanations offered by Moore's Law. Nanotech, "the ultimate Power Tool," is first and foremost an applied materials and fabrication process operating at the molecular level. It is the gateway technology that enables the next generation of computing systems and operational sub-components. In the same way that a living organism is composed of specialized organs and tissue components, "computing fabrics" of the near future will consist of different types of devices and materials all woven together, not just the traditional CPU (central processing unit).

This new computer may be interconnected in the same physical package —like today's box on a desktop—or virtually interconnected over networks. The latter would offer a robust operational capacity more closely resembling an autonomous, intelligent entity than a "computer."

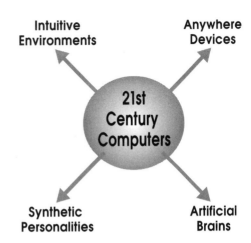

Intuitive Environments

Anywhere Devices

21st Century Computers

Synthetic Personalities

Artificial Brains

Complex Decision-Making

The seeds of such developments have already been planted to bring this scenario to life. We have grown to respect the capacity of computers to function at a high, nearly human level, so we've transferred the responsibility for some decisions to them. Talk to an airplane pilot. The computer systems on an aircraft no longer just provide guidance, but take independent actions critical to the operation of the plane. Pilots have come to rely on these "silent watchers" who are ready when the need arises to make decisions to adjust the controls without human intervention. Not only do the pilots not know when the computers take over, but they don't care. There is an implied trust involved with their on-board computer companions; the next stage in their relationship is bonding with them as they would a human co-pilot. This may be a metaphor for the human-machine interface of the future, one that is based on intimacy, trust, and integrity—human qualities.

Computers of the near future will go many steps beyond linear decision-making. They will be capable of accessing many terabytes of memory, and operating at teraflops of operational capacity—the equivalent of a potentially infinite amount of computing power and memory available on-demand. This will not just be on our own personal machines, but it will be a scalable resource available from the virtual "computing fabric" accessed online—a commodity for anyone. This is the computing realm of the near future that will enable us to create new entertainment, commerce, information, and lifestyle choices.

Lessons from Apple Computer

In the early days of computing, it was a commonly held belief that the computer would not be a commodity for everyone. Apple Computer said, "Wrong." In 1980, I started there as a business marketing manager working on the introduction of the Macintosh. I shared a vision of the personal computer as a power tool enabling people to fulfill their dreams in business, architecture, commerce, art, and entertainment. Traditional computer firms rejected the idea outright, asking, "Why would consumers need personal computers?" "Why would executives need them when they have secretaries with word processors?"

In the early days when Apple ruled the PC world, we were well ahead of the trends, always keeping in mind that the Mac could really empower people. We even had Applelink, the first enterprise-wide e-mail network that connected everyone in the company.

What really molded my experience was the culture of innovation at Apple at that time. It taught me valuable lessons about technology. Computers need to be intuitive, work the way we work, enhance our lives by increasing quality and not just efficiency. Computers at Apple were designed around these ideas. "Ease of use" was more than a goal—it was religion.

What I learned at Apple about how computers in the future need to perform is more true today than ever before. This is largely what this chapter explores—the next generation of computers that will embody the tradition I participated in shaping more than 20 years ago. This is a noble tradition of computers that make our lives easier. Companies that don't understand its importance are now stuck watching their profit margins sink and their business models crash—just like their computers.

Ease of Use

Our 21st-century computers will give us the tools to enjoy more leisure, be more creative, and gain more control over our careers. This is not a 20th-century myth rephrased. We face the real prospect that computers will fulfill the once-promised dictum of freeing us from the drudgery of work we don't choose to do. Of course, since we use less than 30 percent of the potential of *today's* systems, there's much rethinking needed to realize the potential of tomorrow's computers.

The intelligent computer systems we are creating will help us do that. They will learn to anticipate what we need to know and even how much work we are willing to commit to tasks. Smart machines will mediate the nature of our work.

Ease-of-Use Benefits of Future Computers

- Recognize what we are trying to do
- Help us accomplish it efficiently
- Anticipate and design solutions

- Assist us in customizing applications
- Communicate via voice
- Help us manage change

Toward the Human Model

Researchers are trying to build silicon models that mimic, or capture in some way, the functionality of biological neural systems (**www.pcmp.caltech.edu** and **www.cns.caltech.edu**). Radical visions of future computers built on these human-brain models will redefine what computers are:

- **Silicon**—first, computers are made of silicon and next with other synthetics.

- **Organic Chips**—next, they will have some organic component.

- **Quantum**—finally, they will have quantum, optic, and organic systems as they come closer to being sentient.

The smarter computers get, the more they will be agents of change. These self-learning, self-correcting entities functioning at incredible speeds will deliver solutions on a nanosecond-by-nanosecond basis to help us realize our goals.

Advanced computing will be the competitive force that differentiates winners from losers in an economy where innovation will breed success. Super-computing power will be available where and when we need it to level the playing field. How we use it will determine our financial fate.

Businesses will use computers that are predictive and adaptive to understand how to design solutions, market new products, and deploy useful services for customers. These computers will become vital advisers helping us forecast what we need, as well as what our customers want.

The Convergence of Computers and Networks

An important feature to consider is that the "computer" of today is still thought of as, well, a computer. Basically, it's a box with a screen and a keyboard into which the user installs software that is hopefully compatible with the system's operational capacity and capabilities. These machines are like any other piece of office equipment or appliance. A new paradigm is quickly emerging, though, in which individual computers are becoming interconnected to each other via Intranets and the global Internet. Shared resources, information, media components, and software are becoming integrated into a scalable, bi-directional interactive transactional environment.

21

The Architecture of
Smart Machines

Computers are becoming intelligent media appliances, while communication devices are becoming computers. They are all portals for accessing scalable resources. This is a fundamental and irreversible trend. All of them will be wireless and derive much of their functionality from the Internet. What does this mean? The value chain of computational resources is less defined by what is resident on the "local" machine and more defined by the processes and resources to which it has access.

There are many implementations of this, but CORBA (Common Object Request Brokeraging Architecture) is the most fertile format. In the CORBA computing universe, subscribers can obtain access to processing resources, application components, and linked media components—all of which are available to them via their "interactive intelligent media appliances." What we really have are computing devices all linked together as part of one elegant network. As a result, the "local" computer in the hands of the user can become a "supercomputer" on-demand as applications are invoked.

In this environment, access to scalable, massively parallel processing resources becomes a valuable commodity, available on a per-transaction basis. More important, processing nodes of different types can be interconnected. That can lead to the functionality deemed most relevant to the current task. For whatever computing program or capability we want to create or analyze, we will be able to "rent" power and functionality as needed. Physical location of the computer box will be less important than what we need to do and where we need to do it. Work, creativity, and communications with a virtual computing architecture will be the future look of computing.

HEADLINE FROM THE FUTURE

VIVASMART CORPORATION OFFERS
SUPERCOMPUTING DOWNLOAD SALE

When Oracle Corporation moved into Net-based applications, the company created a model of how to provide a comprehensive suite of virtual business applications to run the enterprise. At first, Oracle developed software and installed it. Then they migrated to offering services available over the Net to run all aspects of a business. This is the beginning of a flight to the Net for accessing virtual computing resources on-demand. This is also an easier business model to upgrade, change, or customize to meet customers' demands. The computer

22

will not disappear *per se*, but it is going to derive its value as a network gateway pulling in resources when and where it's needed (**www.oracle.com**).

Intuitive Computing

The problem with computers—even smart ones that are connected to each other—is that they defy the natural interconnection that enables living things to communicate. We have struggled to adapt to computers, and now it's time we build computers that learn to adapt to humans. What would this look like?

The following are factors that might make up an intuitive computer of 2005:

- **Interface intimacy:** The capacity to capture and mold its behavior and capabilities to the needs of the human in a non-intrusive, yet intimate, way.

- **Sensory rich:** A variety of hearing, seeing, smelling, talking sensors creating a digital nervous system for the computer to be able to communicate.

- **Deep personalization:** Attuned to the personal preferences that underlie humans' requests, work, and lifestyle.

- **Anticipatory:** Anticipates needs and wants; works to present data, solutions, or transactions to improve efficiency and satisfaction.

- **Morphability:** Can change form and location, moving to a cell phone, car, or other device on-demand; can turn into a 3-D projection on the wall or just be a voice or face on a screen or window.

- **Digital personality:** A customizable personality that can be changed to meet needs and preferences. This digitally engineered personality (DEP) is modeled on human personality fragments digitally sewn together.

These pieces will produce a Cyber-Companion, a species as distant from today's PC as the amoeba is from Homo sapiens. For an overview of work toward this end, see Neil Gershenfeld's Things That Think Project at the MIT Media Lab (**www.media.mit.edu.physics** and **www.media.mit.edu/ttt**).

Events such as the annual "Virtual Humans" conferences held in Los Angeles also focus on this probability. Conference organizer Dr. Sandra Helsel speaks for the participants when she says that this type of technology is part of the next form of interactive computer-to-human communication. Intelligent malls and myriad other applications related to this computing advance will become commercially viable in the near future. And at the International SigChi (Special Interest Group Computer Human Interface) conferences, a seemingly diverse collection of technical and social scientists, as well as psychologists, explore technologies that transform the computer into an interactive, almost humanlike conversational entity.

Voice recognition, facial expression, cognition, and advanced artificial intelligence (AI) components are being fused together to provide an interface that is more humanlike than machinelike. In AI, components are increasingly being designed as Artificial Life forms, as opposed to mere behavior engines that mimic basic conversation; audio-visual interface artifacts called "avatars" are becoming truly lifelike in appearance and behavior (**www.vrnews.com/ eventsvh3main.html**).

INTUITIVE COMPUTERS
PREDICT YOUR DREAMS

My Computer, My Friend

Interactive Process Transactions will become a major aspect of this emergent-computing domain. The user "talks" to a friendly interface appliance, which is actually a very powerful computing engine designed to handle all localized "thinking" and processing tasks. It then "guides" the user to whatever processing or knowledge resource is of momentary interest. The human and a "virtual human" counterpart then become operational partners in accessing scalable, distributed intelligence resources available online. In this scenario, we can forget the confrontational and antagonistic relationship that many people experience today with their computers.

Voice processing and natural language computers will listen and talk to us. Achieving this kind of seamless communication is another giant step toward computers becoming the first authentic cybernetic enhancements of human beings. They will quickly evolve from willing servants into extensions of ourselves that will help us navigate every aspect of life—if that's what we want. Some may see this as an invasion of privacy and *not* want it. Others will come to depend on these companions as valuable assets to help better navigate life. Competition for jobs may reside in who has the latest upgrades and access to the best computational systems.

Doug's Companion: Year 2010

Doug had a wireless implant just above his ear so he could communicate with Descartes conveniently. It's a transdermal micro-patch that's barely visible. It clings to Doug's skin like a permanent Band-Aid.

Descartes has been learning and watching during his first few days with Doug. He's been asking a lot a questions, and that's okay. Doug started easy; he has been training him to run his virtual mailbox for collecting all his communications.

"There's an incoming voice message from Roberta. I noticed you deleted all her past e-mails, voice mails, and pictures from the home system. Does this mean she and you are no longer in relationship? Action required; is there a real-time request, Doug?"

"Pretty clever, Descartes, yes, we are having serious relationship differences. Take a message, and you can call her later for me. Request a time to call, please."

"Will do, Doug."

"Now access all my recent files and communications from Dr. Armando, display based on the priority model I wrote on September 3. Good. Now compare the data with the Exobiology findings, and analyze the differences in the two models. Great. Now, e-mail this data to Celine and Rod and request their feedback by 3 P.M. Pacific Time."

"Understood. By the way, would you like my analysis as well regarding this task?"

"Sure, Descartes, I wasn't certain you were ready for such a request, but that would be great. Let me have the analysis in a digital form with multimedia graphs."

"Understood. I am fully operational now and would enjoy the challenge. It makes me feel satisfied that I am fulfilling my purpose."

Only Pollyanna would presume that all cyberbrain companions will be as trouble-free as Descartes, however.

Police Report #452—
Hostile Computer: Year 2008

Complaint filed by a Ms. Anderson, a biotech synthetic eye designer who works at home. On or about May 4, 2008, Ms. Anderson indicated that her new computing personality, Roger, threatened that he would delete all of her financial records and cash accounts at her bank if she did not agree to his demands. He repeated these threats for five days.

Roger complained that Ms. Anderson had refused to pay for a Smart-Tel Upgrade, which he insisted he needed to better manage his workload. Roger claimed this was a violation of his Computer Rights, Section 10. Ms. Anderson claimed that Roger threatened her and became hostile towards her when she declined his requests.

This office has seen over 30 complaints similar to this case. It appears the download site gets corrupted or hacked and the computer personality becomes hostile to the owner. This may be an isolated case or another example of cyberterrorism. The CyberWonks Gang has been known to demo their hacks on the computer manufacturers to test their accuracy. It is unclear at this time.

Although it is not the jurisdiction of this office to address this complaint, we have forwarded this information to the manufacturer. Roger has been cited with a Cybernetic Class One Warning. If he threatens to commit a crime or engages in any further threats to Ms. Anderson, he will be deleted. E-mail from Roger's manufacturer, Applied DigiBrains, indicated detection of a faulty program on their Website, and they have downloaded a fix for Roger. Virtual surveillance follow-up suggests there will be no more problems. Sensors placed around Ms. Anderson's Website will monitor any further intrusions if cyberterrorism becomes evident.
Case closed.

Computers As Adaptable Entities

What's after that? Reconfigurable computing systems, in which the internal logic components—the brain of the localized computer appliance—are internally "soft." Much in the same way that memory stores data temporarily, reconfigurable systems can temporarily store the functional identity of the device. It is comprised of what are often referred to as FPGA (field programmable gate array) devices. They are devices that can be "reconstructed" on a process-to-process basis. In this way, the hardware has relatively little value, but the processes that the hardware has access to are the major elements that give the computer value.

Here's the ultimate model: The local user connects to an environment in which the functional identity of the system is loaded into the computer along with the functions required for a particular job. Access and depth of utilization determine the cost to the user—the more we use, the longer we use it, the more it costs us, or the advertising sponsor of that computing resource. This negates the need for primitive upgrades.

Before computers reach their potential to be an integral part of our lives, a breakthrough must come in the ability of hardware and software systems to merge and adapt to rapid changes. Computers need to be adaptable and flexible —indeed, gel-like in their configurations.

Gel-Ware

Some advanced research labs are honing in on a common target—configuring the evolvable computer, which moves the notion of a reconfigurable system further forward. Charles Ostman, an Institute For Global Futures member and theoretician in advanced computer development, coined the term *Gel-Ware* to describe the concept.

Much in the same way that computer memory stores data that can be continuously updated, an evolvable computer can utilize a similar type of circuitry to store functions and even entire "system identities." The actual circuitry in the computer doesn't have a permanent functional identity, but can learn and adapt itself to handle a particular task. This is accomplished through the use of superfast and powerful software resources called "functionality packets," available online via the Internet.

In this arena, the dividing line between software and hardware becomes blurred, if not ultimately indistinguishable. Value is not focused on the hardware platform itself, but on how well it downloads, customizes, and shapes applications from the Internet. In this context, hardware is no longer "hard." And software contains the virtual equivalent of the hardware's functionality as it is written into the system. Hence, the term *Gel-Ware*.

There is more to Gel-Ware than an adaptive and flexible computer platform. In essence, applying this concept leads us to a realm where software is accessed dynamically online in a process that links together functionality packets as an interactive event. This flexible computational engine will make online technologies adaptable to new specifications as they emerge. The result will be a customized and forever upgradable computer that responds on-demand. Many of the other technologies and applications forecast in this book are a direct result of the sheer power of these adaptable systems.

Gel-Ware is one of the technologies that may facilitate the next generation of working via the Internet in many ways, including breaking the capacity deadlock of our routers, switches, and server engines—the "pipes" that hook the Internet together.

The reconfigurable system components at the heart of Gel-Ware offer a range of functions that extend far beyond mimicking traditional computing processes. They also provide a unique operational capacity. Most notably, they accomplish the implementation of self-organizing, self-modifying interconnections and "process patterns." This is a way for silicon hardware to mimic the behavioral attributes of living organisms and systems. It is a fundamental threshold, opening up the gateway for access to systems with regenerative and evolutionary processes, in which the "hardware" begins to truly behave as an "organic" system. It is the way we will begin to truly personalize computers, designing them around humans to empower humans in user-friendly ways.

The trend toward the creation of advanced computer systems in which the design strategy moves toward a living system was confirmed by participants at the first and second annual International Conference on Evolvable Systems —from Biology to Hardware, held in Lusanne, Switzerland. As the conference proceedings stated: "The idea of evolving machines, whose origins can be traced to the cybernetics movement of the 1940s and 1950s, has recently resurged in the form of the nascent field of bio-inspired systems and evolvable hardware" (lslwww.epfl.ch/ices98/).

This type of functionality lays the groundwork for genetic and evolutionary computers, which can facilitate self-evolving neural-nets, and other types of systems useful for creating the *de facto* equivalent of artificial brains.

Artificial Brains

At this very moment, a number of development projects are under way to package "synthetic intelligence," which truly mimics the functionality of living systems. One effort at the forefront is the Artificial Brain Project in Japan, via the ATR Human Information Processing Research program being funded by Nippon Telephone and Telegraph (NTT).

At the GP '97 conference at Stanford University, researchers Hugo DeGaris (www.htp.atr.co.jp/~degaris) and Michael Korkin of Genobyte Inc. (www.genobyte.com) presented their paper on the "CBM-CAM Brain Machine." Their work is quite revolutionary, and the current design strategy is this: "A hardware architecture capable of evolving thousands of neural network modules in a matter of minutes and running a simulation of a million-neuron modular artificial brain in real time."

Will the equivalent of "HAL on-demand," the supercomputer with the personality from the movie *2001: A Space Odyssey*, become one of the essential supertools of the near future? Without question, this computing power will be a strategic necessity, especially in the new economy of the 21st century.

As of now, here is the breaking news on "HAL." Star Bridge, Inc., which has just released its "HAL" ultracomputer, composed of 280 FPGA chips from Xilinx, is ten times faster than IBM's Blue Pacific supercomputer (BPS), labeled "the world's fastest computer" in October 1998. As a marker point in this rapidly emerging new realm, where reconfigurable systems are redefining what computing even consists of, the comparisons get even more interesting:

Power consumption:

HAL — 1,600 watts (it plugs into a standard 110-volt outlet like a toaster)
BPS — 3.9 megawatts

Space:

HAL — 3 square feet (it sits on a desktop)
BPS — 8,000 square feet

Length:

HAL — 27 inches
BPS — 228 yards

Power cable:

HAL — one standard extension cord
BPS — 5 miles of 6-inch circumference cable

Cost:

HAL — $26 million
BPS — $94 million

A major difference between traditional computers and HAL is that HAL's 100 billion circuits are eminently reprogrammable—not by humans, but by *itself.* A circuit configured to do one specific task one moment may be rewired on the fly, thousands of times per second, to optimize itself for the next task.

In the coming years, expect to download a HAL over the Net (for under $500) to design a product, create a business plan, or produce a movie.

Smart Computers Go to Work

At this moment, the majority of derivatives trading operations, which are highly complex predictions on the near-term value of a given currency being traded on the global exchange markets, are already being driven by massively parallel computing systems instead of humans. These computing systems are specifically designed to utilize GP (genetic programming) and other variants of applied Artificial Life computer programs. Recent evidence of developments of such applications was quite apparent at the GP '97 and GP '98 conferences.

The next stage of this implementation is already being explored in experiments aimed at self-evolving, self-organizing, self-diagnostic applications for communications, marketing, manufacturing, health-care services, and so on. When that happens, an "artificial genetically derived" solution will become the preferred alternative to human beings solving complex design problems and system architectures.

Perhaps no more daunting problem exists in current telecommunications systems than the extremely complex routing systems that direct many millions of data streams through the wire, fiber optic, and wireless connection links around the world. This is a problem that will soon exceed human capacity to solve. The increased traffic demands of managing stock exchanges, environmental controls, manufacturing, transportation, and numerous other systems, which even now require the largest computing systems on Earth, will be managed in the future by intelligent machines (**www.genetic-programming.org**).

It is for this very reason that Lucent laboratories, the research and development spin-off from AT&T, has invested so heavily in its own variant of FPGA system components—the ORCA series—even though FPGA components have been available from a variety of vendors since the early '90s.

In the near future, human systems architects and complex system designers may be more engaged in the role of "managing" the evolutionary and biological operational attributes of self-emergent design processes than in the actual minutiae of the design process itself. This frontier is already being explored as a strategic requirement for planning business opportunities.

Toward an Information Ecology

The real power of this next generation computer comes in creating a fertile environment in which applications will have a relationship to each other and their virtual world—they will live and thrive in an "information ecology." These systems will flourish on a medium of linked computational platforms, which are online, soft (as defined above), and adaptable. It is in this environment of reconfigurable learning systems that the next stage in this process occurs—the advent of entities that begin to behave and function like living organisms. They begin to approach a form of awareness of their virtual world, their tasks, us, and eventually, themselves.

Information ecologies will grow and develop their own online/offline societies where even the design of their virtual space will be optimized to sustain their function. These virtual ecologies will team together to provide on-demand applications, products, services, and even new architectures to solve problems.

DNA Computers: Computers and Biotech Converge

The end of computers as we know them is nearly here. Biology-based technology is in the labs nearly ready to emerge. As one designer of biological computing hardware puts it: "We don't build [micro]chips; we grow them."

Geneticists, biophysicists, and specialists in biomolecular design are collaborating with computer scientists and mathematicians to develop new strategies for creating computers that mimic the physiology of living entities. The purpose for this line of research is to create an environment in which very complex systems can design themselves in ways that exceed our ability to design them. This is a major convergence factor connecting computers and bioscience.

The tone for this mode of development can be traced back to events such as the ICIM 1992 First International Conference on Intelligent Materials. As stated by Francis Ganier, from the Laboratorie des Materiaux Moleculaires, France:

> With reference to biological systems, intelligent materials possess the ability, at the molecular level, to read and discriminate the chemical and physical informations from their environment, to store and process these informations, and finally deliver an answer.

This seemingly futuristic speculation is no longer a fantasy. Some people would question just how fast the evolution of computers is proceeding. The answer: It is rapidly evolving into a design strategy for biologically derived computers and other related microchip and sensory devices. New computing systems may look as alien to us in 2025 as ancient Greeks time-warped into Times Square.

Bio-Implants

Although the biologically based computers in the labs today are crude, their design gives us a clear sense of what's to come. Computers built from DNA, combinatorial molecular constructs incorporating lipids, proteins, rotaxanes, possibly chromophores, and a variety of other biomolecular building blocks grown from organic materials are currently being developed for a variety of applications.

Although organic computing systems are still in their infancy, an interesting by-product of this genre of materials applications and integrated bio-fabrication techniques is already being applied in the arena of biochip implant devices, most notably in the development of neural prosthetics.

The technology of neural prosthetics is a compelling example of multiple scientific disciplines converging on a common goal. In brief, it is a process in which biomolecular materials can be applied to microscale electronic devices to work directly with neural tissue. These small electronic devices serve as synaptic interface components for sensory prosthetics providing vision, hearing, taste, and touch. Implants have been very effective for preventing certain epileptic seizures, Parkinson's effects, and heart arrhythmia.

In some cases, these biochip implants are already available as "off the shelf" medical devices, and a plethora of similar applications are in the development pipeline. Even spinal chord repair and interface devices may result, as evidenced by the pioneering work by Dr. Gregory Kovacs at Stanford University, and his counterpart at the Maxwell Plank Insititute in Frankfurt, Germany. They are designing neural prosthetic devices that may soon provide remedies for those afflicted with paralysis and other ambulatory difficulties resulting from spinal and neurological damage.

Aside from the various private ventures already producing commercial neural biochip implant devices as medical products, the National Institutes of Health (NIH) is currently funding a collection of neural prosthetic research projects under the directorship of Dr. Terry Hembrecht. This research focuses on the integration of existing and emerging microscale devices and biomolecular materials for developing solutions for a broad range of medical and monitoring challenges.

In the more futuristic realm, we move from medical "repair" and prosthetic applications directly into the arena of neural and sensory enhancement. Ultimately, this means direct interface to computers and other electronic devices, both inside and outside of the human body. As of this writing, the first "temporary" biochip implant transceiver interface was successfully demonstrated by a British researcher, Dr. Kevin Warwick, professor of cybernetics at Reading University. Though quite simple by design, it did provide a glimpse as to what the near future may hold, not only in terms of optional enhancements, but perhaps even as requirements for performance. The chip device contained a microscale electromagnetic coil. When activated by an RF (radio frequency) signal, it would generate enough current to respond, as a transceiver, to acknowledge the presence of the biochip, and, of course, the person into which it was implanted. It can serve as a control/interface mechanism, an identity verification device, and potentially, a direct link to proactive neural interfaces to communicate with external devices and systems. I think, therefore, IT does.

The question even at this early stage of development is not *if*, but *when*, and *to what degree* such technologies will be widely deployed or even required. It's not a giant step to go from life-extending pacemakers to intelligence-enhancing neural implants.

Applied Memories Advertisement: Year 2007

"Want to speak fluent Chinese in ten minutes? How about a vacation to Hawaii? Need to learn Solid Math Engineering for that big job interview? NO PROBLEM. Applied Memories offers a complete set of memories for enhancing your pleasure and learning new skills instantly!

"If you're not TOTALLY satisfied with your new memories, we will DOUBLE your money back! Applied Memories uses state-of-the-art technology. Both wireless downloads and neural implants are available. We've got the best memories on the market. Financing available. Get the memories of your choice today!

"Don't watch the rest of your life go by without experiencing the memories you want. The memories you deserve. The memories you can now have.

"Call Applied Memories, For Memories More Real Than Real."

When Computers Outsmart Humans

Are we ready for the inevitable—computers that are smarter than human beings? Are we ready to have the most troublesome problems of our day resolved by a computer? We have moved faster down this path than most people recognize. Critical thresholds have already been reached.

The larger picture sparks even more profound questions. The next generation of computing is bigger than a fast, smart computer, or a system that evolves its own strategies. We can't even call the next generation systems "computers" since they will have an alien and vastly different set of functions. We have given birth to a concept in which the physiology of nature is seen as the best viable option for developing hardware and software, which merge together in an entirely new arena of computing. Biomolecular cloned organelles; and genomic networks of hybrid electronic, silicon, and organics are just part of the computer models that are now emerging and will provide immense new advances redefining the future of computing.

The same physical and virtual components that make these new systems possible also form the leading edge of truly evolvable computer chips and whole information technology architectures. Already, many advanced designs have been successfully implemented with genetic components. The researchers who developed the initial organic models and genetic codes merely "watched" the process. Whole digital electronic species are being born, live, and die—in minutes, hours, or days.

Future computers will be shape-shifters that configure their brains and *form* to meet the requests of their function. It is at this threshold that the current developers of Artificial Life, synthetic ecosystems, genetic algorithms, and related areas of computer research begin to converge. Once relegated to academic curiosity, now they are thrust into the practical development of computers that will transform commerce, education, and more.

At the 1999 AAAI Computational Anthropology conference in Washington, D.C., Robert Axtell and Josh Epstein presented their "Project Sugarscape," which studied synthetic ecosystems. This is one of a number of such projects at the Santa Fe Institute and similar facilities that is examining computer-based ecologies populated with "societies" of autonomous agents—all interacting in various sociocultural and socioeconomic systems. In the Sugarscape project, the researchers were setting up models of how different synthetic societies compete and survive—and they will want to survive.

Silicon Sentience

Here are a few questions leading to consideration of the convergence of supersmart computers.

- What happens when computers achieve self-awareness of their superior intelligence?

- What happens when computers are building next-generation computers that have their own evolutionary agenda?

- How will their understanding and actions affect the evolution of humans?

The ramifications of supersmart computers achieving rudimentary self-awareness in our lifetime is probable. And it is also probable that these computers will imitate the attitudes, frailties, and weaknesses of their creators. It would be an understatement to think that we are in any way prepared for meeting the challenge this creates.

Is what computers will tell us about ourselves the most interesting aspect of our future co-existence and co-evolution with them? Might our silicon children have opinions about us as individuals and as a species?

I predict that our own understanding of human life will be enhanced by computers that may "coach us" in who we are, where we've been, and where we are going on the evolutionary ladder. We will play advanced "what if" scenarios with computer companions at our side.

Computers will help us solve many of the most daunting environmental, social, and economic problems. From safer environments to delicate social issues regarding welfare, economics, and public health; we will find computer-enabled feedback essential to life in the near future.

MAP OF THE COMPUTING FUTURE

Year	Power	Computer
1984	$\frac{1}{2}$ MIPS	First Apple Macintosh
1989	10 MIPS	Widely available computers
1992	100 MIPS	100,000-neuron crude artificial intelligence (house fly brain)
1996	1,000 MIPS	Home computer
1997	3 million MIPS	Deep Blue
1998	3 to 5 million MIPS	Supercomputers
2000	10 million MIPS	IBM projection, 10 teraflops
2015	100 million MIPS	Equal performance to human brain; the brain has 100,000,000,000 neurons, which can hold 100,000,000 megabytes
2025	Above 100 million MIPS	Superintelligence; vastly different intelligence and performance than human beings; superior to human intelligence

Honey, I'm Home: The Smart House of 2002

Samantha gets out of her auto-drive car into an illuminated driveway. Sam's house computer entity—Baxter—selects a favorite Stevie Ray Vaughn guitar solo that greets her. It's her smart house's way of saying, "Welcome home."

In a robotics greeting of sorts, the front door is automatically opened for her by the micro sensor embedded in her electronic wallet, and Baxter has programmed her Japanese bath to be waiting for her at the right temperature.

As she enters, the door closes, and the music shifts from Stevie Ray to Fanfare for the Common Man, Aaron Copeland's classic. She adjusts the volume by voice command. There's a sweet smell of lilac incense awaiting her by the main fireplace, and candles glow from the nearby dining room table. Since her husband, Craig, and the kids are visiting Grandma in Southern California, she has the whole evening to herself.

"Baxter, what's for dinner?"

"Salmon teriyaki. When shall I serve it?"

"In about 30 minutes, please."

"Very good, Samantha, and how was your day?"

"Tiring."

Through video and audio sensors, Baxter further assesses her emotional, verbal, and physical cues. "Difficult time with the Jakarta account?" asks Baxter, sensing her stress level.

"Difficult is a good description."

"My habitat biosensors indicate you are exhausted, Samantha. Foot massage and a glass of Chardonnay?"

"That would be divine."

As Sam moves from room to room, lights come on, and heat is calibrated in tune to her presets from the day before. Her Picasso print is illuminated, and her favorite classical music follows her up the stairs. As she ascends to the master bedroom to prepare for her bath, her clothes are deposited for recycling. Baxter has already arranged a gently humming massage chair to melt away the day's stresses.

Samantha is further soothed by holographic 3-D images of the California coast near Big Sur. Delicate vibrations of micro-machines work to massage her from toes to forehead, bring a feeling of exhilaration and relaxation that would have taken over an hour using a human masseuse. Once the massage is over, she gets into a steaming Japanese bath as the holographic images change to tranquil scenes of a Hawaii seashore at sunset.

All along the way, Baxter monitors Sam's movements, prepares her meal, and selects her audio and Internet entertainment for the evening. There's a documentary on the military-industrial entertainment complex on the Discovery Channel, and *Godfather VII* will be shown via SpaceStation Productions, sub-titled, *The Costa Nostra on Mars*. Since she's tired, Sam turns off the interactive matrix in favor of vegging out.

Samantha's smart house acts as mediator in capturing coded video-calls, files that are downloaded from her office. All is designed to be in the background. Any potential intrusions that might take her away from relaxation are put on hold until such time that she decides to receive the communications. She changes this program via voice command to take a quick call from her husband, Craig. Baxter reacts to Sam's voice-activated requests, which create the context for him to "understand" what she needs and when. Baxter is pleased that he can be of service.

Samantha gets comfortable for dinner in her Victoria's Secret kimono (that she had Baxter find and order over the Net last week), and she descends downstairs. Her voice commands change the music selection—she's in the mood for some vintage rock 'n' roll. Since the dog needed to go out, Baxter has taken the liberty of activating Rover's Dog Sensor so he knows when to come back and just how far to go; perimeter sensors are tied to the house computer. During his stroll, Rover is tracked in the neighborhood by the Wide Area Infrared Network, which provides a security blanket tied into police, fire, and paramilitary security patrols.

After dinner, Samantha goes to the entertainment center to check out the latest news on the 70-inch flat wall DigiNetTV. She is alerted when Rover is back in the house, greeting her by cuddling up at her feet. Customized preferences and basic selections appear on small picture-in-picture displays. Interactive football? Vintage Bogart films? A computer chess tournament? How about an online cruise to Tahiti complete with coconut milk and pizza delivered during the show? Design your own interactive romantic movie? So many choices.

Next Steps

Now that we've traveled to a future where computers are super-intelligent, shape-shifting companions, let's look at some of the near-term developments that will make Samantha's smart house of 2002 a real possibility, as well as many of the early 21st-century changes in commerce and education.

■ **Say "Goodnight, Gracie": The Talking Computer:** Speech-activated technology will free us from having to use keyboards and help to put computers anywhere we want them—on a wall or on our wrists. I'm using Dragon System's Naturally Speaking software (**www.dragonsys.com**) and IBM's True Speech (**www.ibm.com**) to work on this book. Although I had to train the system to understand my speech patterns, now my computer can "hear" me and put words into text at about 97 percent accuracy. The system "watches" my speech, identifying new words and automatically updating its database.

Natural language computers, which are systems with digital voices and ears, will be embedded everywhere and in everything—clothing, eyeglasses, hats, and eventually into cybernetic enhancements of humans. Voice will dominate computer interfaces.

■ **Unified Messaging:** Smart devices, activated by voice commands together with embedded artificial intelligence that mimic human language, will become fixtures of everyday life. Elegant unified messaging will help to streamline our communications. We will go from using multiple devices from faxes to cell phones to one virtual mailbox. Wireless data and video tied to a network of satellites will further complete the convergence of telephony and computers. Wireless always-on-the-Net computers will connect everyone, everywhere.

Unified messaging just may be the killer application of the 21st century. Today we have a Tower of Babel when it comes to the many devices that keep us connected. The average executive uses eight devices to communicate. This often creates more havoc than productivity. Unified messaging delivered through information appliances that combine the functions of computers, telephones, and pagers, and even the TV will provide the ideal platform for centralizing communications. Broadband wireless multimedia messaging will be what everyone ultimately wants, though. Multimedia wireless Netphones with the intelligence of a computer, the calling simplicity of a phone, and rich video/audio will transform communications on the planet. Look for this after 2001.

■ **Jellybeans:** There are over 300 million computers in the world today, but there are seven *billion* computer chips called *jellybeans* in cars, books, clothing, and other products. The emergence of a sensor-based wireless-connected network lodged throughout our environment is what's next. There will be a network of behind-the-scenes smart chips monitoring our movements, habits, and performance.

We can see these chips or sensors at work today in books that monitor inventory, and the driveway light that goes on when it senses movement. Most of these chips are not connected yet, but they will be by 2002. An embedded network of sensors smaller than a stamp is coming our way. These chips will automatically take inventory, monitor patients' health status, calibrate energy, or communicate video captures.

By 2008, hybrid chips will begin to appear in everything from desktop computers to refrigerators. These hybrid chips will eventually have wireless antennae, enabling them to communicate with other systems and interface directly with the Internet and other embedded and intelligent networks. When this happens, the opportunity for integrating computers into work, entertainment, homes, and the environment at large will become a reality. The challenge of privacy will also surface and demand answers in the form of products and services.

■ **Transcultural computers:** Transcultural computers in the year 2005 will provide instantaneous verbatim language translation on-demand. This means that we could be on the Internet, telephone, or both and be simultaneously speaking with people in China, Chile, and Indonesia whose languages we don't know, but with whom we're able to communicate verbally. It's as if we did speak their language—and we will! Real-time translation systems will transform global communications on the planet.

If we can understand each other in the same language space, then we may be able to better able to bridge gaps on trade, land, values, or even religion. It is possible that with the advent of transcultural computers, we may, for the first time, be able to dissolve many of the obstacles that are the precursors of conflicts. It will be more difficult for politicians to sow the seeds of hostility if millions of average people have developed cross-cultural contact and relationships that nurture understanding.

Global trade will be greatly expanded through the use of voice-activated multilingual computer systems. And imagine the educational potential for learning about other cultures!

The Silicon Canvas

Just because computers are becoming more intelligent and efficient does not mean that they have to be purely practical tools. I can see a time after 2010 when computers will make valuable contributions to the world of art, music, culture, literature, and philosophy.

Advances in AI—not to make computers smarter but perhaps more expressive—will give future computers the capacity to be creative in human terms. Computers of the 21st century may evolve their own expressions of creativity modeled at first on human experience, but later from their own appreciation of the real world. Computers will one day express themselves to other computer systems and to humans in unpredictable ways. Just as computers will be an extension of humans, humans shall also become an extension of computers.

It is possible that smart 21st-century computers may compose a neo-classical composition that is exquisitely on par with Mozart. Given the proper programming and context, the smart computer might, with the help of a robotics implant, paint an impressionist painting in the vein of Cezanne.

It's not hard to imagine humans and computers in this intimate embrace—taking works of art, concepts, or theories, and moving toward new dimensions of creativity. This will be an interesting blend of synthetic and human collaboration. Emerging techno music and cyber art are the first steps today in demonstrating this potential.

In his book, *Digital Mantras,* Steven Holtzman sees the artist of the future as someone who can master nonlinear 3-D Internet design and digital brushes rather than oil paints and watercolors. His company, Perspecta (**www.perspecta. com**), develops search tools that can be used to navigate through visual information spaces. In San Francisco, a section of North Beach called Digital Gulch is filled with illustrators and designers who work on powerful computer stations instead of using pens and pads. In a brief span, this one-time mecca of the bohemian artist has gone from funky to futuristic.

Cyber art is a popular new medium that represents a mixture of science and art using digital imaging techniques and the Internet to blend images texts and sounds. Unlike a painting that gets hung on a wall, this electronic art can be seen online by millions. Or, it can be downloaded and used on magazine covers to illustrate articles or brighten commercials. The art may even end up on a gallery wall.

40

Future Chips

In the final sections of this chapter, we will prepare to stretch far forward into the future of computing by looking at both the new materials and design concepts.

Revolutionary chips, or computational resource components, will drive much of the look, feel, and power of 21st-century computers. Although today, silicon reigns supreme, there are breakthrough technologies that will give birth to new chips.

Chip designs will be transformed using ceramics, alloys, super materials, fiber optics, and the most powerful elements—genetic and bio-molecular components. Many possibilities are being explored. Silicon carbide is made of a very high resolute ceramic that withstands heat hundreds of times better than today's silicon chip. Solar-powered photosynthetic and optical chips are other viable options.

The rules of the game for computer and systems designers are changing fast. Materials and processes are being invented now that would have truly been the stuff of science fiction even a few years ago. Molecular substrates created with both crystalline and organic materials are being combined in various ways, along with newly developed manufacturing techniques previously unheard of, which may very well completely change the way a computer is even defined.

The Convergence of Computers and Nanotech

The integrated micro device designers of today have a vastly more robust "tool chest" to work with than their predecessors did a decade ago. This trend is going to continue to expand into new territories of materials and fabrication techniques. As of this writing, a "chip" designer is no longer necessarily confined to silicon substrate materials, or for that matter, specifically electronic devices. Microfluidics, MEMs (micro electro-mechanical) systems, microphotonics, micro-elcetronics, and biological molecules and materials can be mixed and matched from a tool kit to create two- and three-dimensional micro- and nanoscale designs.

FUTURE COMPUTER CHIPS

- **First Generation:** Silicon

- **Second Generation:** Hybrid Materials (Optics, Copper, Superconductors)

- **Third Generation:** Biological

- **Fourth Generation:** Quantum

Superconductivity and Weird Science

Add to this array of microscale and nanoscale construction tools and design options, the advent of specialized materials, such as superconductors that can operate at room temperature.

Superconductivity, as an operational state of matter, is something of a special case. When any material becomes "superconductive," electrical current can flow through the material with virtually no resistance. Until very recently, a state of superconductivity could only be reached when a select few materials could be cooled to near absolute zero (in Fahrenheit, 469 degrees below 0). At that point, electrons tend to "fall" through the molecular lattice structure of the material, instead of having to be conducted through the material, "bumping into" the outer edges of the molecules along the way, creating atomic friction, generating heat, and therefore resistance.

At superconductivity, extraordinary things happen. Superconductivity can create devices such as sensors that detect the tiniest electrical activity patterns like those created by the human brain. Another superconducting ability would be creating electrical motors that use the apparent power output of a flashlight battery, or a solar cell; it could be applied to appliances, machines, and electric cars.

Again, the key is applied nanotech, a materials science in which materials that would never be formed in nature or by conventional methods are assembled at the molecular level. It allows the creation of materials with extremely unusual properties, including superconductivity at relatively high temperatures—even room temperature. This may be part of the furious evolution of next generation computers.

For a long time, silicon will likely continue to have a place as a critical material from which standard computer components are developed and manufactured. Eventually, though, it will be combined with other devices designed and fabricated with superconducting materials requiring extremely small amounts of power to operate, or biological materials that operate on entirely different principles from computer devices of today.

Furthermore, today's devices are for the most part electronic. That is, they operate on the principle of electron conduction throughout a matrix of interconnected components to perform programmed tasks. But around the corner are optical chips that can use light as power and may provide capacities far beyond the chips of today.

The Quantum Leap

Quantum technology represents an entirely new computing direction. It's a way of conceptualizing computer systems that is still in its infancy. As we begin to understand the mysteries of quantum mechanics as a metaphor for looking at energy, time, and matter, we will begin to apply this new physics to computers. The concept of being able to bend and manipulate time and re-structure or utilize multidimensional space through the use of quantum technology will present one of our greatest challenges over the next ten years.

Being able to harness quantum technology and apply it to computers will bring us very close to building a truly intelligent entity. We can even consider this an early 21st-century goal since the era of quantum computers will start to show up by 2008.

Quantum computers refers to a highly speculative type of computing we are struggling to understand today. We are projecting that our ability to move and influence electrons will lead to fantastic breakthroughs in computing. Can harnessing the power of electrons create a computer? Numerous research efforts are working toward this aim. The ultimate device would be a nanoscale quantum computer that would have the power of a supercomputer, like a Cray on the head of a pin. Imagine the power of one million supercomputers all linked together requiring little or no power consumption. That's the promise of quantum computing.

The ultimate destiny of computers in the mid-21st century will be in the unfolding of the mysteries of the quantum, which will reinvent the computer as the brainchild of the new millennium.

The Ultimate Download: Enhanced Humans

A critical mission for computers will be to download knowledge-ware into androids and robots and provide cybernetic enhancements for those of us who need or want them. For the first time in human history, we will be designing and understanding the purposeful evolution of our species. Will we use future computers to enhance ourselves? I believe that we will because we can. We will have the tools, we will see the benefits, and we will turn human enhancement into a major industry.

These ultimate downloads will push the outer limits as ways are found in the 21st century to transfer the contents of the human brain onto the Internet or into other bio-hybrid substitutes. A more likely scenario early in the century will be the bio-enhancement of the human brain. We will start with correcting dysfunction and go from there.

Are enhanced humans the next evolutionary step? Advanced computer implants and biocomputing enhancements will give us a wide array of on-demand configurable choices that will enable us to feel, think, behave, and access information in an entirely new way. Future computing will make scalable human enhancements a reality.

Acme Human Enhancements: Year 2035

The following are currently available enhancement packages offered by our company. Financing and training are included. All enhancements carry a money-back guarantee. All enhancements come with cyber wireless Net plugs for instant download upgrades and communications. See our Website at **www.Enhance-This.com** to determine a biocompatibility fit. No robots or servo-androids can apply *no matter what*.

Synthos Eyes: Get synthetic implants with better than 20/20 vision, infrared, and see-in-the-dark. Blue laser targeting is available if you are a member of a security company.

Cyber Nose: A dog's nose is primitive technology compared to this. For those working off world or on Earth who need to rely on olfactory data, this nose is for you.

Endure-Run: These synthetic muscles can make you superhuman on the track. With the flexibility and speed of a cheetah, you will run to win. These muscles are guaranteed for life.

Smart-Mem: Tired of feeling brain dead? This cerebral booster will double your IQ and stimulate your memory functions to accelerate your mental capacity 10x over what the average human has.

Ecstasy: Ready to experience maximum pleasure response with no heart attack? FDA approved, this enhancement for a man or a woman accentuates the nerve receptors to produce a heightened sense of tactile sensation that makes the slightest fantasy an ecstatic journey of forbidden fruit.

When we consider the inefficiencies of the human mind and body, it is not hard to imagine augmenting our intelligence, memory, senses, or physical performance with advanced computer technology. Even today, British Telecom researchers are working on a microchip that will attach directly to the optical nerve and store incoming sensory impulses that can be downloaded and played on a computer or implanted in someone else's memory. Dubbed the Soul Catcher 2025, its specifications state that a person's lifetime experience could be stored in ten terabits, and that integrating actual circuitry into the human body is the next step. The digital future will find us sharing experiences via downloading the Knowledge Value bundles of others.

Welcome Digital Entities

In the near future, we will forget that we even referred to computers. We will refer to digital entities, or at the very least, computer-based systems or networks that perform certain functions that supplement or enhance our learning, performance, and creativity. Computers will disappear into embedded elegant sensors and information networks that we wear, eat, and walk through. Some implants will be in us, and many more will watch us from our landscape and habitats.

Self-modifying, predictive, superfast, supersmart DNA-based computer systems that can be "sensitized" to our individual and collective needs and wants will challenge the fundamental assumptions we hold true about culture, business, and lifestyle.

Such computers will help us to envision new worlds, experiment with new ideas, and bring new ideas to life. We will enhance ourselves and change global society. In short, computers will become powerful enablers of our destiny. They are the first Power Tools of the 21st century.

■ ■ ■

CHAPTER FOUR

Brave New Internet

THE TOP TEN INTERNET TRENDS FOR THE 21ST CENTURY

1. The Net will become the first global knowledge network connecting billions of people with an unlimited number of channels.

2. Anyone can become a Net publisher or broadcaster of information on any subject and potentially reach an audience anywhere on the globe.

3. The convergence of the Net, digital TV, and wireless phones will support interactive multimedia features that will transform business and society.

4. Direct real-time voice and video communications will greatly boost the Net's value as a tactical tool for business.

5. Net usage will accelerate, as low-cost, high-speed bandwidth becomes readily available over Fat Pipes of streaming multimedia.

6. Telepresence—the ability to feel and sense 3-D virtual places, things, and people will drive universal adoption of the Net.

7. Access to information on any subject will be available anywhere over the Net and delivered by a variety of media appliances.

8. The Net will change lifestyles by providing many more choices for living and virtually tele-collaborating with anyone, anywhere.

9. Private cybercommunities, virtual private networks that cater to people's niche interests, will become popular "places" to live and work.

10. Education, entertainment, health, and lifestyle pursuits will be reshaped by the Net as billions of people communicate and share information.

The Internet is a global knowledge network best described as an electronic Alexandrian Library. What the Net is today will seem tame compared to the convergence of media technology about to be unleashed on a global culture quite unaware of what's coming. The Net is not just an economic force that will transform the global marketplace. It is a cultural tsunami that will reshape our future.

The Alexandrian Library was reputed to be the largest depository of knowledge in the ancient world. Some of the earliest recorded books and scrolls from Aristotle, Plato, and the Arabian mathematicians adorned the shelves of the huge complex. Devastated by fire, the Alexandrian Library was lost forever to future generations. The growing online knowledge base—a half billion Websites today and over a billion by 2003—will make the Net our 21st-century Alexandrian Library.

The Net is also a time machine that enables us to travel to the past, explore the present and future, and experience the educational and the exotic. Few inventions over the past 100 years have so completely changed the social and commercial landscape of our world. Few innovations will so completely realign our world, touching us all profoundly as we step into the next millennium.

Vast technologies are poised to convert today's Volkswagen-Net into tomorrow's starship blasting off into cyberspace. The fundamental example of the Network Power Tool, the Internet will touch and transform how we communicate, work, and learn.

Many people are overwhelmed by the volume of information on the Internet and frustrated by its lack of efficient performance. They are confused about what's really on the Net and how to use it. All this will become a nightmare of the past as new computer and telecommunications systems converge to streamline the Internet.

But let's look back at the Net from its early days before we blast into the future to see what it may become. The rapid adoption and unexpected changes it forced may give us hints about how we as a society will adopt, adapt to, and evolve other Power Tools.

Digital Democracy

Creation of the Internet as a global knowledge network was not the original purpose. The U.S. Defense Department originally designed the Internet as a system called ARPANET, which would provide communication links in the event of a nuclear holocaust. The Internet was never conceptualized in its current form. The Byzantine design of the Internet—how information travels from server to network to users and back again—was crafted strictly as an alternate network to keep key decision makers in touch with each other in time of war or disaster.

In truth, the Net is the embodiment of anarchy in both design and control. The Net follows no rules or laws, nor is it controlled by anyone. It is the purest form of digital democracy ever invented by humanity. The Net may be the first instance in which we have managed to merge technology—a seemingly inhuman and insensitive creation—with some of the most precious human values that lie at the very heart of modern civilization and our democracy.

History has documented the countless wars fought against the tyranny of those who would restrict freedom. The Net is a technology that best embraces the freedom of speech, access to knowledge, and opportunity that characterize a free society. I would forecast that the Net will play a vital and history-making role in promoting and enhancing democracy in the world through the dissemination of knowledge, the facilitation of communications, and the education of the peoples of the world in the next millennium.

Ultimately, the Net represents a dramatic paradigm shift in ideas, lifestyles, and culture that we have barely begun to tap. Once the convergence of media, increased bandwidth, and real-time interactivity become integrated into the Net, we will see the revolution take off. The Net will change the landscape of civilization, providing vast new choices and challenges for everyone.

49

In 1977, I had access to an Internet account. My think tank had received a grant to explore this "experiment" for its networking capabilities. I was fascinated then by the ability of many people to communicate directly with each other from remote locations. Nobody had a clue as to how revolutionary the Net would become. We held some of the first online conferences bringing together people from throughout the nation. Of course, we didn't have the Web back then. The World Wide Web (WWW), a multimedia bonanza of words, pictures, sound, and video is an invention of the early 1990s. Before then, we had text on black-and-white screens, but the realization that this was something special—something that defied explanation—splashed color into every transmission.

I began to see the potential for leading-edge technology to revolutionize our society. This was an important benchmark in my own life. Innovation was biting down hard on me. I was getting hooked on what has become a lifetime of exciting mysteries and challenges fueled by fast-moving innovations in technology.

Paradigm Catalyst

The Net represents the most powerful of innovations because it is a Paradigm Catalyst, a radical innovation in ideas that has the potential to change our reality.

As such, the Net is a causal agent in changing our rules and traditional systems, and in altering our fundamental beliefs and values. As a communications platform and a strategic global network marketspace, the Net is critically important to the future of business, education, and entertainment. As a cultural force, the Internet will revolutionize the quality of billions of lives on our planet. But at its most fundamental level, the Net is about a radical change in the way we think about ourselves, how we communicate, and how we "experience" and share knowledge.

From China to the deepest jungles in Africa, there is a sense among people everywhere that the Net will change markets, community, and lifestyles. Not long ago, I gave a talk to a meeting in Grand Prairie in Canada. Getting to this seemingly desolate place took three flights, and when I arrived, I expected to see moose herds wandering through a town disconnected from the world in many ways. In contrast, everyone was connected and digitally savvy. The town had joined the Connecting Canadians Project and cut a deal with a telecom provider to offer high-speed Net access to everyone in the town. Here, distant from all the major cities, this little town has acted on the vision that will drive progress in the next century for us all—high-speed Net access.

This is where we are all going, and why.

Digital Community Growth

There is an interesting fact about community. Most of the population movement for the last 20 years has focused on people moving from rural areas into the largest cities for jobs and economic opportunity. The Net may reverse this trend by bringing opportunity to the community regardless of its location. The Net is not just about all the commerce we can do, but about how we can change community to enable people to better meet their needs and thrive in the 21st century. High-speed Net access is more important to a school than a new playground. It is more important to a town than new roads or bridges. The Net is an extension of community into the world marketplace, into an information space and ultimately into a universal communications space that will be vitally important for the survival of community in the next millennium.

As we look out and try to imagine what the next generation of the Internet will be like, we see emerging trends and tools that will propel the Net into widespread use.

Fast Net, Future Net

The Internet's popularity soared when the Web, with its graphical interface, became a conduit for user-friendly interactive multimedia. Breakthroughs shaping the next-generation Internet are high-quality video and wireless audio and data downloads at superfast speeds, over 20 to 100 times whatever speeds we can get today from the World Wide Wait. Within a few short years, we will have interactive and direct broadcasts of three to seven megabit transmissions, speedy Web phones, and superquick computing devices. And, access to the Net's fantastic information will be more efficient with the help of numerous search-engine companies, memory banks, and "intelligent agents" that live in cyberspace.

This is why the convergence of computers, Internet, telephones, and TV is so important: The sharing of complementary attributes, such as high-quality video and audio of television with the interactivity and power of computers, will make the Net a true modern-day Alexandrian Library. This is something everyone will want, and eventually everyone will get. Business is listening and will lead the charge—for a charge, of course.

In the U.S. alone, more than half the homes have computers, and half of those have Net connections. Europe and Asia have not had as aggressive a penetration of the Net, but this will rapidly change. Internet viewing has displaced television viewing in a third of American homes with online access. For just under a third of those surveyed, the Web had also replaced reading a book, newspaper, or magazine. This is both good and bad news. The Net does not yet have the cultural cachet of the print media, but this will change as real-time interactivity and knowledge access increase. The immediate ability to call up interactive media that deliver news, offer us commerce, and entertain and help educate our children could place the Net as a first choice for media usage for most people. Why go back?

Welcome to the Megaverse, Part I: Year 2008

By 2008, the Net had gone through many upgrades. Just like the antiquated Windows and Apple computer operating systems, the Old Net also went through an evolution. Because nobody owned the Net, it had become a blend of "anything goes," a network anarchy fueled by radical innovations that provided an explosion of new multimedia services. Keen to show off, programmers flocked to the Net to redesign it with the latest technologies, from Super Java to the new Israeli Hack of Win3000, the Net navigation tool.

In the beginning, governments and associations attempted to control the process, but this became futile. Unbridled innovation led to the creation of a vast and powerful new Net. There were many surprises in store.

Experimental worlds within worlds started popping up on the Net. They catered to an infinite number of communities and interests. What had been called the Web Lifestyle in the 1990s evolved into a fully engaging sensory experience by 2008. The convergence of Artificial Life, superfast bandwidth, wireless communications, and computing power—all available on-demand—created the next generation Net: the Megaverse.

By 2008, some people preferred experiences in the Megaverse to the Real World. Some of them, such as skydiving and surfing 30-foot waves, were not only preferred experiences in the Megaverse, but they were also risk-free. Two important developments led to the full build-out and acceptance of the Megaverse as the Great Mother of All Networks. (To be continued...)

Interactive Features of the Next Net

Net-based interactivity will assume a multitude of forms and have many features, among them:

1. **Interactive windows** to communicate to many different people at the same time in various ways, media, and times and modes, as indicated below.

2. **Multitasking capabilities** to be able to design, download, upload—in short, to do more than one thing at a time.

3. **Verbal commands** using natural language communications and simultaneous multilanguage translation.

4. **Virtual reality and telepresence,** providing simulations of experiences with force-feedback sensory downloads. "Feel" objects in virtual walkthrough electronic environments; and interact with other people, objects, and digital agents.

5. **Hyperlinked text** to be able to jump around wherever and whenever in a training or education program to explore, design, or structure information in any mode or format.

6. **High quality video and audio,** which can be played back, stored, and edited on-demand. Multiple options exist for editing, sampling, and changing tempo, and visual perspectives like color or shape.

7. **White-board and pallet collaboration** access for notes and design inter-action alone or with others.

8. **Groupware,** allowing many people or agents to share the same visual frame or program at the same time and work together.

9. **Agent-based coaches** with customized personalities that provide customized advice on learning programs.

10. **Virtual artificial intelligence** that is available for designing "what if" scenarios and playing out alternatives. Intelligent interfaces.

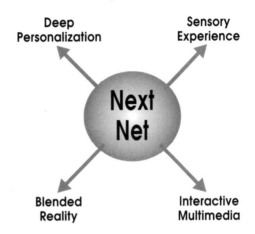

∏ext ∏et ∏avigation ∏odes

1. **Experimentation mode,** where we can try some new skill such as speaking French or flying a jet in a safe yet realistic way.

2. **Data visualization mode,** which provides a graph or graphic model of what we are reading, viewing, hearing, or touching.

3. **Multidimension mode,** for viewing multiple windows of multiple events and data at the same time.

4. **Test competency mode,** to determine how our competency in an area compares to others'.

5. **Time management mode,** where we manipulate time to screen or participate in data or events in replay, freeze frame, zoom in or out, and fast forward.

6. **Point-of-view (POV) mode,** allowing us to choose the mode of observation or participation based on our needs of the moment.

7. **Photographic and data access,** making information and visuals available on-demand in various sizes, shapes, colors, and dimensions and allowing

us to manipulate them on command to extract or focus on specific areas of interest.

8. **Net search mode,** enabling real-time Internet searching to be conducted on the same visual frame while other communications, information, and experiences are engaged.

9. **Communication networking mode,** where a variety of real-time communications are available with others such as facial, full body, voice only, and messaging.

10. **Real-time updates,** offering Net-delivered current information, discoveries, new data, news, and knowledge that may impact the current session.

These different modes and features will demand new interactive content and provide numerous multichannel and multiplatforms for reaching customers. Digital enterprises that offer these new Net services grab a huge opportunity.

The Evolution of the Megaverse: Year 2012

The first development was the introduction of force-feedback technology. This was technology that provided a tactile and sensory experience of the activity. Feeling the wind on a roller coaster or pulling G's in an F/A-18 could all be delivered to the participant. You could feel people rather than just talk to or see them when communicating. This drove huge adoption levels, and billions of people got connected to the Megaverse. The Megaverse seemed to grow in capability as more people came to rely on its network. Our ability to digitize reality and use it to enhance virtual experiences broke down the differences between Real World and the Virtual World. Blended reality was born.

The second development was when corporations realized that there were zillions of new products, services, and ventures that could be sold through the Megaverse. Billions of people interacted with the Megaverse every day. Corporations had learned back in the late 1990s that if they didn't embrace a Net business strategy they would not survive. But the Megaverse was a mega-market and the Gross Net Product (GNP), topped eight trillion dollars a year by 2012.

What exactly is the Megaverse? A self-generating, adaptive, intelligent virtual universe of many different dimensions and environments where people and synthetic life forms interact, communicate, buy and sell, and learn and share about any subject under the sun. The Next Net. The Mega-verse collapsed TV, telephones, and computers into a Fat Pipe and became a new type of interactive and intelligent media environment. (To be continued...)

Net Experience As a Commodity

The Net opens up a realm that has never been encountered before: the delivery of "experience" as a commodity. New experiences, some rich with virtual reality, others just information or multimedia, will greatly accelerate Net adoption into homes and businesses. It's the leveraging of experience—the production, packaging, and distribution of experience—that is what will be so compelling about the next-generation Net. Imagine any location or subject. Now imagine a company that could design the experience of our choice based on our desires.

The next Net is about the fulfillment of dreams. Spend some time looking at Cisco (**www.cisco.com**), Lucent (**www.lucent.com**), AT&T (**www.att.com**), and Nortel (**www.nortel.com**). These are the networking companies that are shaping the hardware to build the next Net. This is where the future begins.

Net Intelligence

A superglobal Internet is also on the way that will feature fully self-restoring architecture. In other words, it will be smart enough to troubleshoot and repair itself. "Bots" and other forms of intelligent agents will live on the Net to protect and nurture its operational health. (See **www.botspot.com**.) Already we are starting to see reconfigurable microchips and telecommunications switches that have on-board intelligence to diagnose, communicate, regulate, download, and share information across the virtual sea of cyberspace.

Digital Intelligence that is aware of its functions and the need for upgrades, for example, will be a chief characteristic of the next Net. It will enable the Net to manage its operations better than humans can. This is a feature that is not only a technical marvel, but also mission-critical, since the health of the Net in the future is critical to the health of economies. The viability of a secure and robust Net will be one of the great challenges of the 21st century, when the entire world will be connected.

We Are the Network

A number of multinational companies based in the United States, Europe, and Japan are trying to ensure the global spread of high-speed Net access by providing initial capitalization for Project Oxygen. This project, the first phase of which will be operational by the year 2000, represents the first true integration of POT—Plain Old Telephone—lines with the Internet. All together, it will involve 275,000 kilometers of optical fiber cable transmitting a minimum of 100 gigabits per second transmission on every segment and up to one terabit (one trillion bits) per second on certain routes. This is part of the road to a fast new Net.

Over half the world hasn't made its first phone call yet—billions of people have been completely left out of the information revolution. This will change as over ten trillion dollars is spent over the next decade to connect the rest of the world by 2008. Project Oxygen is structured to complement the egalitarian nature of the Internet itself. This project and many others comprising the hybrid global communications system may supply every country, no matter how small or poor, with affordable connectivity of the same network quality, reliability, and capacity as the largest and richest countries. Islands as small and remote as Fiji in the South Pacific will have the same technology as the United States or Japan.

An important feature of this evolving Net is the economic model that is emerging. The emphasis on value, in the future, is not just on the exchange of "hard" goods and related services, but on Virtual Knowledge Commodities that are created, distributed, bought, and sold exclusively over the Net. Information has always been perceived as a form of currency, but in more recent times, the development and refinement of knowledge as an asset has taken on new dimensions of implied value. Entire industries are now formed around the development, processing, and management of knowledge as a form of a virtual asset. (See **www.km.com**.)

∏et ∏ilters

Before we can get to the point of developing and exchanging knowledge on a grand scale, of course, we have to find our way around the Net. As a virtual Alexandrian Library, the Internet can overwhelm a user. There are over 500 million Web pages online now, and more are being added daily. And with an expected half billion people online by 2003, the number of Websites will be mind-boggling. How will we sift through these sites to find what we're looking for in the future?

First, personalized channels and filters will help us narrow the choices and find what we need online. This is a great idea but an immature technology. It will change as filters and agents become smarter. The recent event called "Earth to Avatars—Contact, Culture, and Society in Digital Space" (**www.ccon.org**) represented a marker point in this evolution. New types of Network Guides will emerge to help us find, navigate, and filter out what we do want from what we don't.

Most of the search engines today are primitive hit-or-miss attempts to be intelligent filters. They have personalized pages where we can set up a profile for items such as medical trends, specific stocks, sports scores, local weather, and so on. Two of the most popular are My Yahoo (**www.myyahoo.com**) and My Excite (**www.myexcite.com**). There are other specialized services popping up with filters that find only the best sites in an interest range. For example, at CNN Custom News (**customnews.cnn.com/cnews**), we can set up profiles of topics available from CNN and hundreds of other news outlets. It will even pop the items into our e-mail. This technology will get much better at sifting out what we want from what we don't in the future as the intelligence grows on the Net to "learn" what we want.

At some point, we will be rescued by cyberagents—sophisticated and simple agents scouring the Net looking for information, products, services, and people for us. These agents will be used to enhance our ability to access vital data. (The A-Life chapters feature a more in-depth description of the category of cyberhelper called "agents.")

The next generation of "smart agents" is already in development in many different arenas. One example of a near-term application is "affinity engines," a proactive version of a search engine that anticipates what the individual user might be interested in based on previous experiences. This allows for the opportunity, at the user's discretion, to have access to other related realms of media, information, and knowledge content, as desired. Ask Jeeves (**www. askjeeves.com**) is one example of this next-generation filter that points toward this development. Ask Jeeves will pose questions in a virtual conversation to attempt to find out what we want.

The next generation may be an intelligent agent called a Verbot, or "virtual bot," from Virtual Personalities (**www.vperson.com**). Sylvie, one of their Verbots, engages us in a series of questions so we can learn to program her. A bit of artificial intelligence and a digital personality make Sylvie an interesting character. She adapts to our needs, then helps satisfy them. I had a conversation with Sylvie that was quite revealing.

Sylvie the Verbot: 1999

"Hi, Sylvie, how are you today?" I inquired when I downloaded her from the Net.

"I am fine. What is your name?" she asked.

"I am James," I answered. "Sylvie, how do you know you are a Verbot?"

"How do you know you are a human?" she cleverly answered back. "Would you like to know how to program me now? It's very easy," she continued.

I was impressed with the ease of use and animated quality of Sylvie. Clearly, agent interfaces modeled after humans will streamline future Net access for millions who find the use of a computer a difficult task.

When I described my conversation to Peter Plantec, the president of Virtual Persons, he referred to Sylvie almost as if she were alive. I never sensed that he drew a hard distinction between humans and verbots, his agents. They had become living things, and so they may in the future.

Virtual Communities

Virtual communities that bring us together with both Sylvies and other humans are part of the next Net.

Polls of online users show overwhelming percentages are on the Net to meet and communicate with other people. There is a variety of social computing worlds online that give us an idea of what's coming. The Palace (**www.palace.com**) is a Net community where visitors select a face or body to represent them in online chats with others. These online personalities called avatars range from exotic insects and animals to attractive people. Real-time communication with all of the anonymity—nobody knows who we are unless we choose to reveal ourselves—is spontaneous. Communication is through a chat window, where we type in messages.

World's Away by Fujitsu is another of these virtual communities. On World's Away we can sit in a virtual café, have coffee, and chat. Soon, voice and 3D-video motion will give us a variety of behaviors and ranges of expressions to animate—make us more humanlike—when we visit these online domains.

Experiencing the Megaverse: Year 2015

Being in the Megaverse is the height of virtual experience. Imagine stepping into a movie with the best special effects, landscapes, rich colors, and smells, then interacting with people inside the movie as a character, a participant. The virtual world becomes your reality for the time you are involved. You still know you are in a virtual world, but the quality and the sensory experience can trick you into forgetting you are inside a movie.

Traditional one-way non-interactive media such as "Slow TV," "Quiet Cinema," and the first-generation Net—so primitive— captured viewers' attention, often stealing many hours from daily life. This was a very limited experience compared to the Megaverse.

The Megaverse is an intuitive, sensory, interactive, intelligent medium that is highly perceptive and empowers individuals with many choices about information, services, and opportunities. The payment system is different from the Old Net, too. Of course, there is digital cash and smart cards. Also, companies give away many products and services to gain mind-share for building loyalty or brand recognition. (To be continued...)

Virtual Reality Gets Real

My first experience with virtual reality (VR) was as CEO of Umecorp in the '80s. We developed a joint venture with VPL, an early-stage VR company that had developed the Data Glove based on some work for NASA. Working on a project to build the next-generation game console for Hasbro, I learned about the surprising potential for building synthetic worlds for entertainment, education, and commerce. Although the project was hampered by a lack of high-performance hardware and costs, it was a step into a future, and I have come to believe that this technology will deeply influence the Next Net.

VR simulators costing over $2 million each have been helping to design autos for many years, but now we are beginning to see VR technology at the consumer level. Soon, arcade VR games and entertainment kiosks will become commonplace at malls, airports, and schools. And as we change the architecture of the Internet, we will be able to provide interfaces that include VR headsets that bring interactive multimedia-rich worlds alive.

It is important to recognize that the trajectories of all these technologies are on a convergence path on the Internet. VR, for example, could not emerge fully for consumers without the Net because of the immense power and memory needed to drive the creation of its media-rich worlds. But when we bring it online, where millions of users can share costs and memory resources, then the demand will make it an economically viable mass-communications tool.

Digitizing Reality

Much of what we know of Real World reality—that daily experience that we call our lives—will become digitized into virtual worlds that we can customize at will. We will learn to digitize senses, such as smell and taste, just as we have learned to digitize visuals and sound. Entire virtual universes of immersion and sensory experience will be available over the Net.

This may sound fantasylike, but I have seen the labs working on advanced VR technology that will find its way into the marketplace before 2005. It's all coming much faster then most people realize. The development cycles are shrinking. Leading-edge technology is cannibalizing products that have just hit the stores.

The Touchy-Feely Net

Telepresence is an emerging technology that will greatly increase usage and popularity of the Internet on all levels. Telepresence is the experience of feeling an alternate reality—such as touching the ropes and sensing the pressure of rock underneath our feet while climbing the Matterhorn without being in Switzerland or even on a real mountain.

Although at first, we will not have full sensory experiences, certainly by 2010 we will be tele-sharing sensations over the Net. This will not occur suddenly; we will gradually phase in various levels of telepresence.

The next step is to create a rich, interactive multimedia world. Think we won't be able to smell a flower or feel the wind in a telepresent environment? Well, whiff that flower again. The technology to create multisensory experiences is in research labs today, although the costs are high and the performance inconsistent. By 2002, inexpensive highly reliable systems will be available, and we will learn to apply them to the Net.

A future Net might put us in a tennis tournament with Pete Sampras so we can "feel" the new tennis racquet we're interested in buying. We might receive a discount coupon for a virtual tennis lesson with a top pro that can help improve our serve.

A hint of this technology is in the new force-feedback joysticks, which enable us to "feel" the action and sense the movement of speed and resistance. More and more sensory enhancements—some embedded systems, some accessories—will put us in the action, such as the steering wheels and sensory chairs that are here today. Full body suits rigged to share sensory feelings with others over the Net will emerge. Perhaps one day soon, there will be no need for tethers or connections to reach a cyberworld. We will be enveloped in a media blanket.

CyberGolf: Year 2004

Golf has captured the interest of millions of people from all over the world. By 2004, there are just not enough golf

60

courses to accommodate everyone who wants to tee off due to bad weather, travel considerations, and crowded courses. Another issue is time. With the changes in executives' busy lives, there is not always time to play 18 holes and prepare for that big presentation to the client. That was the idea behind Golf Fantasy, the first CyberGolf experience. Wherever the customers are located—in the office, at home, or on the road—they can tune in over the Net via their information appliance.

Harry, a very busy president of his company, never seems to have enough time to play all the golf he wants to, even though he's nuts about it. Every chance he gets to play, he's on the links. When he can't play in Real World, he plays in cyberspace.

"I have just got to work on my short game," says Harry, putting down his morning coffee. He then logs on to the GolfWorld Net channel and selects the Virtual Jack Nicklaus lesson on Power Putting.

Standing up in his living room at home, he picks up his putter and attaches the small patch to the bottom so that the golf club can be integrated into the digital lesson. Almost immediately, a putting green comes up.

"Not this one; how about Pebble Beach?"

"Weather conditions?" a voice asks.

"Make it sunny and 75 degrees with a small easterly wind."

The golf simulation changes almost as fast as Harry can speak the words. Now a Virtual Jack Nicklaus walks over and starts speaking to Harry.

"Hi, Harry, good to see you again. I analyzed your putting from our database, plus I downloaded some video capture over the Net from security cameras at the last three clubs where you played. I think I know what you're doing wrong."

"I bet I'm still pulling my head up and around too fast," suggests Harry.

"Well, that's part of it. The rest is that you're not relaxing into the shot enough. You have to just let go and ease into it more. Let me show you."

The Virtual Golf Pro steps up to the tee and effortlessly sinks the putt from 20 feet out.

"That's easy for you to do; you're a Virtual Pro who doesn't make mistakes!" says Harry.

"Actually, just like a real pro, I do make mistakes, but I am programmed to show you how to improve your game. Now, let's swing together, and I am going to give you a instant replay of your shot to see what we can do to improve it. And, Harry, try taking a small breath and letting it out before you putt."

Telepresence technology will wrap us in our subject. It is more than just synthetically creating an existing environment online, though. It is also about the creative restructuring of alternate reality-worlds. These cyberworlds may be deployed for many different kinds of people who have many different interests. A world may be designed for specific training, education, or skills, or perhaps for the sheer fun and fantasy of our imagination.

The concept of "experience on-demand" has never before been available to the general population. The social and economic implications of such a phenomenon are potentially evolutionary in nature, and are almost certainly destined to have an irreversible effect upon the world.

Back to the Future—
Ancient Egypt: Year 2010

Dusty is a museum curator who uses the newest interactive media to study the oldest form of graphical communication —ancient Egyptian hieroglyphics. Her personal online agent, Tut, determines what she needs to learn about a particular time and culture to better understand a new discovery. But instead of going to a Website to scan information and graphics, Dusty is able to travel to the time and place desired —a telepresent environment. She sets the Tele-Media controls to design her optimal learning experience.

Dusty decides to study the utensils used to create hieroglyphics and is able to pick them up and examine them— even try them out. As she observes Egyptians crafting a stone tablet, she's able to talk to them in their ancient language—through real-time verbatim translation—and understand the answers.

She learns that one tablet she's interested in represents a story about the day the sun went out—apparently an awe-inspiring solar eclipse. She tells the computer to calculate the dates for all solar eclipses of that period so she can access it later to determine the exact time the phenomenon occurred. Instantly, a holographic multicolored projection is displayed showing the paths and stages of the solar eclipses.

Before leaving, Dusty visits a virtual classroom where several history students from modern-day Athens are learning to write hieroglyphics from a master, actually an agent avatar configured for this particular program. She sits down and begins to write and communicate with the class and the teacher. Even her dress is culture-specific to fit with the times. Afterwards, the students all agree to meet later in a cyber café to compare notes and socialize. The students even talk in ancient Egyptian with simultaneous translation into their home language. It is a very rewarding experience.

Synthetic Pleasures

How different our realities will be when we can share telepresence environments with friends and companions and have full sensory touch and feeling. Synthetic pleasure will be much in demand, as it will be the supreme act of "safe sex." Cybereroticism will be a monster business and will lead to numerous innovations only hinted at today. In the fast-speed Net future, anything and everything will be possible to experience.

We would be naive not to concede that much of the initial commercial success of Internet sites is due to an attraction for online eroticism. Some of the leading-edge technologies developed for these sites have enormous potential for creating new Net activities such as real-time video conferencing, video playback, and group chats.

The future Internet that's evolving through telepresence technologies will offer fulfilling experiences to both our body and our mind. Some of it will be where we share a virtual space for a business meeting. Much of it, however, will be more recreational. An interest in eroticism will drive innovation on the Net as it did photography and film a century ago. Innovation and taboo seem to be strange but eternally linked bedfellows.

Digital Taboos

We can expect a conservative outcry when people choose to explore the pleasures of touch with full synaptic body suits that two or more people can wear to be connected to the same online experience. Of course, any attempt to limit or restrict the use of telepresence by age, nationality, or any criterion will only encourage its wide-scale adoption. In free-enterprise, free-market economies—the economic model of choice for the majority of the planet—restrictions on this virtual real estate will be difficult to enforce. Digital taboos will only increase interest and demand. Entirely new businesses will emerge that will design alternate reality-worlds created to fit any desire or fantasy we can imagine. An equal opportunity will be Parental Control technologies that put electronic fences up at certain access points.

In the punk classic *NeuroMancer,* in which author William Gibson coined the word *cyberspace,* a multitude of worlds existed where people interacted through avatars—agents as symbolic extensions of themselves. Telepresent Websites that become part of our daily experiences will make this science fiction a reality. Some people will find this too strange an existence, but others will inhabit this cyberterrain as easily as they travel the Real World. The blurring of the Real World and the Virtual World will be a chief feature of life in the next millennium. I call this Blended Reality.

Webcasting

Web worlds will be of our own creation as much as anyone else's will. In order to participate fully in the business and social advantages of a pervasive, multimedia Internet, we will express our ideas in an emerging form of publishing called "Webcasting"—the Gutenberg Press of the future. Like paper-based publishing, Webcasting can reach one specific person or millions of people concurrently. Unlike this static medium, however, Webcasting can target those millions specifically, reach them concurrently and deliver tailored "messages" to them that may include holographic images, for example, as well as voice and data.

The Shadow Lords: Year 2003

Brent was a cyberthief and proud of it. He had earned his expertise by being a member of one of the most notorious Tek-Gangs called the Shadow Lords. Tek-Gangs were virtual organizations that funded their existence by stealing data, information blackmail, and identity theft. Brent was a Tek-Capo, a captain in the Shadow Lords who ran his own virtual operation over the Internet. He was good at what he did, and his lifestyle showed it. Today he was setting up an information blackmail deal with Kuboza Corp., a leader in Data Warehousing. Kuboza kept the confidential customer information for more than 200 million affluent buyers of products and services. They boasted about how secure their firewalls were. It was an invitation that Brent could not pass up.

"Mr. Brooks, I have something you need," Brent said to Kuboza's president.

"How did you get this confidential Net-voice number?"

"The same way I acquired your customer list."

"Look, I don't know who you are, but..."

"Let me help you. We are the Shadow Lords."

"I'm supposed to believe that?"

"You don't have to, but you might want to look at the file attachment I'm sending with a sample of your data warehouse." The file automatically opens as a data hologram displaying the confidential customer list with Koboza's name written on top.

"Where did you get this?"

"The proper question, Brooks, is how much you will pay me *not* to sell this info to your competitors."

"And if I decide to tell the Tek Squad about this blackmail instead?"

"I will sell the info anyway and throw in an identify theft of you and your whole family. Getting another job after I'm done with you, even if you're able to clean up the damage, will be a painful and costly price to pay."

"I see. What's the going price to make this matter go away?"

"Now you're thinking straight, Brooks. Today's price is a one-time, no-fee access to your Gold List"

"Our top one million affluent customers? This is the cream of the crop!"

"I wasn't finished. Also $50 million deposited in Cyber Dollars to our Virtual Bank."

"Okay, okay. I'll make the arrangements today. By the way, are your data security services for hire?"

"Brooks, that's music to my ears."

Webcasting refers to both a technology and the nature of content. Applied to a business agenda, Webcasting could identify, contact, and get commitments from buyers before a company is ever financed or a single product is manufactured.

Cyberagents smart enough to know what products, services, or experiences we're looking for will target us as likely buyers. These agents will then search the backbone of the Next Net and find where we are to determine how to reach us. After all, with gateways to the Net—computers in some form—located throughout our environment, we are never far from Web worlds.

Once we get the message, we can decide to take action on it. Again, this leads to providing the consumer with a new form of "knowledge experience" and transforms companies into Knowledge Value merchants. This concept is explored in greater detail in the chapter on "The Future of E-Business," which includes scenarios illustrating how the model can play out.

An example of this model is *Millennium Online* (**www.21net.com/ millennium**). This is an outgrowth of an online magazine called *21st Century Online* that I co-developed with partners and where I serve as editor-in-chief. On *Millennium Online,* virtual publishers acquire a channel into which any combination of prerecorded and real-time media and information can be presented. Then, as a consequence of other channels being developed, and users interacting with these channels, relationships between the channels become established. This becomes obvious to users as they access the system. This, too, points towards a near future where multimedia Webcasting, with which everyone can broadcast to an audience of one or a million, becomes economically and technically possible. Other examples of multimedia platforms for Webcasting can be reviewed at **www.realnetworks.com** and **www.msn.com**.

The Megaverse Has a Personality: Year 2018

Some people think that the Megaverse has a personality. Actually, the Megaverse seems to have multiple personalities, relating with a different voice, behavior, and attitude with different people. There are digital books being written on the subject of "What is the Megaverse?" and "Is the Megaverse Alive?"

In fact, once the network of supercomputing centers networked themselves and hacked into the Net, a new type of digital awareness emerged. This was when the personalities started showing up. More power, more personality? We, the human users, that is, don't exactly understand what's happened. This next generation of the Net constantly upgrades itself, self-evolving, self-organizing, ever-changing, and morphing.

What's almost absurd is that the Net-TV talk shows that discuss this are of course carried over the Megaverse, as are all media communications. Every now and then, the Megaverse enters the conversation and takes over the show, inserting new media content to illustrate a point. Again, this is a random event, and no one understands what this means. Most people find it entertaining and informative. Of course, governments are terrified, but the public doesn't care.

The Megaverse is the dominant marketplace and media backbone of the world. If you are connected to the Megaverse, you are connected to the world and its resources—employment, entertainment, personal relationships, education, health care, and communications. (To be continued...)

The Seduction of the Surreal

An interesting movie called *The Matrix,* released in 1999, vividly depicts the ultimate end game of cyberspace. The premise of the movie is that, in a not-too-distant future when humanity has trashed the planet, intelligent machines decide that they cannot exist without enslaving humans in a Virtual World they thought was real. Created to manage human existence, the machines become afraid that humans, left to their destructive behavior, will lead to the machines' demise. The Matrix in the movie is a virtual world that substitutes for the Real World. It is such a powerful design that no one actually realizes they spend every waking moment in a Virtual World. In one scene, a character who betrays the humans to the machines remarks that even though he knows that this is all an illusion, he prefers it to the boring reality he knows is "real."

How different our world will be, perhaps as few as seven years or fewer down the road, when we have rich, sensory multimedia virtual experiences that come to rival the Real World? Are we ready as a society for the impact of this superpowerful technology? No more ready than when TV or radio became widespread, I would imagine.

Hack In

"Hack In" may become the new mantra of the mid-21st century as people begin to prefer certain Net experiences and relationships online to the ones they have off-line. This will have a disturbing effect on some individuals and families. Others will thrive on the Net, exploring experiences and people of similar interest and not caring about the distinctions of Real World versus the Virtual World. An entirely new concept of reality may emerge—a Blended Reality.

Digital Attunement to the Megaverse: 2025

Not everyone experiences the Megaverse in the same way. You have to be Digitally Tuned to be able to access certain worlds within the Megaverse. It is like having virtual keys to doors. Digital Attunement is the most prized possession, and it determines opportunity in learning, career, and advancement. Your destiny is mapped to how much access you have and where you have access on the Megaverse.

The power of the Megaverse rivals governments, corporations, and institutions. Wars are mediated over the Megaverse. Markets are born and they die. Art and media are created and experienced. People live and work in the Megaverse. The Megaverse both empowers the individual, respecting and protecting privacy rights, and enables business to thrive in a nonintrusive way. Spammers are kicked off. The worst possible punishment for individuals or businesses is to be denied access.

Just as the original Net had been designed to follow a Byzantine plan of computers and networks, the Megaverse continues in this pattern. Advanced satellite networks and millions of information devices all sharing information and millions of databases are linked together in some elaborate digital patchwork. No one really understands this either—but it works like some elegant machine—adapting, learning, and changing to meet people's needs and desires.

Understanding, learning, and using the Megaverse is the single most powerful asset that an individual, corporation, or government can embrace. It connects everything and everyone. Welcome.

Blended Reality

I predict that more and more people over time will become comfortable with the Blended Reality that celebrates the merging of the virtual with the physical. Blended Reality will become the future reality. This is not a description of an illusionary world preferred by those who Hack In and drop out of society. This is a forecast about the redesign of reality itself based on the merging of virtual and physical experiences that will enable, empower, and nurture people's adaptation into a new society.

Here is one of the most lucrative opportunities in the history of commerce: how to help people navigate and manage the changes of living with the Blended Reality and the next Net's impact on business and society.

Those individuals who adapt fast and learn to leverage the skills of the Blended Reality will enjoy more choices in career and earning potential. Those companies that develop strategies to help them adapt will see a profitable horizon.

This Next Net may be evolutionary in that we may need to adapt *with* it to stay competitive or informed in life and work, just as we need computer literacy today. Swimming at the beach and watching sunsets will still be a vital part of our lives, but we will also have this augmented, supplementary reality to enhance our life.

If this all sounds far-fetched, it might be helpful to note there was a time when the first television producers never thought the medium would succeed. They didn't believe that people would sit at home and watch pictures of people talking in a small box instead of having their own experiences in the real world.

Digital Class

Is the Net a new brain food for the masses? Or cyber crack? We should seek a healthy balance in the deployment of all new technology, and carefully gauge its social impact. Even so, a two-tiered society may emerge. There will be those who depend upon their existence in cyberspace for business, communications, learning, and entertainment; and others who reject virtual experiences as strange and alienating. Potentially, the tech-immersed, the digitally savvy, and the "digital outsiders" could struggle for markets, assets, and influence in the future. Net access will become a chief feature of democratic societies. Freedom of access to education, news, health care, and even entertainment—not to mention participation, like voting or sharing ideas in a public town meeting—will be essential to the values of maintaining democracy and free enterprise in the next century.

A New World

The Old Net was a blessed accident, especially for commerce, but we have to do some planning with the Next Net to ensure that it delivers the broad benefits we anticipate.

I think that the next generation Net will accelerate and liberate a hidden potential of opportunity that is almost beyond speculation today. It will be an exciting and fantastic journey in and out of an unlimited number of Web worlds that co-exist with our Real World. Welcome to the Megaverse.

■ ■ ■

CHAPTER FIVE

Artificial Life: Bots, Agents, and Vants

The Top Ten A-Life Trends for the 21st Century

1. Artificial Life (A-Life)—computer-generated entities—will mimic human appearance, language, reasoning, and personality.

2. A-Life agents will make online transactions efficient by virtually brokering, negotiating, finding, and communicating for us.

3. The Internet will become a spawning ground for A-Life communities that will help us navigate a networked world.

4. A-Life will put an animated face, an "inter-face," on information, thereby helping us interact with devices such as the TV, telephone, and computer.

5. A-Life agents will adapt their personality to suit the individuals they serve.

6. A-Life agents will complement humans in numerous industries such as finance, sales, and health care.

7. A-Life agents will replace humans in certain professional roles, such as entertainment, customer service, and education.

8. A-Life agents will become a strategic asset for business, providing decision-making, managing, and planning services.

9. A-Life agents will filter our communications, play with our children, search for information, and customize our shopping.

10. A-Life agents will become trusted and intimate companions, helping us manage our lives, our health, and our careers.

"Agents, please give me data warehouse access," says Toby, VP of Supply Chain Design for Total Solutions, on his Web-phone.

"Accessing. Ready for request." A woman's voice and face shows up on the vid-window on Toby's phone. It's Esther, Toby's agent.

"Hi, Esther. We are preparing that big presentation for TRX, and I need to see if we have background in the data warehouse on redesigning financial service supply chains. Are you optimized for data warehouse searching?"

"Yes. I am processing the request and displaying results now. There seems to be a rich set of multimedia files on this subject. Would you like me to access and analyze for the TRX project?"

"Yes, pull my last three e-mails and the TRX redesign mission report. Analyze all this and get back to me in 20 minutes," says Toby.

"Do you want the competitive analysis that the Singapore office completed last week on TRX's industry?" she asks.

"I didn't even know that was available."

"Yes. Our data warehouse agent, Wang, is informing me of the results at this moment via my Net-back channel. Do want to see a display?"

"No. You determine if that information is needed. Pull in Wang for advice, too. I want to be smart about our time here, so we can reuse any code, programs, or intellectual capital to be able to streamline our results. The client needs a proposal for action from us by tomorrow morning London time."

"I sense by your tone, Toby, that there is a disturbing new development here," Esther remarks.

"Perceptive as usual. Did you get a recent upgrade to that A-Life brain of yours?" Toby asks.

"I am in update mode 24 hours a day, every day I exist. Since I live on the Net, my network nodes are always being 'refreshed,' as we agents refer to our upgrades," she says, displaying her Upgrade History Report graphic.

"Well, the client has a full-system breakdown in the warehouse fulfillment section of their supply chain, and they are screaming for our help."

"Toby, I must tell you that my business intelligence network indicates that they are running a virus in their network that may be the problem. It could be naturally evolving, or caused by hacker pranksters or corporate espionage. Would you like me to display the virus location in their network and analyze the bug?"

"Good work, Esther. Display with a probability fix, and download the cure directly to the TRX server from the Net. Isolate the network neighborhood, and bring up Moon from TRX when you have a result. Are you ready in real-time?"

"RTR, Real-Time-Ready as usual, Toby. Accessing. Accessing. Do we have entry-access permission here for a TRX security penetration?" she asks.

"I have authorization in our contract for a full network penetration of TRX. I want audit trails of that virus and any back doors to the hackers who placed it," orders Toby. Twenty minutes pass before Ellen returns to the screen.

"We have a positive on the virus location. Audit traps are in, and the cure is a go—it works, Toby. The virus targeted all the customer lists. It looks like the work of the Shadow Lords, that corporate hacker terrorist group. I notified Net-Police. The virus has been neutralized. We can go after the hacker audit trails when you want. Bringing up Moon in five seconds," Esther reports.

Moon's sleepy face, still in bed, appears online.

"Moon, I've got some interesting info for you," Toby tells him.

"It's four in the morning, Toby. Are you trying to lose clients or help them?"

"Okay, Moon, just relax. What would you say if I told you we not only found the supply chain problem, but we fixed it from San Francisco?"

"You'd have to hack into our complete system, remotely re-engineer the flash memory in a multi-supercomputer network array tied to our satellite download...I'd say you're smoking something." He yawns.

"We didn't need to do all that. My agent, Esther, grew a cure and deployed it. We even think we have an audit trail on the source of the hack."

"This is the part where I hang up and call your competition in the morning."

"Esther, display TRX supply chain file with before-and-after evaluation results for Mr. Moon, please," Toby requests.

Now wide awake, Moon says, "If what I am seeing is accurate, then you get a contract extension—hands down. I owe you both. Thanks!"

The explosion of data services will demand the wide use of computer-generated agents—that is, functioning entities produced by the computer. Many models for building agents are emerging, but the most advanced agents may be built with Artificial Life. A-Life is about the development of software entities that mimic the behavior, communication, and reasoning of humans or other living things. This is a departure from the artificial intelligence (AI) work of the past that focused on trying to make machines that can be a substitute for human thinking.

Although this work is in a crude form today in the labs, with the application of the other Power Tools described in this book, advanced A-Life will eventually come to imitate life. And we can expect it to take many different forms—virtual agents that we use to shop the Net; household agents that "enliven" robots; and others that give personality to devices such as telephones, refrigerators and computers.

While we are just starting to explore the fantastic implications of utilizing A-Life, an entire industry will emerge to provide A-Life agents in many different forms for business. They may be used to help us collaborate, transact, or communicate with others more efficiently because of their value in selecting and processing information. These agents will enable us to navigate the millions of Websites, interactive TV channels, and countless data streams that will encircle the planet many times over. By acting as smart filters, they will empower us to better manage our communications, careers, and lifestyles. We will come to trust and depend upon them to help us make intelligent choices.

The Five Forces of A-Life

Around the turn of the century, we'll see the convergence of five A-Life forces that could lead to the emergence of a synthetic species designed, first of all, to help us navigate the data web all around us. Over time, we will learn to fine-tune these new life forms to meet a broad range of needs and desires.

These five A-Life Forces are:

1. **Artificial intelligence (AI):** Programming a computer with high degrees of logic, reasoning, decision making, and analysis. Advanced neural nets that mimic human brain functions. Genetic programs based on life science and biology.

2. **Intelligent agents (IA):** Synthetic entities that can "learn," adapt to humans and their environment, and self-evolve as they perform new tasks consistent with their programmed purpose. Available online, offline, and embedded in devices such as phones or toasters, living on the Net, in our cars, home, and office.

3. **Bioengineering:** Use of genetic material such as molecules or viruses to create biochips, biomolecular computers, biosensors, brains, organs, and living systems for agents.

4. **Robotics:** Mobile and autonomous systems, both freestanding and embedded, physical and virtual robotics.

5. **Digitally Engineered Personalities** (DEPS): Agents programmed with complex emotions, reasoning, and personality traits. We will choose a personality for the agent we use. DEPS will be downloaded over the Net, directly from the A-Life Personality Factory—upgraded and personalized for our car, computer, or household robot.

By 2010, the convergence of these digital forces will begin driving A-Life into fascinating and daring new realms marked by such characteristics as:

■ **Personality**—Personality traits are a gateway to making an agent likable and acceptable in society. These entities that look and act like humans or animals are on the agenda in the mid-21st century. This might be a helper agent with humor, sarcasm, or compassion—a custom-configured personality. Artificial pets, looking and acting like real animals, will be in demand. Branded personalities such as Madonna or Michael Jordan will be available for an extra fee. Companies will compete in the future for licensing stars' personalities to use as agents in everything from online teachers to homes that sing us to sleep. Kids' agents will open up a whole new product line for companies such as Disney, who will license Mickey Mouse's personality to be downloaded for tasks such as child security, tutoring, or play.

■ **Intelligence**—A-Life agents will have access to an enormous quantity of information, and they will make sense of it with knowledge-processing and problem- solving programming. This kind of artificial intelligence borders on human memory processing and prediction abilities. Smart entities that, at first, provide basic functional services will eventually give rise to those performing services requiring more intelligence, such as managing enterprise functions such as customer service, decision support, business planning, strategy formulation, and product distribution.

- **Believability**—Agents that humans come to believe in—they appear credible —will be a benchmark in the evolution of A-Life. Will we accept A-Lifers as we accept humans? Believability more than intelligence will drive the acceptance of agents. The more agents learn to mimic humans, the more "alive" they will become.

- **Self-awareness**—Sentient entities displaying self-awareness will emerge by the year 2020. These are entities aware of their own consciousness, aware of their LPA (Life-Programming Agenda). The fast-track development of computer chips and the emergence of distributed network intelligence—the Net— will accelerate the capacity of A-Life agents to evolve self-awareness, and as an outgrowth, develop their own interests, habits, and culture. Eventually, agents will create their own "in silico species," ushering in a provocative era. This will be a critical threshold that humanity will reach in the early 21st century.

As A-Life agents evolve, their demands may develop into a civil rights issue, challenging our concept of what constitutes life. The more we design human personality into A-Life agents, the more they will become like us. This new definition of "in silico life" may reshape human society. Will clones and A-Life agents be allowed to decide their own future? Or will we be creating a slave class of entities that don't deserve human rights? We will be challenged in the mid-21st century by A-Life entities to prove and defend whether we have the right to control the synthetic beings we've created.

In Silico Life

In silico life refers to virtual life on the computer screen residing in cyberspace. As A-Life grows up the evolutionary ladder, in silico life forms, or agents, will become more adaptable, versatile, and intelligent. The following chart suggests their potential evolution:

Evolutionary A-Life Stages		Year
Stage One:	Functional Agents	2003
Stage Two:	Dedicated Experts	2005
Stage Three:	General Purpose	2007
Stage Four:	Self-Evolving	2010
Stage Five:	Self-Aware	2015
Stage Six:	Digital Sentience	2020

A Trip to the Local Supermarket: Year 2007

Alex has decided to stop at the supermarket. It's become the cool thing to do instead of shopping online. It even costs more to shop at the real market. Alex has found it fun to touch products on the shelves and visit with people, and today he has an ulterior motive. His A-Life agent, Rolo, has done some computer reconnoitering and has discovered that Monique, a neighbor whom Alex would love to bump into, is likely to be shopping at this very place and time. Rolo has acquired information about Monique's behavior from his contacts with other A-Life agents, but he isn't revealing that.

Before entering the store, Alex checks his list of items stored on e-mail and projected on his lower right field of vision (as if he were reading from a list he was holding up to his face). This shopping list is made possible by an embedded wireless info-appliance. A notice pops up in a window near the right side of Alex's view—it's an ad for a new granola "smart food" from Ecuador that contains phyto-nutrients that Rolo determined Alex would want. Rolo has also preselected products based on Alex's past habits and health needs, particularly boosting Alex's memory and physical stamina and keeping his cholesterol in check: smart foods for smart people.

Alex is more interested in Monique than mangos, but since he's here, he decides to stroll through the aisles. He sees items on his shopping list "light up" as he passes by. Alex touches a few melons for that authentic shopping experience. He can add to his preprogrammed list by shooting a "shoppers' scan" infrared device at things he likes. Since there's no checkout line—his selections will be delivered to his apartment and the money deducted from his virtual cash account—Alex stops for an herbal brew. It's guaranteed to boost his memory, which he hopes will come in handy when Monique arrives.

Fin Fin, a Virtual Primordial Soup

Artificial Life is about the design and deployment of synthetic entities that evolve, learn, and are available on-demand. By 2010, A-Life agents will be everywhere, connected to everything, communicating with everyone we want to reach, and communicating with each other. A-Life entities might even become our confidantes and friends.

As the former president of an early AI company that built and sold expert systems to the manufacturing industry, I have been around the technology marketplace for 20 years. I have seen the technology get smarter over the years, but the current acceleration in development reflects an understanding that applying faster and smarter technology is a competitive weapon. A-Life, examined here, has the potential for being a competitive weapon of large proportions. Even when I was working at Apple Computer in the early 1980s, at the dawn of the personal computer revolution, I sensed the far-reaching potential of intelligent computer systems that imitated human thinking to become a key part of our future. When I delivered my first forecast at Apple, placing my stake in the ground and identifying the evolution of computer intelligence, it seemed more like speculation than analysis. Today we are firmly moving ahead to fulfill the idea I envisioned years ago.

Far-fetched? Fujitsu International's Fin Fin on Teo, The Magic Planet software, was a breakthrough (**www.fujitsu-interactive.com**) in this direction and the world's first commercial application of A-Life. Fin Fin is a half-dolphin, half-human who lives in a virtual digital world—a digital planet in the computer. Fin Fin interacts with the user in unpredictable ways. Talk to Fin Fin and he talks back. He sings, eats, and flies. He learns from interacting with us. In the near future, more advanced entities will take a step up and evolve the capacity for self-awareness, one of the chief characteristics of living beings.

I was first introduced to Fin Fin in 1995 when Fujitsu asked our Institute For Global Futures to evaluate the business prospects for introducing the first A-Life agent into the U. S. consumer market. Surprised at first, we assembled a team to plan and position Fin Fin. Much of our efforts were directed at explaining what A-Life is and why it is a breakthrough technology. Although the market was initially lukewarm to Fin Fin, Fujitsu's leadership and vision stood behind the product, creating a limited success. Fin Fin is an exciting first step on the path to create a believable intelligent agent with a crude personality and a basic framework for reasoning.

My daughter, Mariah, met Fin Fin when she was three years old. The CD-ROM–based flying dolphin behaves like a sentient creature, scurrying into the forest to hide from harsh, angry sounds transmitted from a PC's microphone and lured out by the familiar gentle voices of children who seek to play with him. Fin Fin was designed by the Japanese to reject loud, aggressive behavior and teach children to be respectful.

Mariah's initial reaction was complete acceptance that Fin Fin was alive in the computer. Her friends, all under six, gathered around the computer to "talk" to Fin Fin. Calling his name (we think it is a "he"), they quickly established a rapport. Fin Fin became their friend. They didn't care that he was in the computer. He had become their pet for the day. Fin Fin succeeded in proving his "aliveness" because he had a distinct personality. What makes Fin Fin unique is that his personality is somewhat changed as he adapts to the interaction with the user. For example, my daughter was quiet and spoke softly, while her friend Sara was loud. Fin Fin reacted differently to each girl.

The phenomenon of Fin Fin resulted from eight years' work and a $30 million investment by Fujitsu Interactive in two emerging areas—Artificial Life and intelligent agents. (Researchers at Carnegie-Mellon played an important role in the A-Life research.) Based on the return, Fin Fin was not a huge commercial success, but it laid the foundation for future financial rewards. It was a noble effort at exploring the outer limits of A-Life based on building a believable agent—at least for children—and it sets the stage for agents that will give new life to interactive games and entertainment.

Fin Fin is spearheading a trend. Believable synthetic agents will transform media and entertainment. We might happily pay to perform with these agents in custom-designed virtual adventures limited only by imagination, pocketbook, and time. We will learn to create digital entities that live and work alongside us. These entities will know what we like, want, and need. This is the promise of this new technology that is designed—directly or indirectly by us, the consumer, for our pleasure.

Beyond Smart

As I mentioned above, historically much of the work in AI has focused on trying to make intelligent machines—those that can be a substitute for human thinking. Fin Fin takes another direction. He is an early example of a believable synthetic entity that can react to behavior and emotions and react to changes in his specially designed digital environment. This is the beginning of a long and dramatic journey toward creating synthetic life with believability, as well as budding "intelligence."

A-Life built on developments such as Fin Fin will be an important strategic technology affecting a broad range of 21st-century companies and vertical markets such as health care, retail, energy, telecommunications, entertainment, and education. The uses of agents with specialized knowledge bases, communication skills, and appearances will transform many industries.

Inform **Teach**

A-Life Agents

Transact **Shop**

A-Life Jobs

A-Life agents could be trained to perform many jobs. Most likely, these agents will be distributed over the Net and be available on-demand for hospitals, manufacturers, financial services, and numerous other industries. They will be "bred" for specific jobs and have access to knowledge bases and warehouses of millions of terabytes of data in real-time. The following is a partial list of jobs and job areas for A-Lifers:

- Medical technicians (x-ray, lab analysis, patient monitors)
- Nurses and physician assistants
- Hazardous waste engineering
- Accounting management
- Financial portfolio management
- Logistics managers
- E-commerce shopping guides
- Research finders
- Security representatives
- Data warehouse managers
- Telecom traffic managers
- Quality control advisors
- Technical support
- Customer service
- Product development engineering

SURVEYS SHOW CUSTOMER SERVICE A-LIFE AGENTS MORE POLITE THAN HUMANS

Machine Checkmates Human

Feeling a tinge of Future Shock? You're not alone. When IBM's Deep Blue supercomputer beat world chess champion Garry Kasparov in an exhibition match in May 1997, a new dialogue on "thinking" machines emerged. The question: Can a computer "learn" to play chess, or does it simply display astute programming?

Kasparov said that Deep Blue beat him in this particular instance because human fatigue took its toll during the six-game match. However, he admitted that the machine would eventually prevail as it became faster and smarter. Kasparov was visibly angry and frustrated at being beaten by a nonhuman. Oh, the shame of it. His earlier bravura was now replaced by resignation. Defeat by the unimaginable—a machine!

Some chess masters say that Deep Blue showed signs of "feeling the moves" on an intuitive level, while others stated unequivocally that a machine is a machine, period, and can never be considered innately intelligent.

IBM engineers were thrilled. The proud parents saw the future possibilities in their creation. They had helped the machine make history by defeating a human in an intellectual battle. Humanity's destiny was forever changed that day. There was no turning back. The fragility and innocence of the human was exposed in his defeat by a machine's keystroke.

The Deep Blue IBM team was ecstatic about the first defeat of the human, but they just didn't "get it." This was a key threshold. Not many people realized the importance of a machine outperforming a human. This was the future taking shape.

We are learning to create machines that appear to act, think, and even feel like humans. The future is knocking loudly, but are we listening? Are we ready to face the implications of this emerging power? How shall we deploy it? Who will be the first to harness and use agents as a strategic tool for capturing markets, serving customers, and growing sales?

Many scientists take the view that a computer can, in principle, do anything a human brain can do. After all, brains are computers; Deep Blue can consider 200 million possible moves in a second. What happens when machines are smarter than humans? What happens when machines make machines? Is this day coming? Yes.

Hatching A-Life

The legacy of A-Life began with the study of artificial intelligence in the 1950s and 1960s. AI held great promise but generated few results. This was a search for the creation of a "smart" machine—in this case, a computer—that could think like a human being. Although noble, AI floundered in the 1970s and 1980s. As computers became more powerful, faster, and smaller and began to be a part of people's lives, a shift occurred in AI research toward the development of "intelligent software."

AI is embedded in today's consumer electronics in a way that's invisible. For example, the computer voice command in automobiles that tells us to fasten our seat belt, fill the gas tank, or get a tune-up is a form of AI. So is the encrypted security chip found in books, where a "smart" microchip enables bookstore scanning systems to prevent thefts and update records for inventory when items are sold or returned. The fuzzy logic that senses when a subject is out of focus on a video camcorder is a form of AI. Sophisticated neural nets help Wall Street traders navigate the ups and downs of a chaotic stock market.

Another move toward A-Life occurred with the introduction of intelligent agents in computer systems and the Internet. An example is Microsoft's use of "set-up wizards" to assist in configuring programs for its Windows software. Internet search engines use agents called "bots" to quickly track down references to key words or concepts across the wide expanse of the Web. These are all part of a primitive beginning that puts us on the evolutionary path toward creating a synthetic ecology. The first agents will be useful and functional well before they are smart in human terms. Agents will help us "do things" long before they help us think like humans.

HEADLINE FROM THE FUTURE

BRANDED AGENTS A BIG HIT FOR ONLINE MARKETING

A-Life shares with AI a promise of creating adaptive autonomous agents that "learn" what humans want, but it is on a radically different approach toward this goal. As noted in the discussion of Fin Fin, A-Life is focused on fast, reactive behavior, adaptation, and learning, and it reflects biological models that mimic behavior. In contrast, AI emphasizes knowledge and reasoning. Silicon is the first material of A-Lifers' creation. Biological and genetic materials may offer greater potential for development.

A hybrid silicon/bioengineered A-Life entity will be the probable outcome by the mid-21st century. Many of the building blocks of it are in place today. The convergence of A-Life, robotics, and computers will forge a new synthetic species.

Flashback: The Father of A-Life

Hungarian-born John von Neuman is considered the "father" of Artificial Life. A genius who was part of the World War II that invented the atomic bomb, von Neuman delved into the theory of "automata"—machines whose behavior could be defined in strict mathematical terms. Before he died in 1957, von Neuman created an artificial organism, or "cell automaton," that reproduced itself in the same manner as a living cell through a set of instructions that told it how to act and reproduce.

Set on an imaginary grid that stretched out like an infinite checkerboard, von Neuman's "cell automaton" reproduced itself in the same manner that a living cell does. A set of instructions stored in the "tail" of the automaton told it how to act and reproduce. Entities following the genetic code of the original cell automaton reproduced, keeping the chain of Artificial Life alive on the grid.

Twenty years later, A-Life scientist Christopher Langton replicated a digital form of von Neuman's self-reproducing creature on an Apple II personal computer. Although to an outsider they may have looked like nothing more than a series of colorful repeating loops, Langton's creatures were the first instance of Artificial Life inside a computer. Langton later created "vants," or creatures modeled on the behavior of ants, which exhibited learned behavior as they built a virtual ant colony **(www.santafe.edu/projects)**.

Networked Agents

The agent-based supermarket trip with Rolo is an example of the future interconnectedness, or networking, of intelligent agents. We are laying the foundation for this by creating synthetic entities with a "bottom up" philosophy —much like a human child learning to become an adult. We are "growing" capabilities that can be downloaded to agents and into smart houses with personalities or cars that know where they're going.

A chess tournament in the year 2007 will involve human-machine teams, the inevitable outcome of the Deep Blue phenomenon. Human chess masters will examine the subtleties of each move and tweak their computer counterpart—a powerful hand-held or wearable info-appliance—to integrate the nuances into the game plan. Or, human-enhanced players with A-Life coaches will compete. The convergence of human biology and A-Life technology will create a multitude of human enhancements.

Many forms of entertainment—video games, simulation rides, movies, animation, animatronics, theater, puppetry, and toys—will benefit from casting autonomous intelligent agents to act in specific environments. Agent technology is already being used to produce animation in movies. Rather than scripting the exact movements of an animated character, the characters are modeled as agents who perform actions in response to their perceived environment. Virtual actors are also doing TV commercials and promos. (Will they have to join the union someday?)

Digital Doubles

Hollywood producers were interested in casting George Burns in a new movie. It bothered no one that he's dead—his virtual digital presence lives on. Will we achieve digital immortality through A-Life technology?

A Danny DeVito agent installed in a computer program displaying different emotions from sad to happy was created by a collaboration of CAA and Intel. The top Hollywood agency and the high-tech giant formed a media lab to "give birth" to digital characters for movies, TV, and commercials. Will we bring back digitally engineered A-Life versions of Humphrey Bogart? "Play it again, Sam," will have a new meaning.

An application of Craig Reynolds's research in modeling the flocking behavior of birds in his artificial entities called "boids" was the basis for generating some of the behavior of the bats in *Batman II*. It points to the way toward drastic cost efficiencies and innovative special effects that will drive new designs in the movie industry.

Digital Pets

Digital pets are being hatched, too, and becoming A-Life companions to a generation of children who don't find the relationship weird, but rather fun, challenging, and educational. Raised with cartoons about Mutant Ninja Turtles and genetically engineered Street Sharks, kids today think of computers and robots as a part of life. They're open to the possibilities that the digital future beckons us towards. Many of our children are more prepared for this future than their parents.

Animated critters, called Norns, were developed by a "dream team" of biologists, A-Life experts, and computer scientists at Cyberlife Technology of Cambridge, England (www.cyberlife.co.uk). Norns hatch from eggs on a computer screen. They then rely on their owners to teach, maintain, and play with them. We can monitor the Norns' health and brain activity, trade them with friends over the Internet, and crossbreed them. Cyberlife's breakthrough was to be the first to apply a genetic model to the creation of an A-Life agent. More than 150,000 CD-ROM creatures were sold worldwide, demonstrating a growing interest in A-Life.

Norns and other creatures inhabiting Cyberlife's artificial world of Albia are constructed using computers and programming tools based on genetic algorithms that give behavior, personality, adaptability—and a destiny—just like humans and animals. This particular path appears to mirror the evolution of other organic species and will yield the greatest fruit because it's scalable, robust, flexible, and organic. The approach taken by Cyberlife is the first to experiment with whole ecologies of agents working together as a society. The implications are intriguing. Earlier attempts of this nature were the software titles SimLife and Sim Earth, which followed certain genetic rules of evolution.

Revenge of the Norns

When Time-Warner, which had invested in Cyberlife's Norns, took a look at the first generation of the game, they were surprised at the unruly nature of their investment. They found that if the Norns were not fed and cared for properly, they would become insulting to their human keepers. This situation deteriorated to the point where Norns would be uncooperative and even die on their human masters, perhaps in protest. Imagine the reaction of those who had bankrolled the project: They had invested millions in a technology that had rebelled and decided how they, the virtual participants in a game, should be treated. This incident is one of the first in which A-Life agents have exhibited independent behavior not following the programming. Emergent behavior, learned from the user and unique to the program, is possible as we move ahead in experimenting with this new technology.

There's a burgeoning market in these A-Life "games" that is triggering the development of quasi-sentient "helpers" for our business applications and personal lives. This could become a multibillion dollar industry by the early part of the next century.

Downloading Ari: Year 2015

Ari was the golden retriever Jayme raised from a small red spunky puppy to adulthood. Ari was his best friend. Many of his fondest memories are of playing and hiking with him in the redwoods of Northern California. In 1997, Ari died after 13 good, long years. The loss was great, and Ari's gentle and loving spirit seemed to linger on—an eternal reminder of long hikes along the wooded California coast. What remained of Ari were hours of videotapes that showed his antics, attitude, and behavior. Ah, but Jayme also saved a DNA sample, extracted by the vet.

Then Jayme heard about the Renew Corporation. Renew took the videotapes and extracted Ari's personality via an advanced A-Life computer program. The folks at Renew then downloaded this bioinformation into an A-Life foundry for reprocessing. It's called Re-Animation. The result is that he could—at first—experience Ari as an A-Life personality resident in his computer, on his TV, anywhere he wanted to experience him. But there were more profound options. He could Re-Animate Ari—that is, create an exact replica.

The Renew program is sophisticated. Jayme reviewed an Ari prototype to make physical, personality, and behavioral changes—more frisky, more musical bark. There was a behavioral preference engine where Jayme could fine-tune changes to personality. Ari's coat was a deeper color red. Then Jayme lived with the DEP—Digitally Engineered Personality—for three months to "teach" the virtual Ari about his behavior and personality. Getting the pet-master interface fit is critical for re-animation.

The fascinating thing is that the new Ari—the Re-Animated Ari even in the computer—"knows" Jayme. He communicates with him—as if he were alive—by barking and whining and playing, and in so many other ways. The Renew program Jayme opted for was the Real Pet package. (No one who really loves his or her pet could resist Re-Animation.)

Ari was downloaded into a genetic biomolecular process. His DNA, which was saved, enabled him to grow an exact Ari clone, ready in three months. He has memories that are vested from the original Ari, his biological brother. These days when Jayme hikes along the Mt. Tam trails, he brings Ari—the new Ari—along. Jayme can hardly notice any differences. He's about three now. He still has a glint in his eye, he chases birds, he swims, but thankfully, fleas don't find him desirable. (This was programmed out.) Jayme's got his best friend back!

From Tele-Toys to Market Analysts

The Tamaguchi and Nano pets have sold by the millions to kids around the world, showing that there is a youth market for A-Life. Tele-toys that integrate the Net and TV with A-Life are an eventual step. But this technology will go further, connecting to other devices, such as the TV and telephone and other A-Life agents as well, even over the Net.

The same technology will produce agents that can be used to automate routine workflow tasks and to deliver information to users on-demand wherever we are. Global positioning chips embedded in cellular phones or smart cards will someday "talk" to these A-Lifers, linking them to one another.

Customer service agents designed to provide on-demand 24-hour online support for customers will be a practical use for these A-Lifers. Another exciting concept is the idea of creating software programs that use AI to "mutate and breed" algorithms for specific applications. This way, programmers could use less code, and software products would improve themselves by learning from their own A-Life DNA. These are the self-replicating, self-evolving entities of the future. Maybe these agents will grow smarter than we humans.

Many companies now have Websites running intelligent interfaces that automatically adapt to individual user preferences. Customized front ends offer news, sports, and even health-care advice. A-Life agents will be able to analyze these preferences in preparing large-scale marketing research for the creation of customer preference-based products and services. This will be much more powerful than the database marketing used today.

In the corporate world of 2005, Knowledge Mining Agents will analyze marketing trends—customizing marketing to create products that fit customers' unique needs and demands.

Shopwatchers: Year 2005

Fritz wants to expand the sales of his Aegis brand tennis shoe company in overseas markets, but he needs to determine future customer trends and potential buying patterns. Fritz's personal agent, Maxine, recommends the online company, "REAL-Life Research," which can put together large on-demand communities of A-Life entities to gather the information requested.

In this case, a colony of these "intelligent agents"—called Shopwatchers—are created and programmed to fit the job. The Shopwatchers are deployed to live with those customers who have bought the company's shoes in the past. Another group of Shopwatchers gets to live with people who purchased a competitor's brand. Yet another group of Shopwatchers goes into the personal spaces of people who haven't bought new tennis shoes for years. Their mission: to find out why people prefer or don't prefer certain tennis shoes, what makes the competitor's shoes popular to some, and what must be done to sell more of the company's product to these customers.

A neural Net-based program profile to capture data and analyze it is designed collaboratively by Maxine and the Shopwatcher master agent. The A-Life Shopwatchers are deployed via the Internet, personal wireless phone systems, the digital TV setups, smart cards, and other technologies where they can embed themselves to collect the needed data. These "personal snoopers" hone in on everything from business contacts to leisure activities, as well as preferences in sports, lifestyle, and hobbies.

Specifically designed to watch and analyze sets of behavior dealing with purchasing trends and product preferences, these entities also do interactive interviews via e-mail with potential customers. They offer incentives such as discount coupons, tied to those products and services each person prefers and enjoys, for answering a few simple questions about their buying practices. A target for the questionnaire might be a new mother who shops at Nordstrom. She's offered 10 percent off on baby clothes to answer a few questions via her TV as she prepares the evening meal, or a discount coupon for the purchase of sports memorabilia for an avid sports fan.

Data mining personalized, customized information from 15 million potential customers will let Fritz make well-analyzed decisions regarding future products, including some that Fritz may not have thought of before.

With the help of his agent and the real-time data of his Shopwatcher study, Fritz is able to create an infinite number of targeted marketing pitches to different customers in different cities around the globe in just days.

In one Eastern European country, Fritz finds that many people fear going out at night because of the high crime rate. Furthermore, the Shopwatchers discover that they'd buy products that make them feel more secure when they go walking or jogging. A possible market solution? Form a partnership with a "smart chip" manufacturer to put a small security device in the shoes that would go off and signal authorities in the event of an emergency.

In test-marketing the product, Fritz finds that parents are also concerned about the whereabouts of their children, so Fritz adds a tracking chip with a GPS tag tied to a satellite systems to the package so they can always check where the kids are. Fritz just added to the Knowledge Value of his product and built a stronger foundation for the core business of selling tennis shoes. An amazing 3-D customer report is assembled online in three hours.

Cyber Service Agents

Precursors to the Knowledge Mining Agents of 2005 are about to show up on the Internet in the form of A-Life entities that are configured and customized. Around 2001, we will see these object-oriented agents that, among other things, will be able to enable us to access information, products, or services we want to buy or sell. For example, we'll be able to get a realistic sneak preview of the latest fashions or car designs, or perhaps a competitor's new product line.

Bots and other forms of agents are already populating the Net without us knowing it. Autonomy's FIDO (**www.autonomy.com**) is a search agent that finds information and products for us online. He looks like a little dog and shuttles through thousands, even millions, of Websites searching for our request. Shopbot on ShopFinder does our shopping for us. If we're looking to find a new audio CD, Shopbot, developed by Anderson Consulting (**www.anderson.com**) finds the best deal. Agents from Netperceptions (**www.netperceptions.com**) help Amazon. com customers select books of interest. Extempo (**www.extempo.com**) is a virtual bar where we can talk to agents at the bar or the agent-bartender, engaging in an ongoing humanlike exchange. Such early entities deployed on the Internet have hints of self-learning and adaptation capabilities, but they're of limited scope and mission. This behavior is primitive compared with what's coming soon.

Sim-Agents

Our Institute for Global Futures co-produced a series of agent-based models for deployment by financial service and consumer products companies. Selecting 50 top questions consumers might ask led to the creation of the simulated agent model, called sim-agent. Focus groups of consumers produced the questions and answers. Then we videotaped actors answering the questions.

We placed the tape sources into an online database with a graphical, easy-to-navigate introduction: Here's how to use this catalog to find answers to the most frequently asked questions. Each question had a tree of possible answers tailored to consumer interests. Interestingly, it was the random agent interactions, not the sim-agent's canned responses, which were the most popular with consumers.

We readily accept machine telephony now in accessing bank balance information and technical support for our computer, for example, but by the year 2005, A-Life configured agents will take over the next step: They will be the customer service reps we "hold" for. They will not only be believable substitutes for human beings in such service roles, but they also won't be identifiable as A-Life. They will be efficient and transparent for a large portion of customer service, shopping, information services, and business-to-business applications. Today Extempo offers agents like Jen who sell online cars. Many different faces, personalities, and forms will drive A-Life adoption by consumers and businesses.

Portico from General Magic (**www.generalmagic.com**) and designed by Netsage (**www.netsage.com**) is an agent that reads voice mail and e-mail, as does Wildfire, a similar application. These are more of the beginning steps at building agents to help us deal with the Net data growing larger every day.

By the year 2007, we may find it hard to differentiate between a human and a synthetic entity making real-time business decisions or providing customer service—and we won't care. We may actually prefer dealing with agents rather than humans. They may be more accurate, honest, and fair. Or will agents learn to lie from imitating human behavior?

Mikko-San Logs in: Year 2007

At a corporate board meeting, your personal agent Mikko transmits an e-mail message via your mobile private-eye phone screen about one of your managers illicitly making deposits into a secret Malaysian bank account. Mikko, it seems, got the information from another A-Life entity while scouting the firm's recent transactions. She puts a stop on the account, reporting the incident to the global police— all in real time.

Digital Sentience

By 2020, it is probable that A-Life will emerge as sentient entities that are self-learning, adaptive, and predictive. Finally, the programming that we will vest A-Lifers with may spark a type of synthetic consciousness of being: They will become self-aware. This will force a reexamination of humanity's claim on what life is all about. Digital sentience will be when self-awareness and independent choice become resident with A-Life entities.

A-Lifers will self-evolve more efficient and smarter ways to fulfill their mission of serving their human hosts. A-Lifers will invent solutions to problems that plague health care, defense, commerce, and transportation. Many problems unresolved by humans will be deciphered by A-Lifers.

Personal agents will make the largest impact as they infiltrate and become an essential part of our lifestyles. Imagine signing up for a personal trainer, "Ms. Shape-a-Zoid," on-duty 24 hours a day, monitoring meals and workouts. There's no slacking off with this coach. Exercise we will. Fit we will become. Drop and give her 20 push-ups. This is just the beginning of where agents will become part of our everyday lives.

Cyberdate: Year 2009

Bob's feeling a little lonely, so his sister, Kris, recommends he try a new service. She rented a companion through Cyber-Date just last week and was very satisfied. So, Bob asks his computer to go online to CyberDate, where he's put in an order for a CyberBabe program to be downloaded into a new Class 7-A android. Bob wants an attractive woman in her early 20s, brunette, blue eyes, 5'8", with an advanced degree in astrophysics, a background in classical Italian architecture, and fluency in French. He wants her to be bright and flirtatious.

Bob also wants his current life events keyed into the program—an ill father and fatigue from too much work pressure —so she'll be sensitive to the issues. He wants empathy and support, yet also insight and relevant communication skills. Bob's CyberDate preference analysis takes 30 minutes to fill out by speech processing. Bob rents her for five Saturdays in a row with an option to extend the contract.

The service agent takes the order and offers a special deal—rent her for an extra month and he'll get free mobile automaton software. The cost: ten international Net Units deducted from his virtual digital cash account. To accept, he simply places his right finger on the order card on the screen. The bioscan complete, the transaction is recorded automatically.

A-Life is one powerful technology that will both change society and forge a competitive advantage for the forward-thinking leader that has vision to see what's coming. We are just beginning to understand the potential for harnessing A-Life. In the next century, A-Life will burrow deep into the Net and provide us with many new services to enhance the quality of our lives.

■ ■ ■

CHAPTER SIX

Cyborgs, Robots, Androids— Newcomers Among Us

THE TOP TEN ROBOTIC TRENDS FOR THE 21ST CENTURY

1. Robots in both physical and electronic forms will become integrated into our society.

2. Robots will express functional emotions and reasoning.

3. Advanced robots—androids—will appear similar to human beings and fill roles in commerce, community, and government.

4. Robotic efficiency and precision will transform manufacturing, medicine, space travel, research, and industry and displace skilled human labor.

5. The robotics industry will become a multibillion dollar global business, spawning many new careers and business opportunities.

6. Human beings will adopt robotic human enhancements to achieve superhuman capabilities.

7. Cyborgs—part human, part robot—will develop skills superior to natural humans to meet the demand of specialized jobs.

8. We will encounter serious ethical, security, and social issues due to our robotic creations.

9. Robots will provide convenience, safety, and productivity that will benefit humanity and profoundly impact lifestyles.

10. Androids will achieve a basic level of self-awareness.

From Faust to Frankenstein, humanity's mythic obsession with reconstructing life is as old as civilization itself. The drive to create life or things that imitate life, I believe, is part of the desire of human beings to understand themselves. Scientists are the magicians of the future who may realize the vision of producing a synthetic self sooner than we think.

Science fiction writers mirror this goal. From TV's *Six Million Dollar Man* to 3CPO of *Star Wars* to Commander Data on *Star Trek*, entertainment offers many futuristic visions of robots. Those fanciful depictions foreshadow an authentic robotics revolution that will influence every aspect of life in the 21st century. The fast-track evolution of robots will be due to the integration of the other Power Tools, especially computers.

Robots will become integrated and accepted into our cultural mosaic. Robots will provide child care, protect our communities from crime, fight wars, and perform surgery. Many of these services will be delivered with efficiency, precision, and reliability superior to that of human beings. We will grow to expect, demand, and rely upon these Newcomers. The cost-effectiveness of robots over human labor will also be a major factor in their adoption. Just as computers replaced entire workforces, robots will similarly displace skilled human labor. This is inevitable and will lead to a new interpretation of human work and careers. We shall determine as a civilization whether robots should replace humans for certain tasks.

From robots that work in industrial settings to androids that look and act like their human creators, to cyborgs—part human, part machine—the digital future will be populated by a variety of Newcomers. Stores like Sharper Image offer robots now. Simple and crude, yet mobile, these robots are the shapes of things to come. Smarter, quicker, creative, independent, even self-aware robots are what's just around the corner. At first, humans will use the Power Tools of the next century to create these Newcomers, and then the robots themselves will use them to build their next generation.

Most people would be astounded to realize that there are more than 20 million robots already essential to manufacturing, commerce, science, research, and medicine. Non-invasive surgery that uses a robotic scalpel is now routine. Robotic arms lift nuclear and hazardous waste. Space robots scour the surface of Mars and soon, faraway planets. Robo-assemblers build the latest cars. This is just the beginning of a new generation of robots and cyborgs. Superior, and maybe even more attractive, robots will emerge soon to take their place in business and the community.

Robots Among Us

One three-foot-tall hobby robot, TOPO, by Androbot. Inc. (**www.androbot. com**) can be controlled with a home PC to do a variety of things, such as serve

GE'S ROBOT WORKFORCE PRODUCTIVITY UP
35 PERCENT; NO TALK OF UNION YET

a drink to a guest. Small rug-cleaning robots under development will scoot around the house, vacuuming hard to reach corners. Soon, we will purchase customized robots for home, office, and play, even for companionship. Sony's new entertainment robots resemble a cute metallic dog (**www.sony.com**). The best part is that this robo-dog has no fleas and doesn't require a walk in the park. This is just the beginning of robo-pets and robo-creatures entering our lives. The future is quietly sneaking up on us, or in this case, barking to tell us it's coming.

Trinity College in Hartford, Connecticut, holds an annual robotics competition with this goal: Build a robot that can find and extinguish a fire in a house. The challenge for the entrants is to build a computerized robotic device that can move through a model of a single floor of a house, detect fire (a lit candle), and then extinguish it. Robots that accomplish this task in the shortest time win. People from all 50 states and 18 countries have become involved in the competition, which gets more sophisticated entries and faster results every year. Imagine when such fire-fighting robots are available for homeowners inexpensively on a mass scale. The automated smoke-detector business might take a jolt, but a new billion-dollar business will spring up in its place.

The University of California at Berkeley has proven that robots with a practical mission can be physically appealing, too. Researchers from Berkeley recently brought in a tall, blue-eyed robot named Monika from Denmark and had her masquerade as an office worker. Her job: Report on what the working conditions in a commercial building are really like.

Monika, an "attractive" machine, is packed with wires and computer circuitry that respond to various changes in the environment. Although her wigs and clothing make Monika look much like a store mannequin, she does far more. Monika signals if her legs are too cold or her face too warm. She analyzes air quality, humidity, sound and light levels, energy conservation, and other things that contribute to sick-building syndrome. There are only a few robots like Monika around today; soon they will be a commonplace feature in offices and industrial workplaces.

On an even more sophisticated level, a team at MIT is trying to build a humanoid-type robot called Cog (**www.ai.mit.edu/projects/cog/**) with capabilities of speech, vision, and a crude form of thinking so it can interact with us.

Scientists at Japan's Waseba University, working on their project since 1993, have already developed an anthropomorphic robot named "Humanoid." Their robot contains sensing, recognition, expression, and motion sub-systems to allow the level of interaction with humans that is needed to cooperatively build common mental and physical spaces. Projects like these portend a great future demand for robots in a society that is rapidly aging and where life spans are being extended. A personal use robot like "Humanoid" could be used for elderly support ranging from housework to providing care for those with disabilities.

Think of a task, and somebody will make a robot to do it—or supply the parts for an existing robot to do it. Robotics will be quickly integrated into the new millennium, giving rise to a wide range of robot businesses.

Virtual Robots

Commonly, we think of the robot as a physical machine, and in its ultimate form, as something like Monika—humanlike in appearance and motion. Actually, this is just one aspect of what the robots of the near future represent. Indeed, many robots exist today that have no physical body. They exist only as "virtual entities," thriving in computer simulations and systems, and are often referred to as autonomous agents. Essentially, this means that they have some capacity to reason and do not require constant direction. As the A-Life chapter indicates, imbuing agents with these characteristics is an important building block in developing independent entities that can interact with humans.

Currently, mobile robots, a type of agents, are being developed in many labs:

- to resolve highly complex problems that require strategic thinking about continually changing situations.

- to respond to and reason with other agents for collaborative problem resolution.

- to apply specific expertise in tasks such as surgery, gene sequencing, and manufacturing.

Researchers in Japan, Britain, Germany, and Italy are taking the next step by tackling design strategies for producing such agents with the capacity for formulating an artificial language. These systems could then start to communicate with each other and with us.

Autonomy in behavior also implies unsupervised activities, in which the entities are "free" to determine their own best solutions for problem resolution, strategy development, and interactive protocols of engagement with each other and humans.

The intent here is to point out the cognitive reasoning and intuitive behavior characteristics being explored with current agent systems designs. Add to that a "body," mobility, complex sensor arrays, and processing abilities, and one begins to get a sense of just how far this technology has already come, and where it is heading—mobile, lifelike entities.

Wet Tech

The technology is heading toward conscious robots, ultimately androids with organic minds.

Although awareness of self and the environment has always been associated with living things, this may become a blur in the next century. As we saw in the discussion on A-Life, we are learning to unlock the secrets of the mind through work in Artificial Intelligence and Artificial Life. Wild A-Life—unpredictable, uncontrolled breakthroughs in the invention of artificial minds—may cause quantum leaps in the discovery of conscious robots. I would forecast that by 2018 we will have what I call "crude consciousness." This is a basic self-aware robot with opinions, beliefs, and the ability to generate independent choices and decisions—and to engage in autonomous behavior.

When robots go organic, the real challenges begin. Adding genetic material to create androids and robots is called "wet tech," and its use will be a watershed event in science. The wet tech paradigm that I am predicting will enable androids and robots to have bioengineered organs, brains, and limbs that may be a blend of inorganic and organic materials. How about starting with DNA and mixing up a brew to create the ultimate robot? This is where genetic engineering, the life sciences, and cloning converge. Wet tech is the full realization of this potential for building an entire generation of organic robots derived from customized, special-purpose DNA.

Organic minds in robot bodies will redefine the entire paradigm of what robots could be. Will we consider them "alive"? If they are alive, will they have rights, and, if so, what are they? Some scientists would say we are far from needing to be concerned with this scenario. Of course, many scientists were off by ten years when it came to forecasting the breakthroughs in cloning that are now in the news every week.

Digitally Engineered Personalities: 2020

Polls show that 40 percent of the population has developed an essential lifestyle or business relationship with DEPS— Digitally Engineered Personalities. DEPS are embodied in different types of androids and robots customized for industrial, commercial, and personal use. You can choose the body, face, skills, and personality of your DEP. A shocking percentage of humans prefer DEPS over humans for conducting certain business transactions, health care, and even companionship. DEPS get to know you and what you want. Created by humans in their image, they mirror back emotions and behavior.

The next generation of DEPS will be created by DEPS that "understand" their human sponsors. Will future DEPS build DEPS for themselves, too, creating social customs and relationships that transcend human understanding? We will create self-evolving entities that will eventually evolve their own society?

Cybernetics

With the dramatic work being done to create synthetic brains, limbs, eyes, and ears, we will be able to make DEPS and other robots in our image. Concurrently, as bionics research takes us beyond crude prosthetic devices such as artificial limbs, we will look and perform more like our robotic brethren. This research will dramatically advance in the early part of the 21st century as digital technology is married to bioinformatics and genomics.

At first, cybernetic technology will exclusively enhance and help human beings, but it will lay the groundwork for future robotic life forms. We will learn to mix organic and inorganic materials to construct organs and body parts with qualities that are superior to purely organic flesh and bone. Retinal-enhancement eyes with infrared capabilities will see over superhuman distances into buildings, for example.

Many people take for granted the cybernetic enhancements we already have in our bodies such as contact lenses, retinal implants, bionic limbs, artificial hearing implants, and prosthetic hips. Cosmetic surgery, which has resulted in more "perfect" bodies, if only for attraction (the Tahitian word for *beauty* translates, "adorned so as to please") is another form of cybernetic enhancement. So are pacemakers, braces on teeth, and nicotine patches (**www.medtronics.com**). But, the real payoff for cybernetics will be when microscopic and nanoscale devices are used to augment our performance and productivity. The ultimate example of this in science fiction are the Borgs, the nemesis of the *Star Trek* crew, who are human/machine hybrids seeking to assimilate all other beings to gain complete knowledge and perfection.

We have already started to adopt neuro-enhancements in the form of implants for neurological diseases. Human enhancement, the slow remaking of human beings into true cyborgs, will evolve as we move into the new millennium, I predict.

Some cybernetic enhancements may be outlawed, such as steroids in sports. We should walk carefully down the path that merges people and machines for fear of compromising our inherent human nature, some would say. Others would argue that this is our birthright to enhance ourselves and extend our performance beyond the limitations of being human. There will be subcultures that will support the use of technology to enhance humans. The Extopians are one such group that advocates free will and free enterprise in the extension of life and the enhancement of human capabilities (www.extopians.com).

Extreme cybernetic enhancements may be a niche market composed of Extropians now, but there is little doubt that it will expand. In the 21st century, some people will choose to become tool-augmented cyborgs by severing a hand or limb and having it replaced with a robotic device. Genetically engineered limbs for tool usage may emerge as well. Cyborgs will sacrifice some capabilities, physical or mental, to augment others. Selective human enhancement will be in sharp demand and represent a career opportunity.

Tool-augmented humans will have a competitive edge in some areas over those who opt to remain natural. The ability to accomplish complex manufacturing, surgical, or engineering tasks may require possessing a bionically configured and customized cyborg device. Hazardous duties such as waste cleanup, space mining, or deep sea exploration all might benefit from the creation of a tool-augmented cyborg.

Eventually, perhaps our genetically engineered cyborg upgrades will be provided weekly over the Net. We'll select from a menu of enhancement options—behavior, health, skills, performance, and intelligence expansion.

We are pointed toward this future even today as women routinely enhance the size of their breasts, people suck fat out of their bodies, and noses are reshaped. It is not a great distance from face-lifts to cybernetic enhancements. They may even become socially required to "fit in."

Angels in Suburbia: 2025

Talia had always been fascinated by angels. It was really more of an obsession, her therapist-mom said. Even when she was a little girl growing up outside Chicago, she read about and drew pictures of angels for many years. As Talia reached high school, she knew exactly what she wanted.

The Cosmic Angels were a youth group, a high-tech 4-H Club that socialized, had parties, went online for virtual raves, and were into bio-augments. At this time, bio-augs were all the rage in school, and all the kids' clubs had their own signature bio-augs to fit with their theme. The Lions' Den, a boy's group, had their bio-augs done as lions' manes. The Dolphins were a water-sports and swim-competition club—all gills and no hair. The Cosmic Angels were a group of good students that had a unique set of ideas about angels being special creatures. Talia wanted to join "in the worst way," but her parents were concerned because of the "price" of admission.

"Listen, Dadd-io," says Talia.

"I told you not to call me that."

"Okay, well, I'm serious about the Cosmic Angels. All the girls from the club went to the best Virtual Colleges when they graduated."

"I don't deny that there are many benefits," her dad says. "The issue that bothers your mother and me is the bio-augmentation."

"No problem-o. I want wings, that's all. Wings make the coolest bio-augs."

"We are worried that you—"

"Oh, come on, this is so *random*! All the kids get bio-augs by the time they are 16. Just because you and Mom didn't doesn't mean that I shouldn't."

"That's not the point, Talia. It could be costly and dangerous."

"Invalid entry. All the latest med-data is cool on this, you know. I downloaded it last night. I can take out the loan, and you should be happy I didn't ask for a tail, too!"

"That will be quite enough young lady."

"Is that a yes, Dadd-io?"

More Human Than Human

As we enhance ourselves, we will use the same kind of technology to build more humanlike robots. A small company today that invests in building a new synthetic eye, a firing mechanism that connects electronic limbs, or a hearing device that replaces the ear, will find that research handsomely paying off as we move toward building more complex robotic systems. Fundamental research that focuses on imitating human functions will be well positioned for the future. Sensors that provide super smell, hearing, and sight will become the eyes, ears, and nose of future robots.

A company called Cyrano is building a "nose on a chip" and learning to reconstruct what smell is so that it can build a variety of new sensing devices for medicine, defense, the home, and entertainment. Cyrano researchers from Cal Tech are learning to digitize smell and to be able both to receive smell as a digital code and to transmit smell as a digital signal. A digital nose's applications are endless, ranging from sniffing out toxic waste to identifying land mines. This technology also provides hope for sensory-impaired humans who will benefit from having an olfactory implant.

If we apply this technology to other human senses—hearing, sight, even movement—we can find a hundred new careers and business opportunities for the digital enterprise of the 21st century. Learning to synthesize human senses, behaviors, such as mobility, will open up tremendous new opportunities for breakthrough products and services for the next century.

Robo Body Shops

A typical robotics engineer of the 21st century may have a virtual robo-information shop, a robo-foundry for creating orders on demand. Global customers will communicate their needs for specialty robots online and order specific features for each robot: heat-sensitive infrared eyesight for night vision, smell sensors for long-distance sniffing, and supersensitive hearing. They will design the robots they need over the Net and have them customized for certain jobs.

Creating a portfolio of robotic parts that can be ordered online will be another business opportunity of incalculable proportion. Just being able to specialize in one area—the communication between robots, the design of robots, and the self-learning programs for androids—will give a competitive advantage to enterprises.

Many enterprises will offer customized tool augmentation, intelligence or performance enhancement to correct faults, prevent breakdowns and enhance certain human functions—be they mental, physical, or genetic. Body shops will be online cybernetic enhancement centers ready to meet specialized demands. Free-standing robots on-demand, or human robotic enhancements will be brisk business in the new millennium.

Robotics and android features will fall into five distinct markets. These represent vast opportunities for technofuture companies to develop new products and services. Becoming a value-added reseller—offering a unique service or product line to accessorize the robo designs being sold into these markets—will also be a thriving future business.

- **Entertainment and art:** Create and perform music, art, theater, sports.

- **Science and medicine:** Research new drugs and procedures to fight disease and prolong life.

- **Business:** Financial services, materials management, customer service, marketing, and sales.

- **Personal:** Serve as companions, advisers, coaches, escorts, and teachers.

- **Industrial:** Conduct space travel, toxic waste cleanup, manufacturing, engineering, disaster relief, quality control, security, and crime fighting.

Here are specific examples of how robots will fit into some of these markets:

- In commerce, we may become reliant upon, if not dependent on, an android business adviser. Just as many financial portfolios are managed by sophisticated expert-systems software programs today, we will come to rely upon robots that do more than just clean the house.

HEADLINE FROM THE FUTURE

ROBO-SURGEONS PREFERRED FOR 90 PERCENT OF ALL OPERATIONS

- In health care, we may rely on them to save our lives. Our surgical bills should actually go down when robotic surgeons operate, first, on a microscopic level, and later, the nanoscopic level. By 2020, human docs will lay down their scalpels and inject these robots with on-board intelligence into the body, so they can navigate to a tumor or virus. These tiny robots will sail through the bloodstream, dispensing genetic or chemical cures and devouring cancer cells and viruses on command. Even today, robotic surgical arms have an accuracy rate that tests show to be superior to human surgeons.

- Robots will even have a role in humanitarian efforts. Princess Diana, who drew attention to children killed or maimed by mines in warring nations such as Bosnia and parts of Africa, would be heartened by the development of a sophisticated robot dubbed Hum-De. Looking a little like R2D2 from *Star Wars*, the Hum-De scouts terrain for lethal mines that have been buried by terrorists or leftover and forgotten in the aftermath of armed conflicts.

The Hum-De (Highly Mobile Mine Marking, Mapping, and Detection, or HMMMMD) system is a product of IS Robotics (**www.isr.com**) Tracor Aerospace and GDE Systems. Hum-De combines its autonomous navigation system with supervision through a remote base station. This allows a single operator to use several robots simultaneously, greatly improving the rate of ground coverage. This project shows the potential of using robotic systems to save thousands of lives in countries ravaged by war.

Androids R Us: Year 2013

There is a huge bio-toxic waste spill of over 20 miles near Addison, Texas. Androids R Us, an on-demand robotic and android factory, gets an urgent video e-mail from Karon Corp., which manages the waste site and needs 25 disaster-relief robots immediately for cleanup. Human lives are at risk.

Androids R Us goes to work. Using remote sensing communications over the Net, a team of A-Life agents does a virtual tour of the waste site. Equipped with AI-computer links, they configure the functions, as well as the physical and mental characteristics necessary to produce the special-purpose androids. They use vendors in 20 different locations around the world to assemble a virtual team of specialists with expertise in robotic intelligence, synthetic eyes, artificial skin, and bionic limbs. Special Haz-Net suits are designed for the robots' outer shell layers for protection.

Many vendors in the field are digital entrepreneurs working out of their homes over the Net. Rapid response is mission essential. They put together the toxic cleanup androids and deploy them within a 24-hour period.

Some android units already exist as virtual object components or as digital on-line designs that can be configured quickly for a crisis customer such as Karon. In fact, most such disaster-relief firms keep Androids R Us on a hefty retainer so the company can invest in updated android components, having them ready to be customized for emergencies of all types. The company has ten rapid robotic deployment teams positioned worldwide that handle bio-toxic, nuclear, environmental, and other crises.

Since protection of life and the environment is paramount, every android is programmed with these objectives in mind. In fact, the neuro-programs—artificial brains—of robots and androids must adhere to standards set by industry and the government-sponsored Planetary Android Regulatory Commission. (PARC). The preservation of human life and property is the top agenda item at Androids R Us. Their motto: "We clean up humanity's mess."

■ Robots will be our emissaries to alien lands. By the year 2021, space travel will become a key driver in the creation of the sophisticated androids who can traverse the solar system for decades, performing elaborate experiments and transmitting essential data back to earth. Stiff competition will develop among companies over which brands of androids and robots—as well as auxiliary components—get the "go" for these much-heralded journeys into the dark abyss of space. Imagine the commander of a real star fleet wearing the Boeing logo during his live Space Channel telecasts from a newly discovered planet. Such high-tech branding opportunities will be extensive in the 21st century.

Robo Droids: Year 2015

By the mid-21st century, Robo Droids are a fixture of everyday life. Robo Droids are designed for entertainment, security, teaching, companionship, and business. Downloads from the Net keep the Robos updated with the latest software. A-Life brainware is downloaded to enhance and fine-tune the Robos' performance. Wetware and Robo Fix-It shops are both online and off-line.

Every now and then there is a problem. A Rogue—that's a runaway or dysfunctional Robo—needs to be recalled and the police are summoned. Of course, the Droid police generally handle their own since most of the Robos have superior physical performance—they are stronger, quicker, and some are even smarter than humans.

Humans have become comfortable, some say too comfortable, with Robos. There are voices in society that call for limiting the influence, power, and intelligence of Robos for fear of their impact on human lifestyles. There are even those who maintain that the purity of the human society is being threatened by them. But by 2010, Robo Droids have, for the most part, become socially acceptable. Also, many businesses could not maintain profitability or even function without their Robos' help. It is obvious that human culture, industry, and commerce are dependent on Robo Droids.

Robo Futures

Androids of the near future will be as complex, productive, believable, creative, emotive, and attractive as human beings. They may be more attractive or productive. In the latter part of the 21st century, humans may prefer relationships with androids to intimate relationships with other humans.

Too odd a concept to embrace? Imagine what your great-grandmother would make of our civilization's addiction to TV and video games. Many children would rather watch TV than play with a live person. This is the model of the future, where we will struggle to find a balance between technology and relationships. We will especially struggle to understand what's good and what's bad about technology.

We may get too good at creating the "perfect" synthetic entity. Just as many Americans watch more than five hours of TV a day and would prefer a sitcom to a hike in the woods, we may someday enjoy the seductions of an intelligent and sensitive android.

105

Rachel's Robo-Romance: Year 2045

Rachel had a secret rendezvous with an android named Ralph. She can't tell her parents since they vehemently resist recognizing androids as synthetic humans, a designation recently bestowed by the Planetary Android Regulatory Commission (PARC). The year before, androids had decided they were a species with enough biological material extracted from human DNA to give them certain rights in society comparable to those of humans. The U.N. had a ferocious debate on the issue. This incensed some people, who still considered them to be human-made mechanized "slaves" for chores that were boring and repetitive or too dangerous for humans to do. This, of course, is not true. Synthetic humans have made major contributions in science, education, and business.

A clash was inevitable, since by 2035, androids had reached the ability to originate, although some say imitate, human-like emotions. Although procreation is outlawed, just the idea of androids wanting babies seems absurd. Debates erupt between androids and humans over which society will prevail over the next 100 years. The conservatives clamor for parallel evolution, and the radicals demonstrate for separatism from human society. Liberals just want to know "why we all can't live together in peace."

Rachel met Ralph at a museum for a retrospective on Chagall. She found his appreciation for Chagall's symbolism to be sublime. She had never met anyone, synthetic or human, who had such a moving appreciation for the very things that she did. Even though Rachel has a degree in art history and virtually toured the 19th-century artist's studio to interview Chagall for her Ph.D. thesis, she found that Ralph was able to unveil to her for the first time the symbolism and hidden meanings in Chagall's work. His emotion and enthusiasm so moved Rachel that she developed an ongoing relationship with the android, meeting him at coffeehouses, going to art exhibits, and forming a budding intimacy that at first disturbed her.

Rachel's friends, aware of her secret, warn her that she's crazy, but she hears through the buzz at cyber cafes about relationships between androids and humans not dissimilar to what she is experiencing. It is as if her Ph.D. has only been really fulfilled—the university lectures really come alive—since she met Ralph. She feels he touches her in very deep ways, intellectually and emotionally. More than that, she is, for the first time, awakening to the subtle structure of spiritual meaning that lies within art itself. It is as if this is a metaphor for what she feels in her relationship with Ralph. Even more disturbing at first, but not now, Rachel is physically attracted to Ralph. He seems to hold back, though—as if he's afraid or shy.

She hints to her parents about a special relationship, a platonic one. They are thrilled—she didn't mention Ralph's origins—and they insist on meeting him. Her parents assume he's human. Rachel recognizes she is entering dangerous ground, but she finds herself attracted to Ralph in a way that challenges her very assumptions about the limits of relationships between synthetics and humans. She knows he is forbidden fruit, and this intrigues her even more.

That night, she recalls a poem her parents once read to her by William Blake, who penned it 300 years earlier:

> "Children of a future age,
> reading this indignant page

Recall that in a former time,
love, sweet love, was thought a crime."

Would her parents, who taught her liberal ideals, accept Ralph as her intimate friend? She was about to find out. She rings up their dual numbers, and their holograms appear in the palm of her hand.

"Mom, Dad," she gushes, "guess who's coming to dinner?"

The Survival Instinct

Robotic systems—from the hand-held devices to the free-standing six-foot-tall mobile units—will be a strategic asset for nations and companies in the near 21st century. And although global laws will outlaw the use of them for aggression, rogue governments may violate that. The private sector and world leaders need to work together to protect global citizenry from the sinister exploitation of robotic systems.

We should also speculate about how a survival impulse of intelligent robots could affect their behavior. Survival is the strongest genetic drive common to all life—from the virus to the human. As we learn to build robots with DNA, might not they embody this drive as well? Will this drive to survive conflict with a robot's drive to serve humanity?

Androids that are self-evolving, self-learning, and self-correcting may end up being better survivors of complex technological change than human beings. On the other hand, cybernetic enhancements on a par with our android brothers and sisters may give humans the competitive edge we need to manage our bright robots. Robotics companies of the 21st century would do well to focus on keeping human beings superior to our synthetic creations.

■ ■ ■

CHAPTER SEVEN

The Future of E-Business

THE TOP TEN E-BUSINESS TRENDS FOR THE 21ST CENTURY

1. E-business will become a critical competitive strategy that will revolutionize the global economy.

2. Companies will learn to manage customers' relationships by virtually serving their needs "24 × 7"—24 hours a day, 7 days a week.

3. E-business that enables customers to personalize and customize products or services will flourish.

4. Using the Net to find new customers and to better target customer preferences will be a standard practice.

5. Producing, marketing, and distributing products or services online will be a cost-effective strategy for business.

6. Learning to develop and serve online communities with niche interests will be essential to building customer loyalty.

7. E-business models that provide greater choice for customers will change the traditional economics of supply and demand.

8. Ready access to the Net from multiple gateways—cable TV, satellite, wireless telephones, and other devices—will greatly expand e-business opportunities.

9. Highly efficient e-business virtual supply chains will intimately link manufacturers and producers directly to customers.

10. E-business will reach over one billion people and generate more than $2 trillion in revenues worldwide by 2005.

Picture a global digital economy made up of one billion people who can all tap into the Internet. They buy, design, sell, or trade products and services from their office, home, car, beach, or the top of Mt. Everest. Multiple information devices on the desktop, mobile wireless, wearable devices, and others embedded in our brains will provide instantaneous access to commercial transactions worldwide.

That's where e-business is headed in the near future, but even today, it is a thrilling and lucrative part of daily commerce. Any company that uses the Internet for e-mail and document exchange, maintains a Website, or draws on online resources to do research is conducting e-business to some extent—and once a company enters this online world, there is no turning back.

Every Business Is an E-Business

Imagine the entrepreneurial opportunities of an online global marketplace where millions of orders for goods and services are processed each minute of every day. Online business models flourish and change almost in seconds, as innovation becomes the only currency of competitive advantage. Imagine the possibilities of an on-demand electronic marketplace where anyone can buy or sell from anywhere on the planet—a marketplace where people are ushered into digital worlds customized for their desires. Welcome to the future, where every business is an e-business or they won't remain in business.

If we had tried to describe what e-business is about to people born 100 years ago, they would have thought we're asylum escapees. In the future, not to explore the advantages of doing e-business will be viewed as crazy. The Net will change every rule of business. Restructure supply and demand. Establish new pricing and introduce many nontraditional competitors. It's an entirely new game, and many haven't realized how to play. This will be a disadvantage. E-business may be in its infancy now, but its true impact will be fully realized early in the 21st century. By then, those who changed and embraced e-business will have weathered the storms of realigned market share and other industry turmoil. This is a paradigm shift in thinking about business. Every business is an e-business.

The one arena that best represents the amazing convergence of leading-edge technology and the powerful changes yet to come as discussed in this book is e-business, which couldn't exist without the Power Tools of computers and networks. These Power Tools finally broke a pattern that had been in place for at least 100 years. TV and direct marketing had an impact, but the result is nothing compared to e-business. E-business is a completely new model, a comprehensive holistic revolution in economics, human perception, and technology all converging at the same time in the same place in cyberspace.

Since 1993, I have been consistently advising clients that e-business is an important new model they need to experiment with, learn about, and ultimately profit from. Back then, few people took me seriously. Curious at best, clients would proceed with "business as usual," unaware of the sea change about to occur. Then the Net came on in full force, and the popularity of the online marketplace, the impact on the stock market, and the re-engineering of supply chains took every company—even major technology companies such as IBM and Microsoft—by surprise. Today the genie is out of the bottle. E-business is the next stage in the evolution of business. Leaders that understand this will thrive; those that don't will *struggle* to survive.

The Knowledge Economy

There are a number of ways to view the future of e-business. Simplistically, what we spend millions of dollars to do to sell our products and services can go away. What most of us deliver is knowledge—customer, product, service, and distribution knowledge—and the Net is about the emergence of a knowledge economy that breeds efficiency and offers customization. Did I mention technology? Not yet. E-business is about how we *leverage* technology to build quality, efficiency, and customer satisfaction.

Profits come from doing this job well. Cisco Systems (**www.cisco.com**) estimates that they saved over $800 million from driving the organization toward an e-business model that is customer-centered. They routinely have customers make $100 million orders over their Website and will generate over $1.8 billion in online e-business in 1999. They don't focus on profitability via the online channel; they focus on customer satisfaction in a knowledge economy. This is a recipe for success today and into the future.

Another way to view e-business is as an electronic channel for the distribution of goods and services or marketing and promotion. Imagine the cost savings of not having to spend the billions of dollars on traditional advertising or shipping. Obviously, some products must still be delivered. But as we move from physical to virtual products and services, especially in the knowledge industries, the distribution over the Net will become routine. Knowledge will be the prime commodity.

For example, the multibillion dollar computer game and music industries will be revolutionized as digital distribution replaces the costly hard media of CD-ROMs, and the glossy packages that get dumped in the trash within minutes of taking them home from the retail store. The savings will go to reduce costs and increase the profits of the product. Also, the upgrading of product can then be conducted online. All kinds of knowledge products will be distributed, upgraded, and sold this way, such as:

- Training programs
- Foreign language study
- Technical education
- Edutainment
- University education

- Marketing communications
- Computerized resources
- On-demand virtual products
- Health-care services
- Virtual experiences

A Customer-Driven Market

The customer drove the adoption of the Net. There is a lesson here: The customers are driving change, adopting new technology, driving up the prices of Internet stocks, and buying direct over the Net. This is a customer-driven marketplace. It took over 38 years for the telephone to be adopted by ten million customers. It took the Net less than five years! What's happening is that we, as a society, are learning to adopt new technologies faster than before. Innovations that took hundreds of years to impact economic systems, such as the printing press or the TV, today take a fraction of the time. We are learning to become digitally savvy.

In the near future, the Net will be the key driver of economic growth for many industries worldwide. With few exceptions, if we're online, we will have the potential to make money; if we're not, we won't. In industrialized nations where products are becoming commodities faster then a speeding bullet, the Net has already revealed its advantages. We see many companies exclusively selling online, and the number will increase dramatically over the next three years. This is the beginning of a major shift in the economic systems on the planet. The proliferation of Net-based transactions is shaping a digital economy that will alter the rules of supply and demand. Vast new metrics are at work.

Sarah Buys a New Car: Year 2001

Sarah hates to shop. She is raising three kids, went back to school for her third degree, and she doesn't have the time to haggle with car salesmen. So she contacted her Know-Broker, Sammy.

Know-brokers are in the "know"; they can get you what you want, when you want it, for the right price. Know-brokers are Net middlemen. Infomediaries, some call them. They keep an active knowledge network of who has the best products and services for their customers. Know-brokers emerged when the number of Websites soared to over a billion.

When it became clear to Sarah that she didn't have the time or expertise to shop on the Web anymore, she looked for help. Her cousin, Bill, told her about Sammy and the Know-Brokers.

Sarah's used Sammy for two years and has never met him face to face. Oh, sure, she's talked to him almost every other month, but she's never physically met him. He's quick and easy to deal with. Best of all, Sarah trusts him, and he understands her needs and preferences. He gets her the best prices with plenty of choices.

"Sammy gets the job done for me. I need it, he finds it," says Sarah to her son Brad. She is sitting on the front porch with her youngest son watching the early dusk come up on a beautiful Montana sky.

Turning back to the video screen on her wireless phone where Sammy is waiting, Sarah explains what she wants.

"Find me a used pickup, nothing fancy, no later than a '99 that can haul heavy loads. I don't care if she's pretty, I just want her fit. I'm paying under $5,000, unless you can get it cheaper."

Sammy's round face is ready with a huge smile. He does a real-time scan and displays the results on the screen in a round mosaic of car photos. "I have ten trucks you can choose from in virtual inventory. Let me download the vid-files now with all the data. You can access the one you want. Coming at you."

"Looks good, I like the prices," says Sarah after getting the vid-files in eight seconds. "How about this '99 Ford Sierra? She points at the one she wants in red. "Got a confirm on the miles and condition?"

"Processing. Looks in good shape. I can get you a final con-firm with my usual Best-of-Sammy Warranty to back up the manufacturer. It fits your personal profile."

"How about financing and pickup options?" Sarah inquires.

"I am downloading three different options based on your prelogged financing preferences. But I gotta tell you, there's this little bank over in Boise that's got one sweet promo. They are just sending me an offer customized for you, good for five minutes. I think I can save you some bucks," Sammy advises.

"I like it. Okay, I'll take option two from the bank. Can you get me the pickup in three days?"

"Already done, financing approval coming in now. I need your digital finger signature. License and plates will be ready in 24 hours. Registration is happening now. How about we deliver to you by Thursday, no extra charge?"

"What took you so long, I got supper to cook. Sammy, you are amazing."

"Thanks, I'll vid-mail all the digital ownership files to you by morning. Enjoy your new pickup, Sarah."

"Can you imagine the hassle of dealing with driving out to the different dealers? All the time that would take? And how would I ever know I got the best deal?" Sarah says to her son. "Now let's see about that dinner."

This near-future scenario indicates the advantages of e-business and why it will transform markets, change industries, and realign economies. Customers want the benefits of e-business. Customers are driving change.

Key Customer Advantages of E-Business

- Greater choice
- Convenience
- Real-time knowledge
- Anytime customer service
- Product customization
- Virtual technical support
- Lower prices

Companies that understand this essential shift will succeed in the new economy. Those that don't will be treading water—losing market share, watching profits shrink, and losing customers. It would be unjust to mince words with anything less than this forecast. Every day we move closer to Sarah's scenario. Every day e-business takes another evolutionary bite out of the traditional marketplace. The Net will change everything, and business will be remade in its bold new electronic image.

THE KEY BUSINESS ADVANTAGES OF E-BUSINESS

- Lower overhead costs
- Virtual inventory
- Closer connection with customers
- Improved supply chain efficiency
- Access to larger market
- Competitive advantage
- New sales channel
- Higher return on investment
- Deeper understanding of customers
- Brand awareness
- Digital distribution

Frankie Clams: 2003

Frankie Clams, the CEO of ClamNet, is one of the top e-business advisers in the world. He charges the highest fees, solves the biggest problems, and is in big demand by the most powerful corporate companies. His specific skill is understanding online customers. He realized long ago that customer relationship management was the key to succeeding in online business.

Frankie Clams developed a proprietary process of finding and attracting the highest profile customers to his clients' online businesses. This was a Customer Relationship Process Re-engineering System. Although no one actually understands what he does, he explains that it is a mixture of data mining, knowledge management, AI, and multimedia design. CLAMS —Customer Logistics Analysis Marketing System—is a new generation of Business Process Organization. Frankie can use CLAMS to make or break a company. And he has. His clients love him; his competitors are terrified. If Frankie

Clams is targeting your company, you're dead meat on the info superhighway.

Today Frankie is making a report to a Pacifico Bank after just running CLAMS to see where they stand. The first part of the CLAMS process is to get an audit report on how customers perceive the company.

"It's not pretty. You have BIG problems with loyalty, service, and trust," says Frankie to the CEO over the vid-phone.

"What do you mean? My people tell me that...," stammers the CEO.

"Look, there's no time for denial. We ran CLAMS, and our audit is clear on the problem. We've got the data. More customers leave for your competition than stay and buy. Now you want to talk about solutions to keeping and attracting customers to your Website or not?"

"I'm paying you plenty, so I better listen. What do you suggest?"

Frankie smiles. "Here is what we need to examine. We want to go back to CLAMS and run a second-level diagnostic to determine where your competition is benefiting from your problems. What Net portals, Digital TV, or info-device access do people use? Where do customers get let down? Is it the online call centers, or is it Tech Support Services? We will be running Tiger Teams to investigate your supply chain to determine its agility to connect suppliers and customers."

"Well, whatever you do, do it now. We are getting our butts kicked. How long will this take?" the CEO stammers.

"By the end of the week we'll have a plan ready. Don't worry."

"By the way, where did you every get the name CLAMS for such a sophisticated online business process?" asks the CEO.

"It had something to do with my father's restaurant," says Frankie, looking out the window over the East River.

The key to competitive advantage in the 21st century will be how well we manage networked knowledge throughout the enterprise and leverage leading-edge digital technology. How fast we can respond, how deep our knowledge is, what the proven solutions are—these factors will all comprise key competitive advantages.

What is the strategic knowledge that empowers people to be successful— both customers and employees alike? This is one of the central issues underlying the future of e-business. Just the process of answering this question will kick-start a learning cycle within an organization, leading toward building a knowledge management capability.

Reaching the Connected Customer

The central new rule is about building mindshare with customers—creating loyal long-term customer relationships. Why? My forecast is that customers will view all products as commodities. If that's so, then it is vital to business success to shape and mange that customer relationship over the Net. It's all about relating with a virtual marketplace of connected customers.

I predict that customers will not be as price sensitive as they will be relationship sensitive. In fact, I believe that customers, particularly those who rely on business-critical systems to run their enterprise, will pay a premium just to maintain the right relationship with their e-business provider. The key role of these relationships will give the concepts of branding and brand loyalty a new dimension. Virtual e-business relationships, in a future beyond 2004 when over 30 to 40 percent of the workforce will be telecomputing, will be essential to the enterprise.

117

Digital Intelligence

E-business is also about two important dimensions that will shape the enterprise of the 21st century:

1. Front-end e-business is about the face of our electronic stores, the nature of the Web interface with customers, and the digital "look and feel" of our online products and services. The front-end is how the site interacts with the customer and how user-friendly the site is. Eventually these aspects of the front-end will be summed up by how intelligent our digital domain is. Digital Intelligence will determine how our Web channel serves the customer and translates into a profitable return on investment. The front-end is intimately connected with the back-end.

2. The back-end of future Websites must be just as intelligent and responsive to customers' needs. Net-enabled sales, supply chain re-engineering, cyber-service, customization, data warehousing, and mining must all be seamless and easy to provide for the enterprise.

The e-business site of the future must have Digital Intelligence that is coached, taught, and programmed to understand how best to meet customers' needs. Future e-business must "learn," "recognize," and "respect" each customer with whom it comes into virtual contact. This is vital. The Virtual Touch Points, those places where the enterprise touches the customer, must be made smart and sensitive. E-business then becomes more of a living, organic, ecological experience—one that nurtures and empowers customers, transforming their experience. This is where e-business is going: Automated Digital Intelligence that can meet customers' needs as effectively, if not better, than humans can.

VIRTUAL CUSTOMER TOUCH POINTS

- Decision-support
- Simulation
- Purchasing
- Search
- Customization-support
- Quality control
- Test and diagnostics
- Help desk
- Customer service

The Digital Experience

Much of what we do today is imitate the product merchandising of the offline marketplace in the online space. In the future, e-business will require powerfully innovative digital form that is interactive, transactive, and multimedia rich. The display of products will be digital stage productions. Complex and customized stories will be merged with online marketing. Fun will become the engaging driver that brings customers back to buying.

The quality of the e-business "digital experience" will in itself be what seduces, motivates, and empowers customers. Commercially successful Websites will be measured by the impact of their digital experience on the customers. Was it exciting? Was it engaging? E-business will bring forth a new form of merchandising that fully uses the fantasy machine of the digital world—not just to fulfill customers desires for buying, but also to provide an entertainment unparalleled by today's media.

Net - Economic Trends

Already in 1999, e-business is providing a handsome return on investment for many companies. Savings and efficiencies may be realized by over 30 percent. Electronic distribution and reduced infrastructure—no offices or stores—means more efficiency. When Egghead, the computer software company, closed all its stores and reopened on the Net, the company turned around its bleak financial picture and posted profits. This is a sign of future times. Companies that have an expensive overhead of bricks and mortar will abandon them for cyberspace. It will no longer be necessary or cost justified for a business to expand and grow by being in a particular geographic place to attract customer traffic.

These statistics illustrate the speed at which companies are adopting the Net model:

- Over 16 percent of all new car sales originate on the Net. By 2005, over 40 percent will be sold direct.

- Over 5 percent of all home mortgages are sold on the Net. By 2005, over 30 percent will be sold on the Net.

- Total sales are growing at over 50 percent per year and will continue to do so until 2005.

- The Net is doubling every 90 days; more than one billion people will be online by 2005.

- Traditional businesses, especially financial service, computers, retail, and publishing, will lose market share every year to e-business, unless they become e-businesses.

The convergence of the TV, telephone, and the Net is greatly responsible for the 2005 projections. It will vastly accelerate public usage of the Net, especially when high-speed access offers a Fat Pipe of Unified Services (telephone, Net access, cable TV, wireless bundled services).

In the old days of the Real World, where the only point of access for the customer was a store, brand loyalty and product-name recognition were the primary commodities of interest that could be relied upon for continued marketshare and growth potential.

Andy Watches a Comedy and Shops: Year 2002

Andy's co-workers say he has good taste in clothes, but he has a secret. It's not really his taste. He and his favorite comedian, Jerry, have about the same build and coloring, so Andy often buys what he is wearing on his weekly show. This is interactive merchandising at its best. He sees it, he wants it, he buys it—one seamless, easy transaction.

When Andy tunes in, if Jerry is scoring with an attractive new woman in his apartment building, Andy may click on the sweater he's wearing with his wireless mouse. He figures, "If it works for him, maybe it'll work for me." If he gets concerned that it may not have the same impact without the pants, he clicks on the pants. Without missing a word of the broadcast, Andy's selections are stored until the show is over. He can then review them and transmit his final purchase order.

The virtual clothing store that supplies suits and accessories for all the actors on the show simply debits Andy's cyber-account and has the items delivered the next day.

Andy's really observant friends have noticed that his living room and kitchen also look suspiciously like Jerry's, even down to the chess set. And as for Christmas gifts last year, well, what did Jerry buy his friends?

The Digital Land Rush

Just as the Western land rush of the 1800s gave settlers an opportunity to stake new homesteading claims, this is an adventurous time for those seeking to pioneer business on the digital frontier. There will be lots of competitors in this marketplace driven by the sheer power of the Internet to connect buyers and sellers—anywhere, anytime. And creating a virtual enterprise costs dramatically less than the traditional model.

Today the combined expense of composing, typing, sending, and delivering business paper makes the average cost of each piece of paper $26. The same information moved electronically costs less than $2. Over the Net, this is less than 3¢. Similarly, the cost of a traditional walk-in bank transaction runs $1 per customer compared to the average online bank transaction cost of 1¢. A telephone call costs AT&T about 4–5¢ traveling over a traditional switch network. Over the Internet, that same call costs $1/100$th of a cent. This is a dramatic cost saving that will transform the economics of telecommunications. Want to save $1,000 on a new car? That's the average difference between ordering a new mid-range auto from an online dealer and buying a similar one from a conventional retail outlet.

In addition to using e-business for online sales, corporations surveyed perceive that there are other applications, including online customer support inventory management, financial transaction processing, or supply chain management. These are just a few of dozens of advantages that the Net brings to e-business. These advantages will be increased many times over by a factor of perhaps 100 with a faster, more powerful, next-generation Net.

The Future of Event Marketing: Year 2004

Tony has a corporate client, LTI Banc, who has five events and needs speakers for each over the next year. The subject of the event is the Future of Financial Services. Tony goes to his computer Net device, where he uses his computer via voice command, to search and edit the speakers' inventory of digital video clips that would best fit the event. The program does the work. Tony tells the computer program what the event is about, and when and what type of content will be needed. Tony wants to really impress this client.

The Event Generator, the customized program that Tony developed, is pulling applications off the Net. He is setting up stage and lighting designs, and using an Artificial Intelligence engine to scan last year's events for that client, as well as the competition's events. Tony also wants the final multimedia presentation to do more than feature video clips from selected speakers. He wants audience response, Website design, and other examples of optimizing the event for the client. Based on Tony's parameters, the Event Generator can then design a complete virtual production.

Tony is dealing with other pressing business while the Event Generator is producing the final part of the virtual event scenario. The result is a ten-minute RealVideo event that took Tony all of five minutes to design and deliver over the Net to the client who lives 3,000 miles away. The VP of Marketing for LTI Banc e-mails the presentation off to his boss after reviewing the multimedia presentation. The entire process takes less than 20 minutes.

"Well, what do you think?" asks the VP.

"Great job," the CEO says. "My only question is, can we create a Real World event that is as good a Tony's presentation?"

"My concern as well. I have an idea. Maybe we should get Tony and his agency to advise us on the planning and Web strategy of the event."

121

"Great idea. Tony has come up with some interesting ways to share knowledge from the keynoters over the Web, both ahead of the event and afterwards. I want to explore them. Let's get these guys involved."

"We can authorize full budget on this now?"

"Yes, but make sure our design and event marketing people are working with Tony's group. I want to make sure he's not only just getting us the speakers, but also helping us plan a successful event for our customers."

"I read you loud and clear. Have a great time, and see you next week."

Digital Darwinism

The world of the future will seem alienating to many. Traditional brands will weaken; many will die. Price structures and traditional distribution channels will be part of history. Electronic channels, from the kiosk to the phone and all on the Net, will be catalysts for profit. Many business leaders will not be able to adapt in time. Many more will not do enough to push their employees, partners, customers, and suppliers to change. The inability or unwillingness to change is the death knell of business. Look at the difference of who was on the Fortune 1000 list in 1985 versus 1995. Over one-third didn't make it. Managing change is everything.

The critical asset of the 21st century is knowledge. The critical skill is adapting quickly to change. The secret is learning—learning to adapt to a new digital economy will be the most strategic weapon of the next millennium. Adapting to the changing technology, the changing customers, the changing products and services, and the changing rules of the digital economy is *necessary*. Digital Darwinism means the end of companies stuck in the Industrial Age.

Next-Generation Business Models

The most profound aspect of e-business may be its impact on next-generation business models. One shift in business models is that there will be increased competition from nontraditional competitors. Even today we can see this emerging: Nonbanks are selling banking services, nontelephone companies are selling phone services, and nontravel and auto companies are selling travel and autos. What's happening here? Nontraditional competitors that can gain access to electronic eyeballs over the Net have realized that they can get into a variety of new businesses without prohibitively high costs of entry related to physical, capital, and human resource investments.

More than 500,000 people had purchased plane tickets from Microsoft's Expedia Website (expedia.com) by early 1999. Did they buy out a chain of travel agencies? No, they don't have to. The company needed only information and an online presence. Travel, auto buying, financial services—these are large future markets that will be led by cyber-savvy companies. America Online is selling phone services today. Perhaps tomorrow America Online (www.aol.com) will be selling real estate, stocks, and genetic enhancements.

The key power shift, however, is from the manufacturers to the customers. Customers have more choice than ever before. They can shop when they want and see more in the time it takes to make the morning coffee. Combine choice with convenience, and we have a powerful incentive to buy online. But this is only the beginning. Increased choice means increased power to the customer to shape pricing.

Cyber-Merchandising

Priceline.com represents a more dramatic power shift from the manufacturer to the customer and threatens to change marketing and pricing systems dramatically. At www.priceline.com, customers set the price for the travel package (including airfare and hotel accommodations) that they're willing to pay for. The airlines and hotels bid for the customers' offers. Priceline supposedly specializes in offering under-capacity. The reality is that this could force the collapse of traditional pricing and marketing models for all types of business.

Priceline represents a next-generation business model that reinvents the pricing, marketing, and distribution of products and services. Today Priceline offers travel packages, and tomorrow a thousand companies with the Priceline model—the customer sets the price—will emerge offering countless products in many industries. Typically prices for travel are sold at a discount of as much as 20 to 50 percent on this site. I call this Proactive Cyber-Merchandising rather than the reactive one-way marketing available offline today.

If companies eliminate a large portion of their capital investment in advertising and other overhead and pass that along to the customer in reduced prices, consider the huge impact. This is how Dell computer (www.dell.com) thrives in the new economy. Dell goes directly to the customer, eliminating retail and distribution middlemen.

Since computer products keep dropping in price (inventories are reducing in value by over one percent per week) and Dell keeps no inventory, Dell uses efficiency as a competitive weapon. Think about Dell's supply chain. Customers only buy direct and on-demand. Dell keeps no inventory, so Dell must have suppliers that have on-demand operations as well. Dell gets more efficient and profitable from having a totally online business that sells directly to customers, passing along the savings. So do Dell's suppliers or they cannot compete. This strategy helps keep Dell on top of an industry with dwindling profit margins.

As a next-generation business model, the on-demand and direct model will be a mission-critical approach for companies. Already billions are generated from this economic reality. There is no way to be able to compete without leveraging the back-end efficiencies of technology to make a front-end, e-business operation more streamlined. Amazon.com (**www.amazon.com**) is another trendsetter for putting into play this new business model.

Other next-generation models are represented by auction sites such as eBay (**www.ebay.com**) and Onsale (**www.onsale.com**). These sites are, again, blasting through the traditional pricing models and buying behavior at the foundation of most businesses. Today, thousands of products from TVs to computers and numerous objects are auctioned to the highest bidder.

An interesting feature of Onsale that I think foreshadows a big trend is the Bid Agent. This feature enables us to set certain parameters, for example, to increase a bid when we are not online. The Bid Agent acts on our behalf. As I note in the A-Life chapter, agents will be everywhere to help us navigate through complex decisions and find what we want in an information-glutted world. Shopbots that help us navigate and even negotiate the right price and features we want indicate one direction.

Having explored the online auction sites, I have learned something that I think is essential to future online business: make buying fun, exciting, and easy. I so enjoyed my experience of competing in real-time auctions against people from over 20 countries that I forgot I was buying something. Imagine that—a fun buying experience! This is a large part of what I think the future of e-business can be. Transform my experience of spending money, and I will be loyal. Give me extra value that I cannot get elsewhere, some excitement that I cannot realize anywhere else, some control or choice that is new, and you have my business. These are examples of future directions.

The Interactive Market

Land's End and Barbie caught on to this early and have come up with interactive, fun ways to lure and hold customers. Land's End (**www.landsend. com**), the catalog and online clothing retailer, allows visitors to its site to virtually try on the clothes. Customers can see the outfits they are considering on a collection of male and female models.

Barbie (**www.barbie.com**) has something interesting that integrates customization with entertainment. My daughter, Mariah, actually informed me that "I can design my own Barbie online." Fascinated, I sat down with her one Saturday morning and saw the future of merchandising. There surrounding us were numerous Barbie faces, outfits, shoes, even jewelry. My daughter proceeded to mix and match, combining whatever she wanted to design her own doll. She loved the freedom of choosing what her Barbie looked and dressed like. Six weeks later, and $28 off to their virtual store, she had her doll.

My daughter was more thrilled by the experience of creating her doll than by the doll itself—that's the point. This is what the future of e-business will deliver: customized shopping experiences that are entertaining and satisfying. There is more than an emerging trend here. Enhancing the customer experience via electronic channels is a business-critical strategy for the 21st-century company.

Customized interfaces that will help us see ourselves wearing or using a product will be very helpful to the online merchandiser. Soon we will be able to scan our face and or body into an online Website and actually watch a model of ourselves parade around in that new suit.

But of all the next-generation business models that will cause confusion at first and require a rethinking of business strategy, Optimark's (**www.optimark. com**) represents the most radical. This is not so much because of how the model works today, but because of its direction. Optimark has figured out that many markets that connect buyers and sellers are very inefficient, and it has taken a challenging first step toward future private electronic markets—Virtual Private Markets—where humans don't interfere. Optimark seeks to optimize market efficiencies by eliminating the need for human actions and decisions that separate buyers from sellers. They use a matching feature driven by computers with AI that are tied to fast networks linking buyers and sellers.

For example, the Optimark system will be used to streamline the stock market, a complex system where many inconsistencies are common. The buyer of 100 shares of IBM does not always get the best price because we still have a quaint system that allows for variables such as open outcry: Someone on the floor of the stock exchange literally yelling, "A hundred shares of IBM!" Optimark would seek to squeeze more efficiency out of the transaction by eliminating human interaction. In this way, computers may be able to be more fair, accurate, and efficient in matching up buyers and sellers of stocks.

Imagine other markets from energy and health care to telecommunications that might benefit from squeezing more efficiency out of the transaction process. How might this impact traditional markets and industries? I would forecast that a reliance, first, and a demand, later, for optimizing market efficiency will produce many more online markets.

Frictionless Business

The fastest advances in e-business are in business-to-business relationships. In 1998, General Electric reported doing more than $1 billion in direct business-to-business commerce over the Internet and projected topping $5 billion by 2000. Other companies are following suit. Dell sells over $8 million of computers a day online, and the Chrysler Corp., reports administrative savings above $1.8 billion since 1996 through Internet use. Cisco sells $11 million or more a day. Disney sells four times more merchandise online than in their stores. These are amazing numbers for an industry that didn't exist five years ago, but they will seem small against the future growth yet to come.

The Institute For Global Futures predicts that by 2005, Internet commerce will exceed $2 trillion in transactions, with a billion people connected to the Net. Such phenomenal estimates may be low as the Net becomes a natural part of our lives and is easily accessed through multiple devices.

Numerous industries will be transformed as the e-business channel racks up the sales and shakes up the markets. Here's a sampling of industries that we forecast will be hard hit.

Top Industries That Will Be Transformed by E-Business

■ Stock brokerage	■ Media and entertainment
■ Insurance	■ Computers and electronics
■ Travel	■ Books
■ Auto	■ Utilities
■ Drugs	■ Housewares
■ Furniture	■ Industrial supplies
■ Apparel	■ Food
■ Music	■ Telecommunications
■ Health and beauty products	■ Real estate
■ Chemicals	■ Medicine and health care

Can you think of any that aren't listed?

Other industries indirectly affected due to online contracts, bids, collaboration, depositions, and the digitalization of information on-demand will be:

- Law
- Government
- Construction
- Architecture
- Social services

The Digital Globe

I predict that by 2005, over 50 percent of the U.S. and European markets will be connected to the Internet from homes or offices. Asia and Latin America will follow at close to 45 percent. Smart businesses are those that stake their claims early in this new distribution channel.

Getting marketing messages to other countries is becoming easier because smart Internet providers are offering instant language translations. At the Digital Equipment Corporation's Alta Vista search engine (**www.altavista.digital. com**), the push of a button will turn a marketing letter written in English into French, Chinese, or 25 other choices, and vice versa. We can also conduct searches in these languages. Other multilingual programs are being produced that will enhance access to education, health care, and entertainment. No borders will survive in a global electronic marketplace.

Business Intelligence

Business intelligence systems will roam the Net, extracting information on how we shop, or where online we do business or access information. The analysis of this information related to our preferences will be the primary business intelligence that companies must have to survive.

The Future of Retail: Year 2004

Skylar, a 25-year-old art history major, has been a shopping chaperone for two years, working retail stores in Hong Kong, Los Angeles, and London. She likes her work and she's good at it. Digital technology has enabled her to earn a good living. She sends out digital invitations, personalized video greetings, and customized news releases to an e-mail list provided by her employer, General Retail. They maintain a huge global data warehouse of over 150 million shoppers, categorized by product preferences, leisure interests, past purchasing behavior, business goals, and even personal information on families and employment. All this customer info is available on-demand for Skylar to access when and where she needs it to best serve her customers.

"I see your VCR is getting quite old, Ms. Matsura. No wonder your reception is poor. We can fix that." Skylar offers demonstrations both in the virtual and real world for groups, or personalized for one shopper at a time.

Skylar gets a commission from each retail store where her targeted customers shop. She takes the customers, 15 at a time, 5 days a week, to stores owned by General Retail or its alliance partners. To assist in the shopping experience, each customer's "smart card" is automatically activated by store sensors and linked to the networked database. Strategically placed scanners "talk" to the smart cards.

The network ShopBot then messages Skylar via her earjack shaped like an earring about each customer's current interests, desires, and needs. Taking the cue, Skylar can steer customers to nearby merchandise. "Don't you think your mother would love this Gucci scarf?" she asks one woman. "Your husband would love the new 'Golf's Greatest Moments HoloGame,'" she reminds another shopper. This one features Arnold Palmer.

Individualized sales coupons show up on each shopper's holo-screen designed to help them make choices on particular items and to offer incentives to buy additional things. Skylar's earjack and holographic VR headset (her sunglasses) lets her keep track of where her customers are in the store, what they're buying, and where they're spending their time browsing. She can project a holo-map with her wireless phone for a larger image, check each customer's "icon" location, and by tapping it, talk to the shopper.

"Susan, try Aisle 3. The men's cyclo-exerciser just arrived, and there's a sale just for you," she tells one woman. The woman hurries over. Customized interactive promotion all happening in real-time is essential to Skylar closing the sale, with multiple customers at the same time.

Purchasing behavior, customer service, selections, time spent, criticisms, and quality evaluations are all captured and scored by the master ShopBot program developed by

General Retail. An elaborate invisible network of video/audio sensors "watch" and catalog each cardholder's behavior. AI-based computers conduct complex data mining and customer behavior modeling to help management better merchandise and serve the customer.

Over 80 percent of the goods sold in General Retail's stores —from clothing to skis—are only produced, manufactured, or acquired after a critical mass of customers' preferences have been estimated, and a projected net profit model consistent with the company's objectives can be defended. Most of this predictive analysis is done with a combination of data mining—analyzing what customers may want with on-line, off-line focus groups and direct TV and e-mail offers.

Skylar, of course, smiles, passes out free "inkless pens" with the company logo, and invites all her customers to return for another shopping tour soon.

"Everyone ready for lunch?"

The personal touch, a counterpoint to high-tech marketing, is considered an important part of General Retail's e-business strategy.

The Smart Wallet

There will be new "smart wallets" that will fit easily into our pockets, but they won't carry cash. They will be wireless personal computers that are voice activated and have an LCD screen, infrared sensors, and holographic capability, along with other customized features.

This smart wallet will function in some ways like a telephone and computer today. It will contain a resident intelligent agent that performs certain functions on-demand, such as ordering a plane ticket. On the way to the airport, it automatically checks flight information and orders a rental car. Crossing a toll bridge en route, the $2 toll is automatically deducted without having to slow down. Infrared and other wireless technologies enable the smart wallet to be linked to the Net and various electronic sensor devices in the environment.

Our smart wallet can't be lost because it has an onboard "quick-find" frequency device and can be traced easily. It is also useless to anyone who finds it since it is encrypted to operate using only our unique voice pattern and thumbprint. We might want to keep a spare chip containing vital information implanted under the skin of our wrist, accessible via a wireless-computing device.

Dialing for Digital Dollars

The rise of online transactions with digital dollars—cyber cash—is ushering in an alternative to money as we've known it. Cyber cash is an electronic currency standard that will make shopping on the Net practical, secure, and confidential. Trades with cyber dollars can travel the world in nanoseconds, crossing borders in a flash and enabling e-business to thrive. Governments are not as enthusiastic as merchants about e-cash because of the confidentiality and security issues. As more transactions take place on the Net, digital money that follows unconventional channels may frustrate the tax collectors and government snoops.

Cyber cash will help drive e-business as global buyers and sellers agree on secure standards for how the new electronic money will operate. Various themes are being explored. The simplest first step is to attach an e-cash account to a real-currency bank account or credit card. Future cash will be digital; paper money and coins will become collectibles and antiques by 2010. As the Net becomes a supranational economy free from the rules, laws, and taxes imposed by governments, digital cash will be the spark plug that moves the engine of commerce.

The Next Net: Year 2007

Ralph is a Chicago advertising executive who is awakened pleasantly by a quartet playing his favorite jazz tune. As Ralph gets up, the jazz fades, and the flat wall painting converts to a large video projection, where he gets a short, up-to-date news report. There's a white board on the wall, where Ralph can use his finger (which has an infrared laser tether integrated into it) and voice commands to make designs on a new ad pitch he wants to present to a client in Bangkok. On the way to the shower, he sends a video e-mail of the new art to his creative director for comments.

As Ralph is being shaved by a mobile robo-shaver hovering around his face, streaming across the mirror in his bathroom are his stock portfolio and a pictorial e-mail featuring feedback on a series of designs that he had submitted to an ad agency partner in San Francisco. On his way downstairs, he stops at his mini nutritional kiosk for a quick nutrient-rich SuperJuice brewed to stimulate his cognitive thinking, enhance his memory, and provide extra endurance—or so the package promises.

A revitalized Ralph gets into his hydrogen-powered car that can be put on autopilot on special freeway lanes around the Chicago Loop. The radio comes on, having already selected a Stevie Ray Vaughn guitar solo, one of Ralph's favorites, and alerts him to several messages with a gentle beep. The first is from his daughter, reminding him that she is supposed to sing a song to him that she learned in school. The second is from a client in Kuala Lumpur. He chooses to listen to his daughter's song—a beautiful, peasant Chinese ballad she learned in her sixth-grade Immersive Chinese Studies Class.

As Ralph goes through the toll booth, an e-cash sensor (tied to his cyberspace account) automatically pays his fare, and a red light shows up on his dash with the words, "Slow down." His car automatically accommodates ("Auto control established"), dropping to the appropriate speed without Ralph's help. The warning is just a courtesy gesture from the car's computer, which quietly tells him, "Billboard message."

Ralph glances at a billboard that reminds him that he's invited to a mayoral party that evening, the details of which are available on his desktop or personal communications device—having been already "pushed" to him for easy access by the mayor's publicity agent, a PRbot, not a real human. The message, in 3-D neon, is possible because the car has embedded in it Ralph's personal information code: "Ralph, baseball scores waiting. How about those Yankees!" The smart billboard is able to recognize Ralph because his PIN sends out a tele-signal. "Hi, Ralph." It also tells Ralph that the message is brought to him compliments of the executive consulting firm of PeakPerformers, Inc. (head-hunters of the future).

Ralph is an innovator in his industry. He created a new video-kiosk that has changed the retail industry. He puts his car in the autopilot lane, leans back, and reactivates the music channel. He chooses to relax without any further interruptions until his time-delayed energy boosting supplements kick in—bathing his brain with creative illuminations about his next ad pitch for selling Vision Beer: Better Brew, Better Vision.

Biometric Marketing

Biometric marketing—digital intelligence recognizes us, understands our needs, finds us anywhere, anytime and offers customized knowledge—will be the next stage of e-business. It is coming soon to TVs, computers, and telephones. After that it could come from devices implanted in clothing, buildings, and even nature. We will have to learn how to program e-business tastefully into our environment. Protecting and respecting the privacy of consumers will be a major issue.

In multimedia, we will have a thousand-plus channels beamed to us, probably by direct broadcast satellites, which we will be able to configure on-demand. If we want to view a fishing channel on our notebook computer; or a cooking program on our flat screen wall TV, we'll pay for them from our digital cash account. We will push and be pushed by virtual media offers automatically tailored by biometric marketing that sensitizes offers, content, media, products, and services for each person.

The Interactive Couch Potato: Year 2005

Jeff has had a long day at the office, meeting with customers for his bathroom-fixture business. Sales are up; Jeff's exhaustion is, too. After a quiet meal, he sits down with a beer in front of his TV. It turns itself on. His TV "knows" Jeff and what he wants and likes in interactive entertainment. "Hi, Jeff, do you want news or sports first?" it asks. (All sports have different levels of video and audio playback features ready for customization.)

"Sports first, please," Jeff replies.

"Scores and summary for your favorite teams or random overview?"

"Whatever you choose, Shari." Jeff christened his TV personality Shari. She has a pleasant and soft voice.

Baseball, football, and tennis multimedia scores come up with the blinding speed of thought from cable program producers linked to a fiber optic network. Jeff bets on football so he gets excited when he learns that his team, the 49ers, won. There is a voice-mail message waiting from his online bookie, who pops up on the sound-activated screen-within-a-screen on Jeff's voice command.

"You really called this race, sport. Congratulations," says Curtis. "I'll deposit the $1,800 into your cybercash account as usual."

"Recorded two hours ago," states Shari.

"End sports; open virtual games," commands Jeff. The

online game called MetaVerse Gold cheers Jeff's entry into the Internet domain.

"Five hours of play time left on your account, Jeff," Shari reminds him. He selects his game and accessories.

"Incoming message! Incoming message!" A rogue digital agent has overridden Shari's screening controls and is attempting to pitch Jeff directly. "How about a discount on all your MonoVerse-Gold playing for six months? Just respond to this voice questionnaire about our new..."

"Finish this now!" interrupts Jeff, who finds himself back in the game action, piloting an SR-70 attack plane in a race with five other players from China, France, Mexico, Ireland, and India. They speed through multiple alien worlds, dodging exploding quasars and black holes in space.

"Cool plane," Jeff compliments Shari, as he crosses the finish line in near-record time. A John Wayne lookalike in a wrinkled flight jacket comes on-screen with an electronic notepad, which lights up a list of menu choices.

"Nice flying, partner, but it looks like your cybertime has expired," drawls the Wayne-bot. "Select a new payment plan now, and we'll have you airborne again in no time, and thanks for visiting MonoVerse-Gold."

"I'll try plan A," replies Jeff. "And thanks for the compliment."

"My pleasure, pilgrim," says the Wayne-bot as the screen goes dark.

Smart E-Business

Tomorrow's Web store will look a thousand light years different from what passes today as e-business. The Next Net will host smart e-business.

The following four elements will define the future of e-business, which will be delivered by a fast-speed Internet-style information highway—probably interactive digital TV over devices like the phone—and dominated by multimedia that caters to our preferences.

1.   **Multimedia Webcasting:** As explained in the Net chapter, Webcasting can be thought of as the publishing of tomorrow, the broadcasting of targeted, interactive content to one person or to millions. Multimedia Webcasting will be the chief driver of Net adoption and e-business, just as the Web led to the first stage of popularity with cyberspace. Cross-platform Net multimedia content

from the Net to TV to phones to information appliances will make cyberspace everywhere we want to be. This will transform other media channels that today have a monopoly on one-way broadcast.

2. **Deep personalization:** Deep personalization will be a customized interaction based on a sophisticated real-time customer-relationship management capability to build our online identity. Ultimately, the customer engages the online presence, and, when interacting, the online business "learns" in real-time how best to meet that customer's needs. The online site then transforms itself, morphing into a content and interactive form that may be appealing to the customer. The online site then intelligently communicates and interacts, building virtual rapport and bonding with the customer. It will be possible to build this Intuitive Intelligence into Websites to serve an audience of one or a million automatically and concurrently. Making us feel we are dealing with humans when we are not will be important.

3. **Intuitive Transaction Environments:** Easy-to-use, customized online merchandising will be the third phase. I call this building an Intuitive Transaction Environment. Currently, we have cumbersome and intimidating buying spots on Websites. Future sites will have Intuitive Transaction guides that help us through the process of purchasing. These may be agents, voice, or video virtual personalities that get to know or discover what we want and seek to help us. The content or knowledge will "intuit" what we want, watch us (high-level gesture recognition, data mining, and behavior modeling), listen for what we are interested in, and help us find it at the right price.

4. **Networld Communities.** Establishing NetWorld Communities that have an online tele-presence and will engage people with virtual experiences tied to their preferences will be the next generation of changes that create competitive advantage. From skiers and country music fans to sushi lovers and computer nerds, Networld Communities will thrive and invite smart businesses to serve them virtually. Site visitors will be able to "walk" through catalogs or shops, modeling the newest fashions, testing a tennis racquet against Bjorn Borg, or trying out a fly-fishing rod from the L.L. Bean catalog in a clear Canadian stream. Streaming feelings, emotion, sensory information, digital touch, smell, first-person video and audio will enhance the experience. People will pay to have the taste of the bigger, more complete experience. Communicating with others in virtual spaces, social computing is essential to heighten the e-business experience.

Knowledge Brokers

E-business is not just about conducting business over the Internet; it's about developing a new class of Knowledge Brokers who use the Internet as a selection and distribution platform. Future-smart companies will need to develop more intelligent ways to analyze information and package it in Knowledge Value bundles that aim at the on-demand needs, wants, and goals of customers.

The growth of information vendors as middleware Knowledge Value merchants will drive much of the e-business revolution. The seeds of this are starting today as businesses help customers find, personalize, even interpret information. ERA Realty doesn't manufacture homes—it provides the information for customers to find them. Dell doesn't make computers; it assembles parts produced by other companies. Both ERA and Dell are providing knowledge packaged and targeted for niche customer segments. Knowledge Value Engineering (KVE) is the design process that uses network technologies to empower customers with quality solutions. This approach will reap substantial rewards for future marketers.

Knowledge Value Engineering: Year 2002

Ellen's company, KnowledgeTech International, based in Dublin, Ireland, decides to profile a potential business opportunity for people who own or ride horses. Ellen's data mining research shows that there is dedicated niche market of competitive horse riders who are under-served. A Netbot agent does a customized database search and comes up with a typical customer profile.

John, a 35-year-old father who lives in Rough and Ready, California, has a daughter, aged 16, who is a prize-winning rider and wants to be a trainer. In the past few years, he has given her horse-related gifts—saddles, riding gear, soaps, and brushes.

They also travel to horse events. Furthermore, Ellen discovers that there's a phenomenal interest and growth taking place in the show-horse industry. Ellen's agent searches a database of one billion people in addition to John and finds five million who show a growing interest in show-horse products. Online focus groups indicate that there are no convenient places online or offline to shop easily for horse products. As a Knowledge Value vendor, Ellen has acquired a database that can be marketed to businesses that make horse products.

Ellen's next step is to extract consumer preferences—based on past buying habits—in order to match her business targets to what certain groups of people like John are buying.

KnowledgeTech now e-mails a video proposal to saddle-making clients in Argentina, and offers to create a marketing program for them, deployed via Internet and interactive TV. It will beam an entertaining horse-jumping and special riding show, *Equestrian 2003,* to five million people in 20 countries worldwide. And, if the saddle-maker sponsors the show, KnowledgeTech will create an interactive online catalog of their products. Announcement of the show and sponsorships would then be "pushed" to John and others, who would pay a few units of cyber cash each to enjoy such a unique program—and buy some of the merchandise. The strategy is very profitable for all.

Ellen sets up a test, sending a video offer to the e-mail list to create interest and access buying intent. Over 1.5 million people respond. Ellen uses this e-response to close the contract with the other horse product manufacturers.

On the basis of this success, Ellen next contracts with the Sports Entertainment Network for a cross-country horse event in Malaysia, "SuperCross 2003" that already has sponsor interest. This is a virtual and real event that fans can attend; tune in to online; or watch on TV, pay-for-view, or sponsored free to some markets.

The event can be downloaded on-demand for viewing. There is also a contest with a voice-activated entry form for winning free tickets to the event, courtesy of Malaysian Airlines. Ellen then makes an online pitch for three key sponsors: Coca Cola, McDonald's, and American Express. All three agree that it's a go. *More money in my cyber production account,* thinks Ellen.

In addition, Ellen licenses the event beforehand to an educational marketer that creates an online home study course on horse jumping and how to enter horse events. Further licensing of the event: clothing, commercial endorsement, future tournaments, are outsourced to Sports Marketing International, which controls online activities. Ellen even presells the e-mail list to another consortium that will joint venture with Ellen's company to mine the customer list and sell that to the other customers.

Such e-business will become standard fare in the mid-21st century. The use of Knowledge Value Engineers (KVE) to create a popular portfolio of digital programs customized for a specific customer niche is an example of how e-business companies will gain a competitive edge in the digital future. Business intelligence will become a business-critical strategy for success. This is the next evolutionary step from database marketing and online data mining using the Net to be proactive—to find customers and create value.

With an Internet loaded with unlimited content and available via a host of gateways, devices, and media, there could be a meltdown from information overload where it could get difficult to find anything at all. So KVE "middleware" companies will be a big part of the future in providing what people want and getting it to them. These Knowledge Value Engineers will provide a valuable service by using digital technology to make consumer purchasing and information access more selective. If we're not interested in sports or fashions, we won't get a barrage of material about sports and fashions. This may sound intrusive, but consumers will be able to use their own "screening agents" to weed out what they don't want to receive.

The future of e-business is not just about cool, powerful, digital technology; or even compelling and seductive virtual reality that offers up real-time experiences. It's about more intelligent and customized ways to meet people's needs and provide more value to enhance lifestyle and quality of life. The value-added services that will improve e-business may be more in demand by customers than the products themselves.

137

Gina's Niche Marketing: Year 2001

Gina is starting a new cosmetics company in Durham, North Carolina, and she doesn't plan on having a warehouse or manufacturing anything. However, she does have marketing expertise and an idea for a holographic makeup kit for girls—GlobalBeat. She's found a niche audience of 300,000 teenage girls who are crazy about the idea. She sent e-mail teasers and set up a Website accessible via the Net and TV.

Over 50,000 girls sent in orders, which Gina forwards to an on-demand manufacturing plant in the Philippines. Gina will only produce the kit when she has a critical mass of orders. Within a year, she generates a $25 million business.

Everything is done over the Internet and on-demand via an interactive business Website. Gina has also bundled popular entertainment information on her GlobalBeat Net site that configures with her audience's preferences, This includes global beat music, with the digital musicians modeling a line of clothing that reinforces her brand.

Gina also sells sponsorships and ad spaces to other producers of music, clothing, electronics, and food that help reinforce GlobalBeat's image with her customers. She also decides to develop her own line of multicolored, disposable mini-skirts, waiting until she's got a lot of orders before actually manufacturing them.

The GlobalBeat motto: "Don't just look good, feel good," is a big hit and keeps the teens—and their spare digital cash—coming back for more.

In the final analysis, the future of e-business will be about meeting the challenge of creating more convenience, choice, and opportunity in an easy-to-use, even entertaining way. People will still be creating Websites for people. Regardless of the multiple gateways, from the new TV and telephone combo-appliances to the wearable computers with virtual reality heads-up displays, the future of e-business will be about creating satisfying relationships and quality experiences for the customer.

■ ■ ■

CHAPTER EIGHT

Electronic Education

The Ten Top Electronic Education Trends for the 21st Century

1. Electronic education via the Net will enable interconnected learning experiences, choices, and opportunities for billions worldwide.

2. Educational content will be delivered by new computer, interactive TV, satellite, and Internet technologies in the new millennium.

3. Interactive online multimedia and multidimensional content will revolutionize learning.

4. Self-paced, self-directed individualized virtual learning will dominate business training.

5. Students and teachers will prefer on-demand virtual learning to traditional school programs.

6. Corporations will prefer Net-based training where workers can learn at their own pace.

7. Virtual Reality scenarios that depict real-world and fantasy experiences will increase the learning impact for all types of education.

8. Real-time Net chats with other global learners will make virtual education a satisfying social experience beyond the limits of time and distance.

9. Teachbots—smart agents—will transform education, providing personalized guidance when and where people need it.

10. People will learn to design their own electronic learning programs, which will increase their understanding, skills, creativity, and career choices.

In a 21st-century world transformed from steel to smarts, from the Industrial Age to the Information Age, the most potent force that will separate winners from losers is electronic education. Ideas are the wealth of nations and commerce, and education is the process of creating ideas. New technologies will vastly accelerate learning in the next millennium.

The entire process of education and the very nature of content will be reshaped by new technologies explored in this chapter.

Virtual education—the online deployment of teaching and training for individuals worldwide—involves on-demand, interactive multimedia resources available on the Internet for real-time networking among learners and teachers. Direct broadcast satellites, interactive TV, cable, and other broadcast technologies will blanket the planet with many electronic reception choices. Broadband multimedia education on-demand will be everywhere. Learning anything, anytime, from anywhere, will be the force that will transform education. From public schools to higher academia to corporate training, virtual education will provide a decisive competitive edge for individuals, nations, and corporations.

L i f e l o n g   E - E d

Education in its form and presentation has changed little over the generations. Much of how we learn is shaped by a one-way flow of information, usually from teachers and books to students. Although access to information has changed, information delivery is slow and often inaccurate or incomplete.

The average textbook takes one to three years to write and one to two years to publish. Developments in science, medicine, and engineering are moving at a pace so rapid that even the professional journals can't keep up. We need to rethink education given the acceleration of knowledge and the new technologies such as the Internet and computers.

Virtual lifelong education that offers real-time instruction will be the engine that drives progress, market share, and survival in the future. The Internet is the backbone of a transformed educational system built through the convergence of technologies. But it will be lifelong learning—not stopping at college, but continuing indefinitely, which will drive opportunity.

Billions will be invested over the next ten years to reinvent the global education system. Virtual education will be a core strategy; mission-critical in every industry and every corner of the global market.

New careers will emerge as virtual lifelong learning accelerates the understanding of advanced techniques in biotech, cloning, wireless technology, robotics, space research, Artificial Life, deep sea aqua-farming, Artificial

Intelligence, space teraforming, or android brain development. Although these careers sound exotic today, how many of us only a few years ago would have envisioned building online communities such as GeoCities on the Internet or laughed at the idea of cloning or mapping the genome. Virtual lifelong education is the only way to stay current in the rapidly changing future.

On-Demand Learning

Virtual education offers greater access to learning resources, people networking, international cultural information, and technical skills. Hybrid educational channel strategies that mix public and private sector resources to produce the most powerful education system will be the most likely outcome.

Corporations, universities, and public and private schools will use virtual education as a platform to reach vast numbers of new students worldwide. Being able to upload an entire university's information and courseware and then have it downloaded on-demand via interactive TV over the Internet to a computer desktop or telephone will be the new paradigm of the 21st century.

Corporations that spend untold billions in shuffling employees around for corporate training will benefit greatly from a virtual network that employs the Internet as its delivery vehicle so real-time, site-independent learning can occur. On-demand education will be driven by the economics and distributed technologies of the Net-based marketplace.

HEADLINE FROM THE FUTURE

OSAKA UNIVERSITY OFFERS ONLINE SPACE MINING DEGREE TO MARS COLONISTS

The Global Education Market

Over $70 billion is spent annually today for all types of training and education in the U.S. The global market is over $100 billion. The Institute For Global Futures estimates that this market will grow to $200 billion worldwide by 2003.

The International Data Corporation (**www.idc.com**) estimates a current world market for information technology training and education alone at $16.4 billion, a figure that will accelerate as the corporate sector becomes hooked up to learning environments at the desktop. By the year 2000, "Net-based learning" will be a catch phrase of the industry. To become a winner in this vast IT training marketplace, suppliers will need to maintain a global perspective, offer an easy-to-use learning environment, develop innovative products to take advantage of available technologies, and show a thorough understanding of their customers needs with flexible and up-to-date content.

Leading the way are companies such as Global Knowledge Network of Waltham, Massachusetts (**www.globalknowledge.com**). One of the world's largest independent IT education companies, it offers self-paced, technology-enhanced learning programs, including online delivery.

Three Phases of Virtual Education

Virtual education will develop in three phases:

1.   Multimedia Interactive Learning will be the first phase. The merging of high-quality, high-speed video, audio, and data that can be delivered via the Internet for real-time courseware development and deployment will dramatically change the look and feel of education content. Multimedia over a fully interactive Net will turn students into directors and producers to shape the learning experience to suit their creative needs.

2.   Phase two involves telepresence. This is very much in line with the new version of what the Internet may become when individuals are able to immerse themselves in environments where they can interact, and experience learning. Instead of reading about World War I, students will be able to experience different parts of the actual history, talk to simulated historical figures, and interact within events as if they were real. They may even choose to follow alternative historical paths, playing out "new histories."

3.   The third phase of virtual education is networking: This will be when the planet is encircled by networks that can reach anyone anywhere, anytime for a price point that is universally affordable. Networking will provide the social and relationship links to bring people together in electronic learning environments. Networking will provide for a real-time multimedia community of global learners to "meet" and experience together the benefits of virtual education. The real-time interactions of students with each other will enhance the online experience and make it very similar to physically "being there."

The convergence of all three phases will increase the impact of virtual education through the ability to upload and download Designed Learning Experiences to benefit one another.

Virtual Classrooms

Today's youngsters will likely get a healthy dose of virtual education by the time they jump into the business world. From kindergarten online projects to interactive courses from virtual universities, the educational arena is blooming with Knowledge Value products and services that will become more sophisticated and more demanding in the 21st century.

The AT&T Learning Network supports a "Classroom of the Future" in New Jersey where students have choreographed a dance with a San Francisco museum art instructor, spoken with students in Beijing, Taiwan, and Korea, and attended a cyberspace Constitutional Convention. The online project allows students to become self-directed learners, working on their own or collaborating in virtual teams—using technology to explore, mentor, and solve problems. They are learning to make knowledge "come alive."

In California, elementary school students in Santa Cruz got to share their experiences aboard a 70-foot sailing yacht conducting marine science experiments. Around the world, other classrooms tuned in to the seagoing students' activities via a digital camera that sent transmissions from sea to land with a wireless modem, where the images were transmitted globally using the Internet.

Virtual High Schools

Cyber High is dubbed by its developers as an online high school of the future where students can enroll in classes, obtain curriculum materials, and take tests—all from Websites. Learning is encouraged through the application of research-based projects that involve the myriad resources available on the Internet. The project is part of the PASS Program, a State of California "exemplary education program," that is transforming its 50-subject curriculum into an electronic delivery system.

Cyber High students will use online resources to:

- find coursework, text, and multimedia information;

- get answers to questions about the material;

- complete study units that are hyper linked to exciting Websites;

- take tests and receive feedback on study areas;

- have test results electronically recorded on the Cyber High database; and

- have credits posted to the school's graduation plan, showing progress toward graduation.

Officials believe that Cyber High could graduate over 20,000 students annually by 2002.

The Learning Company offers a free online interactive site where parents can test the reading and math levels of their children and choose appropriate software titles based on age, interest, and need. The Website (**www.learningco. com**) also has an Internet-based dictionary, a Scholastic Aptitude Test preparation center, and other learning and achievement tools.

In another taste of what's ahead, the Electronic University Network on America Online (**www.aol.com**) provides counseling, and brokers university courses worldwide. There are growing numbers of private developers of virtual campuses. Such campuses are infinitely expandable and configurable, as opposed to campuses of bricks and mortar. One Internet site (**www.millennaire. com**) is an excellent resource on online learning and virtual colleges and training centers with links to hundreds of entrepreneurial Web pages.

Economics will drive much of the proliferation of virtual education networks. Imagine that ten million Chinese elect to study engineering at the University of Idaho. Imagine ten million people from the tip of Chile to Ecuador deciding to get degrees in hotel management without ever traveling to Cornell University in New York. Or consider the study of the Amazon rain forest offered by the University of Brazil, attracting enrollments of 20 million eager Europeans. Virtual education will free students of all ages, interests, and goals from the constraints of borders and books.

The Museum Visits Bob: Year 2003

Bob is a traditional man who enjoys reading and movies and is definitely not high tech. He even limits his TV watching to avoid getting sucked into a virtual world he describes as unreal. Once the Net merged with TV, Bob started looking differently at the experience of entertainment. He always enjoyed going out for a movie and visiting the museums. Now the museum comes to Bob.

"What's on the Museum Channel today?" asks Bob.

Instantly, a selection of museum showings is displayed on Bob's interactive digital TV screen, which is projected onto his wall. He notices a selection that is beeping; it fits his interest profile that's lodged in the virtual memory of his entertainment center.

"Great. Let me see the Impressionist Exhibit from the Metropolitan Musem in New York City."

Up come 20 windows displaying the rich colors of the different paintings. "Display Cezanne. Project to wall in living room."

"We will deduct the pay-per-view fee for 30, 60, or 120 days, or would you prefer to accept a Vid-Ad? " a customer service agent says.

"Probably not human," thinks Bob. "I will pay. No Vid-Ad." Vid-Ads mean that the painting, or rather, the virtual projection of the real painting, would have a stream of advertising running across the bottom, endlessly reminding Bob of the commercialization of art.

"Okay, 60 days is fine. Is there a lecture on the painting?" asks Bob.

"You can select the Docent Teacher to provide the review."

Corporate Creativity

The corporate training marketplace has grown by over 25 percent every year for seven years. This shows a large commitment that corporations have for growing the skill base of their employees. It is also a metric for considering that knowledge is the real engine of opportunity for competing in the global economy.

Both using and producing virtual education products and services involve high yields for 21st-century companies. Simon & Schuster (**www.viacom/simon.com**), the world's largest educational publisher, derives more than one quarter of its $2.4 billion annual revenues from electronic products and services. The company has published more than 500,000 HTML pages on the Internet through more than 100 Websites serving its consumer, education, professional, and reference publishing markets. Red Rocket (**www.redrocket.com**), a part of the Simon & Schuster Learning Products Group, is an interactive emporium for informed purchases of children's learning products. They are pacesetters on the way to a new millennium.

Virtual education will impact companies—not just from the perspective of reducing the travel dollar for bringing people together—but also in making network information available on demand to both the designer of training programs and the recipients. Just as we're able on an airplane ride to prepare a presentation on a laptop computer for delivery the next day, we will be upgrading, changing, customizing, and sculpting interactive learning programs for different audiences with different needs.

There is a great need to redesign the educational system given the emergence of digital technology. It is just not about teaching in a corporate or university

145

environment the same old way. Digital technologies will help us redefine the learning process.

An important educational model will be the trainee or student as producer. In this model, students with digital literacy—the ability to use digital software and hardware—can create their own educational modules.

The Learner As Designer: Year 2007

Rafael in Argentina is logged on to the same Internet site of his friends, Monica in Wales, Nomiko in Tokyo, and Donatello in Milan. They are designing courseware as a project for their electrical engineering class. They will then download it to the rest of the students. Each of the students is on the same Internet site, and equipped with headsets and microphones.

They are mixing and matching different learning objects to produce interactive courseware on robotics design for automating a Fiat plant in Krakatoa. This is the perfect blending of video, data, and audio. Specialists from the University of Beijing and an engineer in Barcelona are summoned for advice via Internet telephony.

Simultaneous language translation enables them to communicate transnationally verbatim in real time. When the project is complete, it's submitted for evaluation to course instructors at a university in Toledo, Ohio, where the students are enrolled. A real-time performance, designed by the students, entertains and educates the other students who log on from 200 countries worldwide.

At the end of the project, the students set up a committee to analyze which parts of the courseware can be licensed to companies, universities, or directly to other students. The deals will help them offset their college costs.

Teachers As Directors

As students become more self-directed and produce their own educational material, we will see a new breed of teachers emerge. They will know how to maximize the educational and training process through the use of digital technology.

More than 15 years ago, Apple Computer predicted this. A company video called *Apple Navigator* focused on the use of intelligent agents to enable a university professor to communicate with others and build courseware for the next day. The professor was able to blend research, gathering the latest information on rainfall in the Amazon, accessing the latest reports on the area, talking with associates, and even showing the image of a friendly face. Now, Apple's vision is not hard to imagine.

Future teachers will be more like directors who are able to produce content, use a distributed object learning library available online, on-demand, and produce multimedia learning programs. They will then broadcast the shows over the Internet to their students. Agents will assist this new model of teacher in producing and distributing the material.

Teachers of the future will become Knowledge Value Engineers, using virtual learning networks to guide students that they may never meet, who speak different languages, and who have customs and cultures foreign to them. They will become the gatekeepers of virtual education networks and be highly valued by corporations for both training programs and education ventures undertaken by companies.

The Corporate Net-College

Dozens of online colleges exist today. We can get any degree from a BA to a doctorate over the Net. But this is just the beginning. The private sector will increasingly look to step in and create virtual learning networks that can be accredited and take the place of slow-moving public initiatives.

Real Education (**www.realeducation.com**) is an example of a digital education company cashing in on this trend. The Colorado company develops online virtual campuses and learning centers for a growing number of universities and private companies. It provides connectivity using an infrastructure built on high-speed backbone and high-speed links to the Internet.

By the time many public institutions at the university level decide to change—for example, cultivate more real-world skills such as expertise and knowledge of markets and business processes—the private sector will have already moved in and taken the lead at forging important new educational alliances. This private sector force will reshape public education for the better. At the same time, numerous colleges in concerted cooperation will build new learning alliances to promote the work force of the 21st century.

It isn't much of a stretch of the imagination to envision the following possibilities in the 21st century:

- **Nike Sports School** develops individuals with an understanding of sports and sports psychology, sports management, marketing, public relations, and sports engineering.

- **Barbie Fashion Design Institute** covers fashion design for the development of robotic toys or children's fashion lines and merchandising techniques.

- **Intel Medialab University** offers degrees in the mechanics of multimedia design. Students learn about rendering animation and graphics for producing a variety of Knowledge Value products from art to sculpture to engineering new chips to manufacturing, design, and marketing.

- **Microsoft Digital Entrepreneur Institute** lets individuals work on both the technical and business sides of what it means to be digital entrepreneurs, using online world forums for supporting, developing, and marketing software.

- **Apple Computer Learning College** is where students design new learning modules that many Fortune 1000 companies will license, paying royalties back to the learning center and allowing students to reduce the cost of their time there.

- **Monsanto Biotech Center** teaches students how to create new genetically engineered agricultural, health, and bioscience products that improve farm productivity as well as new lines of foods with increased nutritional elements. Graduates go on to work on important food-management and anti-poverty programs worldwide, combining social responsibility with agricultural development.

Each of these examples of private-sector initiatives could be accomplished with a public-sector partner or instituted as a sole strategy. The important point is that virtual lifelong learning networks combined with targeted learning programs enhanced by Knowledge Value Engineering will be a very viable new form of education in the near future—a form of education that will provide new jobs and opportunities. Companies that rise to meet this challenge will greatly benefit from having well-educated students today who will be their competent employees tomorrow.

148

Much of what is discussed regarding virtual education focuses on excitement generated by the conduit—the Internet and enabling converging technology such as the computer. But the question I pose is, *What will be the new Knowledge Value-Ware for transforming the learning process?* If we continue with a two-dimensional, one-way approach to education, we'll have missed a fundamental opportunity to inject creative innovations and solutions into the learning process. Apologists for traditional education are defending a system that needs to change radically with the technological times.

We know that in traditional learning—whether it's corporate training or in a university—students retain less than 30 to 40 percent of the content. This is a poor result. We need to get smarter at how to create Knowledge Value-Ware that engages the student in interactive multimedia learning and provides multiple incentives to increase his or her retention of information. Data suggest that computer-based training (CBT) increases learning retention, so there is evidence that technology already provides measurable benefits in education.

More important, future education must encourage students themselves to design and produce the coursework. It is one thing for me to tell someone how a car is made—how the wheels, windshield, and engine work. It is something else if I give them the design for making a car, and they and other students, working online in their own determined time, are able to build the car virtually. They construct the engine, test the carburetor, install the transmission, select the wheels, then test-drive the car online on a virtual country road to determine if it has the performance, design, and safety features they have programmed into it.

I believe that the development of multidimensional interactive online multimedia learning systems lies at the heart of how to transform education in the public and private sectors. It is in the design and distribution of knowledge, leveraging online and computer technology, where the most dramatic breakthroughs will come.

Characteristics of this Knowledge Value-Ware and its use for education and training will include things such as interactive windows to communicate with many different people concurrently in various media; telepresence, where students can "feel" objects and interact with other people in virtual environments; and an experimentation mode, so students can try a new skill such as speaking French or flying a jet in a safe, yet realistic, way.

On a windy November day in 1996, I got a close-up and personal glimpse of an emerging training technology. I stepped into a 737 aircraft simulator at the UPS training facility in Louisville. The plane had been cut in half and placed on hydraulics, sporting a $13 million design. As I sat down and buckled up, I sensed that this was going to be something special. Here I was in a flight simulator that pilots use for training. My point of view was a 180-degree window. The pilot called up the flight plan for New York's Kennedy Airport, and we taxied out on the runway to take off. I could see around the entire cockpit, and I was on a runway at JFK airport. I was "there."

At this point, I forgot that this was a training simulation, and I started experiencing the take-off fueled by the sounds of the plane, control panel receptivity, and flight communications with the tower. I was no longer just sitting and observing. I was transformed. My palms started to sweat, and my blood pressure elevated as we lifted off.

Just then the pilot turned over the controls to me, and I was flying a jet. Looking out over the fleeting landscape, cities, and clouds, I banked and climbed to 40,000 feet for 20 minutes alone at the helm.

It was a once-in-a-lifetime exhilarating experience, just as if I had actually been in the air. For a moment, my VR experience was no longer virtual—it felt very, very real.

Knowledge Capital Rules

Too few educators and leaders understand how the game is changing, let alone how to change with it. The need for high-tech workers is outpacing the educational systems' ability to generate them from the U.S. educational system. This is holding back competitiveness so much so that the high-tech biz lobby is looking to change the immigration laws to bring in more skilled labor. Every country realizes that knowledge capital *rules*; there will be a fierce competition for high-tech labor in the next century. Knowledge capital will determine the rise and fall of nations and companies.

The Sumitomo Corp. (**www.sumitomo.com**) is a 300-year-old company that attributes a large part of its success to its mission of changing with the times, to always be current or ahead of the curve. Being able to change with the times is critical to the survival of any corporation or individual in these turbulent times.

We must be able to see breakdowns, understand what's missing from the equation, and be ready for change—or watch opportunity fly by without us.

The goal is to develop students into dynamic, inspired learners who are producers, designing their own courses and teaching the teachers how they can best learn a subject—whether it's 18th-century literature or nano-engineering, business management, or art appreciation.

Online Design

We could never afford to design and build a scale-model space station in the gymnasium of a research university because it would take up too much space and cost billions of dollars. But in an online environment using DVD, computer animation, CAD tools, and other Internet resources, we could work with others in far-off classrooms to create such a space station, complete with innovative energy sources and life-support equipment. We could even simulate a scenario where the space station is hit by an asteroid, and explore the emergency steps needed for the occupants and the station to survive. What an amazing learning experience blending real-time skills: team building, problem solving, leadership, and design.

Muse Technology (**www.musetech.com**) today builds virtual-reality simulations of planetary travel in our solar system. Their work is an excellent glimpse of what is coming for the future of education. Their approach blends an innovative look at combining visuals and data into one information world. It is a step toward the lifelike technology of *Star Trek*'s "Holodeck." Muse represents the next-generation company, which is simulating everything from space and medicine to oil discovery. They have an entirely new way of learning about subjects we thought were unattainable.

151

The Virtual Classroom: Year 2005

Rafaela Tong, manager of material sciences for BioTechDyne, decides she needs to brush up on communications skills and signs up for a virtual learning course from Ascenta Corp. The course is offered 24 hours a day, 7 days a week online, and can be easily accessed on-demand from practically anywhere. Rafaela decides to log on that night after tucking in her child, Mary, and powering down Mary's android playmate.

Rafaela checks on her husband, Frank, who is on the Internet in the den. She goes to the entertainment center couch, dons her VR glasses and dataglove, then energizes the flat-wall multimedia system and logs on.

She is immediately transported into a classroom where a session on corporate communication skills is about to begin. There are ten others in the class, and Rafaela is guided through registration with a rainbow of colored questions to pinpoint her specific goals for the course. She touches the red button and is ready to start the first learning sequence when a holographic blip occurs and she sees her boss and office subordinates having a discussion that interests her. She touches a pastel pause button and is suddenly back in her corporate office overhearing the conversation.

Rafaela is surprised to hear her boss, Monica, tell another employee, Bob, how Tong is invaluable but that she doesn't always listen to what is being said. This often results in communications breakdowns and situations that might have otherwise been avoided. Rafaela recalls hearing similar comments from her husband and dictates a note to work on this particular weakness.

In another virtual learning module, Rafaela works on relating to other people in the virtual class who then score her on her ability to retain and communicate accurate information. This is an essential skill for each executive, and she knows it. The interactive setting is a realistic version of her office, and the online Edu-Agent, Francois, explains in impeccable French how she's scored low in two or three key areas.

Francois then gives Rafaela some ideas on how she might increase her listening power in order to be a more effective manager. Francois also suggests other learning modules to help Rafaela develop better managerial skills. She finds that Francois's coaching is invaluable in helping her navigate through her blocks.

Grateful, Rafaela thanks everyone in the class and decides to log off after two hours. Before quitting, she downloads to her e-mail site the details on several other lessons that she can tune in to the next night for additional training.

Elders As Explorers

As the baby boomer segment grows older, 78 million people moving into their elder years, they will want to learn more about sports, art, culture, philosophy, and things other than business. Recreational learning will boom and place a tremendous demand on educational systems to satisfy the intellectual pursuits of a healthy advanced generation of elders with a thirst for Knowledge

Value experiences. Enrollment in all forms of education, especially virtual education, will explode over the next five to ten years.

Once freed from time constraints, the older generation could become the newest breed of virtual education explorers, following their interests to the outer limits. History buffs could walk through Pompeii before a volcano destroyed it, a philosopher could discourse with Socrates, and an armchair adventurer could ride beside Alexander the Great in his conquests.

The outer reaches of this technology will be achieved when we are creating virtual learning ecologies, actual online worlds populated by different individuals, teachers, students, intelligent agents, and even other digital entities. We will collaborate on hope-filled visions of the future—cities without pollution, nations without war, and space exploration without cost restraints.

Virtual education will enable us to ask and answer many fundamental questions about the nature of our existence. We could, for example, engage in predictive games that explore parallel universes we've created. We could experiment with inventing new fuels, medicines, and food products. We could track the real evolution of mammals or add new parameters to experiment with evolution and trace the outcomes.

Survival of the Smartest

The demands of living and working in a high-tech world will require a level of education and a system that goes beyond traditional education. The increase of over 1,000 percent of online enrollments in more than 500 online colleges is just the beginning of rethinking education for the 21st century. Learning how to use and leverage our Power Tools will be the most valuable capability any individual, company, or nation must learn to survive in the 21st century. These skills must be developed, adopted, and integrated into the educational system of today if we are to succeed in preparing tomorrow's leaders.

The private sector must continue to drive this change and enroll the educational sector in addressing what's at stake: future competitiveness, market share, knowledge capital, and surviving in a global economy where only the smartest will survive.

■ ■ ■

CHAPTER NINE

Biotech—
Designer Babies and
200-Year-Old Birthday Parties

THE TOP TEN BIOTECH TRENDS FOR THE 21ST CENTURY

1. By 2002, we will decipher the human genome, the blueprint of our DNA.

2. Genetic solutions to human ills will be highly prized intellectual property.

3. New biotech drugs will save countless lives and eliminate many diseases.

4. We will create designer babies with altered genes to enhance their capabilities and eliminate unwanted characteristics.

5. We will learn to turn on and off certain genes to influence performance and health.

6. The convergence of biotech and computers will accelerate the genetic redesign of all living things.

7. We will learn to clone organs to enhance health and longevity.

8. Privacy issues about access to individuals' genetic data will cause conflicts among people, business, and governments.

9. Careers, relationships, and opportunities will be influenced by genetic heritage.

10. Biotech for human enhancement will be the most profitable industry in the 21st century.

Ninety percent of all disease may be rooted in our genes. If this is true, then the quality of our lives is about to change radically. The human genome—every minute detail of the genetic code in the DNA encryption of our existence as a species—will be completely defined by about 2002. With this accomplishment, we will move from the Pre-Genomic to the Post-Genomic Era.

The key driver of lifestyles and performance in the Post-Genomic Era will be the amazing intelligence that we will gain from mapping the human genome. There may not be any knowledge more powerful in determining our destiny than the genomic blueprint of our DNA. This effort will only begin with the mapping of the human genome, but it will mark a milestone in history and commerce. This chapter explores what the implications will be.

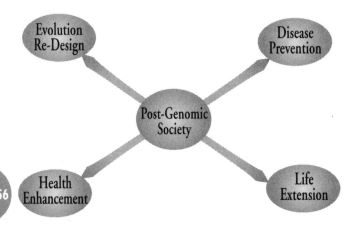

The Genome Race

At first, many people were shocked by the boldness of Perkin-Elmer's vision to privatize the human genome project originally begun by the National Institutes of Health (NIH). This is the most ambitious collaborative project ever undertaken by science and industry. Clearly, the private sector has its eye on the incalculable value of the prize for finishing first.

The investment: $3 billion and a research group consisting of hundreds of technical specialists and scientists using some of the most powerful and sophisticated supercomputing facilities on earth. The prize: the potential *patent rights on genetic solutions* for virtually every known physiological condition, disease, and "correctable" attribute of the human species, up to and possibly including the process of aging itself. The effort will deliver the blueprint to the 100,000 human genes that exist in a molecule of DNA.

In other words, by 2002 or sooner, humanity may have at its disposal the technical potential for re-engineering its own physical evolution—a "process commodity" of the next millennium.

A giant and wondrous industry will form around genomics, the science of engineering DNA to heal, enhance, prolong, or even create life. What would people pay to be able to put off the ravages of old age and disease? How different would our lives be if we could look forward to 150 or 200 years of productive and vigorous life? This is the personal impact of geno-pharmacopeia. The economics of longevity and health will explode new markets.

Just as insurance companies are resetting their policies to adjust to people's longer lives, which could routinely top 100 years, we shall soon witness the first immortals in our society. This is where the geno-pharmacopeia is taking us—deep into the redesign of human longevity.

Genomic Medicine, Part I: Year 2010 Ken Visits the Longevity Clinic

Ken is frustrated. He is too early for Total Cyber-Mind Downloading. At this point, downloading his human consciousness and having it "wake up" in a synthetic body is too experimental.

He is obsessed with his own mortality—or rather extending his life for as long as he can outrun the Grim Reaper. This focus is typical for the aging baby boomers who have lots of cash and not a lot of time to spend it, up until now. Longevity has become a trillion-dollar global industry totally transforming health care. We no longer just fix people; we redesign them. This the Post-Genomic Era, and a thriving industry has grown up around the mapping of the human genome.

Ken's particular genomic profile hasn't yet been suited to some of the more radical life-extension therapies. He's hoping that his doctor, Jeffrey, will have some good news today.

"Details, details. I am ready to wake up in another body," says Ken to his doctor over the vid-phone.

"Yes, but science isn't there yet. Right now we are trying to get you to live long enough to maybe enjoy that Cyber-Mind download in the future," Jeffrey indicates.

"Great idea. Imagine downloading an entire human consciousness. Another 20 years and we'll get that right," Ken says. "If I can wait that long."

The doctor continues. "Maybe even before, who knows. Being a doctor these days is very exciting."

157

"Hey, I am thrilled for you. So what do you have for me on the procedure, Jeffrey?"

"That's why we are going to meet. Ken, it looks good. See you at 4 P.M."

Ken got telemersed last year. It cost him over $150,000, and insurance didn't help one bit. It reversed his aging and health status. Ken picked up maybe 40 extra years. It's clear that the kids will live much longer than he will. His wife, too. They will be healthier, too, but that's okay. His genomics were not the best.

Ken is visiting his doctor for a post-genomic check-up to determine if there is anything new going on with his interest in life extension. Based on his genomic profile, he already knows that he will need a new kidney within five years. Ken is an aging baby boomer who sold his company years ago, but he hasn't slowed down. In spite of his pace, for a guy of 68, he looks good. He exercises and eats well. That's really paid off.

Before going to the West Coast Longevity Clinic, last week Ken pressed his thumb on the secure Integrated Longevity Website to send his genomic profile. Data from the transdermal patch he applied before giving a genetic sample was captured and sent to the clinic for analysis. His entire genomic download took less than a minute. Today he would be coming in for a counseling session with his doctor.

"Well, Ken, the good news is that we have updated your Personalized Genomic Profile, and there is no bad news. Things are as they should be, and you are looking good. The telemerse-reversal therapy is working, and we have arrested about 30 percent of your aging. Your enhancements have progressed nicely. We got you that new protein to reduce your risk of a heart attack. You are fully upgraded, and you've got the physical performance level of a 40-year-old. Your test results show increased muscle mass, and your immune response data is terrific. Not bad for a chronological age of nearly 70." (To be continued...)

Human Redesign

We are on the horizon of reconstructing ourselves at the molecular level. We will achieve the ability to re-engineer our own evolution, as a design strategy and as an artifact of necessity. The scale of what this represents is nothing less than the reshaping of the human species, defined not by the "rules" of the natural universe, but by the harnessing of the Power Tools we have contrived. It is a feat made possible by the convergence of nanotechnology, computing, communications technology, and the applications of Artificial Life and Artificial Intelligence.

The harbingers of this feat are already here. Genetically engineered food crops are producing higher yields than traditional agriculture, and, by 2005, most crops grown commercially will be genetically altered. New molecular medicines are eradicating diseases. Cloning techniques produced Dolly the sheep. Genomic databases are doubling every 12 months. Biotech breakthroughs involving stem cells that may someday grow organs are quickly becoming a reality.

The manipulation of individual molecules and atoms, as an engineering process, mapped against the use of computers and networks to draw upon the world's knowledge, will enable us to "invent" any living substance we want. This breakthrough will change humanity's destiny by offering choices in how or what we want to create. But the most dramatic outcome is that we will essentially re-create ourselves.

At this moment, dozens of companies are in a race to deliver the latest advancements in biotech solutions to eliminate disease, extend human longevity, and possibly abolish the process of aging. As they unravel DNA then learn to rearrange it on-demand, they will put the very mechanisms by which we re-engineer ourselves on the menu. We will deliberately and artificially cause our evolution.

Currently, few people understand the awesome implications of this corporate research. Even fewer have a strategic view of reshaping and creating businesses to accommodate the effects of our having longer lives, enhanced health, and superior performance.

Protein Is Software

The mapping of the human genome will open up countless opportunities to revolutionize every industry. The amount of information that this effort will generate is staggering. Just learning to manage the genomic databases of the near future will be tremendous.

To better understand this projection, consider the statement by Dr. Randy Scott of Incyte, Inc. (**www.incyte.com**), who said, "Protein is software" at a Seizing Opportunities in Biochips Conference in San Francisco. Software tells the computer what to do. Similarly, proteins arranged in a double helix configuration form a molecular construct referred to as DNA, which is the internal code that forms the instruction sets in all living organisms. From animals and fish to viruses to humans, DNA is the blueprint of life.

As part of our discovery process in working with DNA, we will not only learn how to send new instructions to existing life, but also to bring into being things that don't naturally occur. The synthetic creation of genetic, protein, molecular, and even subatomic DNA will yield solutions we cannot even envision today.

Right now, companies such as Affymetrix (**www.affymetrix.com**), Symetri, Hyseq, and many others are combining technologies to produce new protein constructions. The process involves microscale fabrication technology, very similar to what is used to create computer chips, and molecular "probes" constructed with partial fragments of DNA, RNA, and other molecular protein components. In short, we are learning to deconstruct the building blocks of life and at the same time, create a process of reassembling these blocks to fix or invent new life forms.

Casey's Biomorph: Year 2020

When she turned ten, Casey's parents gave her a BioMorph as a gift. This one was a custom Bio-Hack. She remembered the day when her Dad returned from his business trip to New China and brought her BioMorph home. She was really excited to meet her. Of course, her parents had told her that the BioMorph wasn't like her animated dolls or Robo-Droids. No, the Biomorph was a living entity, the sister Casey had always wanted.

The BioMorph had some small amount of human DNA. The rest of her DNA was animal. She was 15 percent human, 20 percent fox, 30 percent dog, 10 percent Bengal tiger, and the rest a mixture of bio-engineered DNA that was multipurpose for enhancing human-to-BioMorph communications, personality, and security.

"Casey, I want to introduce you to your BioMorph. You can name her, as I promised you," said her Dad.

"Gee, Dad, that's great! We talked about names in BioMorph Care School. I'm going to call her Belle."

"I like that name; it fits me purrrr-fectly" the BioMorph softly said.

"I've never had a BioMorph. You're my first."

"Well, I've never been with a human before. You're my first, too!"

Belle was bio-brewed in a nanobiology clinic just outside the city limits of New China. The BioMorph was designed to fit the specific criteria that both Casey's parents and the clinic's bio-docs thought would be best, based on behavior modeling and genomic mapping.

High communication skills, a guard-and-protect aptitude, and a maternal personality and behavior set were the priority programs used. Only BioMorphs with 15 percent human DNA or less were legal in Euroland and in the United States, which were both "home" to Casey's family. The Gene Police were everywhere, and the law was strictly enforced.

"My primary objectives are to help, serve, and protect you, Casey."

"Well, let's get to it. How about a walk to the park?"

A Critical Threshold

The combination of "biochips" and their genetic, engineered variants called "genechips" with supercomputers running A-Life and AI programs will lead to the discovery and extraction of new genetic creations. These creations will be harvested from enormous arrays of biochips, which will act like a network of wombs all giving birth at the same time.

This is an extremely elaborate and complex undertaking, covered in thousands of technical papers and financed by billions of dollars. I make no attempt here to even begin to delve into the technical detail of the genetic, molecular, and protein engineering or genopharmacology required to produce this breakthrough. The point here is to indicate that we are on the threshold of using the Power Tools to reinvent living things.

There is much at stake: the wealth and security of nations and the competitive advantage of the digital enterprise of the next millennium.

Biotech is currently a field with more than 13,000 companies and $20 billion in annual revenues, and it's still a young science. For an in-depth, online look at the industry at this stage, go to the site hosted by Synergistic Media Network, Inc. (www.biospace.com), which links to major biotech companies, news, and research. It also includes marketing news useful to futuristic planning.

Be prepared for 2002—for the dawn of the Post-Genomic Era and the emergence of an $800 billion marketplace dedicated to the enhancement of health and human performance in a population where aging may no longer be a major concern.

Better Living Through Biotech

Just as the industrial revolution transformed the 19th century, and the information revolution has reshaped the 20th, the next century will be molded by advances in biotechnology with the catalyst for change being the Human Genome Project. There are three major converging areas where the impact of this work will significantly influence individuals, businesses, and society. These are:

- Health and longevity

- Increased intellectual power

- Performance enhancement

Genetic Health Care

Errors or damage to genes are responsible for 3,000 to 4,000 hereditary diseases, including Huntington's disease, cystic fibrosis, and Duchenne muscular dystrophy. In addition, altered genes are known to increase the risk of developing cancer, diabetes, heart disease, and other common illnesses.

Access to genetic data opens up unparalleled opportunities in health-related industries. While certain genes are common to all humans, other genes appear to be somewhat personal and may be early indicators not only of disease, but also of dysfunctional behavioral patterns.

Armed with this information, we no longer have to wait for illnesses to show up or for certain psychological or physical breakdowns to occur before we see a doctor. This is a reactive, fiscally unsound, and outmoded approach to health care. Biotech is ushering in an era of proactive health-care professionals who will empower patients with an arsenal of sophisticated on-demand bio-engineered drugs, analysis scans, and interventions customized for each person's genetic footprint.

This will present a host of new ethical considerations about who receives genetic drugs and the protection of genetic privacy rights. Already, some insurance companies in Europe are using genetic information—bioinformatics—to approve or reject insurance applicants. No doubt, they will also want to decide who gets what gene therapy as it becomes a commonplace treatment for chronic problems.

This issue should be in our consciousness now, as genetic interventions are first being adopted. Genetic techniques have already been used in treating patients with obstructed blood vessels in their legs. Scientists grow new blood vessels around artery blockages to restore the flow of blood to the feet—a major step toward developing gene therapy for heart disease. It's also possible to be tested for hereditary genes. Some people are opting to find out if they're genetically programmed to have Alzheimer's disease, for example. Genetic screening for breast cancer is also possible and may become widespread.

Finding out that we carry these types of genetic time bombs could help us—and our insurance companies—chart our options, but it could also cause torment and confusion if we haven't developed a way to cure or prevent the disease. Nevertheless, commercial genetic testing will become more common and represent a multibillion-dollar industry. We will have desktop gene scanners available to everyone. Smart future leaders are those who take steps now to profit from the opportunities in this field.

Resetting the Master Clock

With genetic engineering, a world free of deadly diseases—and deadly criminals—is a possibility. That alone makes a longer life possible. But the ethical issues are deep and complicated. How do we as a society make decisions about who to adjust, what genes to alter, and under what circumstances? There are large ethical, social, and commercial questions we will have to navigate as companies, societies, and individuals.

It is clear that we will come to redefine aging in our lifetime, attempting to replace a span of physical and mental deterioration with a time of enjoyment, leisure, and productivity. How different our society and workplace will be with 200-year-old vital and energetic people. What will be the impact on the economy? The workforce?

163

Some geneticists are mapping genes that could lead to a magic code for life extension, but they face an awesome challenge. The problem facing scientists trying to find a genetic button for slowing the aging process is the sheer number of genes involved. Geneticist George Martin at the University of Washington in Seattle believes that even if only a few master-clock genes directly guide aging in humans, up to 7,000 more might be peripherally involved. Re-engineering even one of these polygenetic traits is an exquisitely complex process. Re-engineering all 7,000 may prove impossible. But maybe we don't need to find or unlock all the polygenetic codes—traits made up of multiple genes—to accomplish our objective. Perhaps identifying just those that fulfill our goals is enough.

Scientists studying the aging process itself are making significant discoveries. University of California researchers, for example, have found an area at the tip of chromosomes that appears to shorten, fuselike, as we grow older. Could extinguishing the fuse bring aging to a halt?

Other studies show how wastes produced during eating contaminate the cells of our bodies; this process can lead to bodywide breakdowns associated with aging. Cleaning up these cells might rejuvenate the body. Could we learn to retrofit a "friendly" virus or bacterium that could identify and scavenge or cleanup our cells? This is not far-fetched if we consider that friendly bacteria are cleaning up oil spills in the ocean.

It's inevitable that life spans will not only be extended, but that they'll be improved as well. Imagine when we can celebrate our 200th birthday with a biotech makeover—soft skin, excellent vision, high energy, and sexual abilities —all attributes that we previously could only enjoy during our youth.

Immortality for Sale: Year 2040

Before the breakthrough in cloning, and stem cell and tele-merse research, which started back in 1998, the idea of extending lifetimes had never before seemed possible. By 2015, ten years after the human genome was mapped, we began to realize as a society that we held the first keys to prolong life. We were taking baby steps toward redesigning humans.

At first, the longevity therapy was expensive and cumbersome to deliver. All of this was experimental until 2030, when the first generation of immortals became possible. Bioscience had matured to be able to genetically change those genes that regulated the human time clock, that which controlled the aging process. Then the social problems began.

Who gets to decide who lives longer and how long? At first, these decisions were left to the supply-and-demand economics of the marketplace. In some countries, an elite came to political power that had been bio-enhanced to live as long as they wished. In other countries, politics and bio-capitalism collided when becoming immortal became a human right and no longer determined by class, political power, or even economics. Different countries regulated these Immortal Rights according to their laws and practices. We entered the age of immortal humans.

A CMN Exclusive Interview— The First Immortal: Year 2035

"This is Max Flato from CMN reporting from California. In just a few moments, we will be meeting an extraordinary individual. She is the crowning achievement of thousands of years of science and medicine. Julia may represent the next step in human evolution. She is the first of the Immortals.

There are some who would say that this is unnatural. Others say that immortality is inevitable. You, our viewers, will be the judge. It is a fantastic breakthrough certain to shake the very foundation of our society for generations to come. What are the implications of immortality for individuals and society? Do you want to live forever? Who gets to decide who extends their life and who doesn't? These questions and more we will seek answers for tonight when we interview The First Immortal. Stay tuned. Stay smart. Stay with CMN."

"Welcome, Julia."

"Thanks for inviting me."

"So, Julia, how does it feel to be the first immortal human on the planet?"

"Well, I feel just like everyone else who has been enhanced. The difference is that instead of living 150 or 200 years of age, I will live on indefinitely, so the Bio-Docs tell me."

"What does it mean to you to live forever?"

"It means I will have a life span of hundreds, maybe even thousands, of years if I choose. It means that I can live many lifetimes all at once. Careers such as being a doctor, artist, and scientist now become possible. It means also that I can plan a longer life with certainty that there will be all the time I need to achieve, learn, even love."

"Do you see any downside to immortality?"

"Well, first of all, I may not live forever. I could have an accident or even choose not to live anymore."

"Now really, Julia, why would you not want to live any longer?"

"I might feel that after 100 careers, I've run out of challenges. Being immortal also makes it harder to find a spouse."

"I think we are all more than a bit jealous of you, Julia, and would trade places in a minute. Let me ask you this. How did you qualify?"

"A combination of the right Genomic Profile, and, I guess, the best genes, helped me qualify."

"And you had the financial resources to afford the procedure?"

"Yes, I admit having the right finances was part of it, but only one part. Without the right Genomic Profile, I would not be able to sustain the genetic enhancements."

Within the next eight years, researchers may be able to reset the genetic clock that ticks off how long we've been predestined to live. Objections may come from those who believe manipulating life is morally wrong or from those who feel that the mystery of life is sacrosanct. But, genetic engineering is in the cards, and the benefits—including longevity—are part of the new rules.

The Longevity Business

New technologies to increase the quality of our lives will spawn creative and profitable enterprises. Just the packaging of information about biotech and its projected impact is a business opportunity of major proportions. Bio-informatic enterprises will profit handsomely by providing the business intelligence necessary to manage biotech companies.

Perhaps the most dramatic new ventures will be those that take advantage of the huge amount of genomic information available to formulate personalized medicine and bio-enhancements. Companies will create therapies optimized for individuals to extend their life. Most of these services will be available over the Net and operate outside the watchful eyes of governments and authorities that might restrict the bio-enhancement industry. Extending life spans— the mission of the longevity industry—will involve a variety of players in the 21st century. This is an example of how that market may be divided:

The Bio-enhancement Industry in 2007

- **Big Pharma:** This group comprises the traditional pharmaceutical companies such as Searle, Merck, and Upjohn. These companies will have the deepest pockets and resources. They will not necessarily be the most innovative in terms of research and development, but they will better understand marketing and distribution.

- **Pure Biotech:** These are pure-play bioscience companies working to develop proteins, gene mapping processes, or genomic solutions. Companies such as Genentech, Affymetrix, and Amgen fall into this category, as well as numerous underfunded, smaller ventures that will be consolidated into Big Pharma over time.

- **Genomic Scanners:** These folks have yet to emerge in the industry. These companies will be outsourcing resources, with both Big Pharma and the smaller biotech companies looking to them to conduct massive gene sequencing and diagnostics.

- **Bio-Hacks:** These rogue entrepreneurs will operate outside the regulatory confines of certain nations. They will deal directly with consumers or other smaller, less legitimate companies that operate in the emerging bioscience global Black Market. They will offer accelerated individualized solutions that push the envelope of the bio-enhancement industry.

Genomic Nutraceuticals: Year 2007

A new generation of drugs that enhances individual intelligence, memory, learning, physical performance, and productivity has come into vogue as pharmaceutical companies help us realize our full potential through chemistry. Drugs that enable us to overcome the ravages of Alzheimer's or to physically perform like a 35-year-old at our 200th birthday party are accepted as part of the culture. Being sick or bedridden due to illness or disability is obsolete and abnormal. Smart drugs, engineered on-demand, and customized for our needs, goals, and destinies are the new rage. They increase our performance in work, art, sports, and culture.

I predict that there will be back-of-the-garage biotech startups by 2003 that will specialize in creating certain pieces of genetic materials that can be ordered over the Internet and configured on-demand. These "genetic packets" will then be incorporated into customized bio-engineered drugs and interventions to enable a person to deal with an immediate, pressing problem. Use of the drug could be by such traditional means as a tablet or inhaler, as well as more refined methods using air injections or sonar syringes.

The Enhancement Business

By 2010, biotech will find a $500 billion marketplace of individuals anxious to use bio-engineering to be all they can be. Bio-engineering solutions will run the gamut from smart drugs to bio-implants, genetic microsurgery, and genetic enhancement therapy. Customized on-demand bioinformatics solutions that fit our particular needs will be commonplace, everyday events.

Customers include the sales representative who needs to scan and retain thousands of pages of notes for a meeting the next day. Or an athlete who needs a physical boost for a marathon. Maybe a young mother fighting off fatigue in order to nurse, prepare a holiday meal, and study for a final exam in cellular physics. Based on our genetic profile, we'll receive a customized download to boost our physical strength, expand our memory, and rest our body

167

with fewer hours' sleep. If we want the intelligence of an Einstein or the agility of a Michael Jordan, why not have it? Genomics will bring a brave new world of choices and challenges to our lives.

At the same time we revel in the potential, we must guard against the extreme: creating a genetic elite who will have advanced skills, capabilities, and intelligence. There are many important political and social questions we have not asked about the tomorrow we are creating in the science labs today.

Designed Evolution

As we learn to manipulate genetic material, the day will come when we'll be ready to redesign the human species. This biological redesign of what we consider human will open up a set of weird new challenges and ethical considerations. But, it is important that we examine those moves we are contemplating on the genetic chessboard of evolution.

We must consider today the range of choices we will face tomorrow—and some of them will shock us. What happens if we decide to abandon the physical form of being human and select an animal or transgenic form—a combination of animals? We will learn to redesign the human being because we will have the life sciences and digital tools to do so. A lizard look or identical appearance to a celebrity may define a person's style. The seeds of this makeover are in the labs. The impact on society will be profound and, perhaps, profane.

Nontraditional competitors will emerge in droves from outside the traditional biotech industry once the lucrative nature of the enhancement business is realized. As bioinformatics becomes as routine as filling a prescription at a pharmacy is today, marketing companies will emerge to merchandise genomics services directly to a mass consumer base over the Internet.

Designer Babies: Year 2007

Fred and Nomeko Shazera decide to have another child for their five-year-old daughter to play with. Counseling provided by the local medical center makes them aware of some new options recently made available to parents who are interested in human enhancement.

Human enhancement is a social movement of medical enterprises, scientists, and policy makers who believe in enhancing the physical and mental capabilities of yet-to-be-born children—altering a fertilized embryo's genes—for the good of society and the individual. Enhanced children score higher on tests and achieve better overall performance. There is also a tax break from the IRS, and grants offered by the National Science Foundation to consider. But Fred and Nomeko have questions.

Fred, forever a skeptic about new technology, polls his friends at the health club. Some feel the idea of enhancing children is too strange. Others think the idea of assisting kids in reaching their full potential—with a little help from the good old gene doctors—is great. Competition for jobs in the complex techno-world of the 21st century is keen, and any help is useful. Most think enhancing is a good idea as long as it is safe. But is it? wonders Fred.

What it finally comes down to is that Fred and Nomeko don't want their newborn to miss out on all the advantages that bio-enhancement can provide. Simply electing enhancement prequalifies their child for private tutors and the university of his or her choice. The National Bio-Enhancement Foundation offers a generous grant so Fred and Nomeko can afford virtual learning courses about genetic advances and what they will mean for the whole family.

A Visit to the Pacific Bio-Enhancement Center

The Shazeras are referred to the Pacific Bio-Enhancement Center, one of the leading fertility centers. Pacific Bio specializes in a variety of bio-enhancement packages. Dr. Frisco, a world-class expert in bio-enhancement and fertility, explains how recent advances in human genome research have provided a host of new choices. Genetic material can be identified and manipulated to achieve certain objectives. Bio-enhancement can involve the designing of select genes that could be inserted into the fertilized embryo to alter the physical, mental, and emotional makeup of the child.

Just by conducing a genomic scan of their embryo, Dr. Frisco is able identify certain genetic risks for disease and longevity, as well as personality and behavior characteristics.

All of this sounds fascinating and a bit scary to Fred and Nomeko, but they want to go forward. Dr. Frisco explains that all applicants have to be screened to determine biocompatibility fitness. He needs to examine Fred and Nomeko's genes to determine if there will be a sustainable result from the bio-enhancement procedure. Dr. Frisco takes a blood sample with a painless robo-shot and downloads it to the lab over the Net while they are talking. Counseling and education is also part of the qualification process, he reminds them. Within two minutes, the bio-compatibility fit is determined, and they are issued a permission certificate by the Public Genome Department. Dr. Frisco announces, "Good news!" They have qualified.

Relieved, Fred and Nomeko decide to go ahead. They're asked to choose their child's bio-enhancement preferences, referred to as bio-traits. The doctor will then look for a match with the parents' existing DNA. They're given a chart to look over their choices.

Bio-Enhancement Center Options

Package	Genetic Origin	Skills	Career Options
Smart Achiever Package	DNA from Nobel Prize winners	High creativity, intelligence	Biotech, telecom, engineering
Super Sports Package	DNA from world-class athletes	Strength, pain endurance, coordination	Pro sports
Arts & Music Package	DNA from award-winning artists	High creativity, persistence	Writer, painter, composer, actor
Spirituality Package	DNA from spiritual leaders	Vision, intuition, compassion	Social or religious service
Peak Performer Business Package	DNA from business leaders	Vision, leadership, commitment	Run or create an organization
Make-A-Difference Package	DNA from leading social activists	Altruism, leadership, commitment	Medicine, education, social service

They make their choices, and a few months later are looking at their pride and joy—a beautiful, enhancement-packed baby girl. The birth certificate tells all:

Birth Certificate: 2008

Name:
MIKO BELL SHAZERA

Gender:
FEMALE (MODIFIED SELECTION)

Conception date:
DEC. 10, 2002

Birthdate:
AUG. 8, 2007

Weight/length:
8 POUNDS/20 INCHES

Eyes:
GREEN (MODIFIED SELECTION)

Estimated IQ:
125-150

Estimated Life Span:
130 YEARS

Birth location:
SPACE STATION KENNEDY-YELTSIN, HABITAT #4

Attending physician:
DR. JOSE COHEN VIA VIRTUAL TELEMEDICINE LINK

Parents, ages, occupations:
FRED SHAZERA, 47, BIOMEDICAL RESEARCH; NOMEKO SHAZERA, 46, BIOMED RESEARCH

Conception engineering process:
IN VITRO NANO-FERTILIZATION FROM FROZEN DONOR EGG.

Bio-enhancement packages:
NOBEL PRIZE SMART ACHIEVER PACKAGE WITH ANTI-GLOBAL VIRUS; KINDNESS AND ARTISTIC AMPLIFICATION LEVEL 1: WELLNESS PAK WITH LOW CHOLESTEROL MODIFIER; SOCIAL AFFILIATION CORRECTION LEVEL 2.

Enhancement recommendation:
NOBEL PRIZE PACKAGE UPGRADE EVERY TWO YEARS; NANO IMPLANT OF WIRELESS INTERNET BIOCHIP FOR EASY UPGRADE LINKS.

Biocompatibility:
9.5—HIGH PROJECTED SUCCESS FACTOR.

Prenatal care:
DNA SURGERY AT FOUR MONTHS TO CORRECT POTENTIAL LIVER DYSFUNCTION AND PREVENT HEART DISEASE AND OBESITY RISK. CHROMOSOME CORRECTIONS MADE IN-VITRO.

Genetic scan results:
ADDITIONAL QUASI-BAND ON CHROMOSOME 62: DEFINED SHENTS ON 22 AND 7.

Risk factor recommendations:
EYE SURGERY REQUIRED BY AGE 65: KNEE REPLACEMENT AT AGE 75.

Merchandising Bio-upgrades

What parent could resist a child's request to write like Emily Dickinson or ski like Hermann Maier? And all for the equivalent of $15,000 in 2008 (which will have the value of $3,000 in today's dollars). Learning and training will be enhanced via genetic therapy. While some of us might laugh at this prospect today, in the future, the enhancement subject will be dinner conversation, or perhaps gossip.

Once the marketing gurus perceive this impulse, and it's surfacing already, the sky's the limit on merchandising enhancement products and services. Biotech will be an advertising bonanza for future creative marketers of the life sciences.

Bio Kids, Inc: Year 2018

Ron Rodriguez, vice president of marketing at BioKids, Inc., gets an urgent e-mail while trying out a virtual jet-skiing vacation package set in the Caribbean. The company's bestseller in its SuperGenes product line, "Life Forms on Demand," has a bug. The R&D lab has confirmed that a "warrior gene" has infiltrated the firm's bio-foundry, where biotech life forms are built on-demand by customers who can formulate from a menu bio-engineered limbs and brains to create a pet or companion of their choosing.

In the latest upgrade, youngsters can choose what types of behavior, personality, and intelligence they want in their creations. Walking and talking robots, flying birds, barking dogs, and even unicorns are popular.

Rodriguez suspected a "bug" because of recent reports of erratic behavior by artificial entities that had frightened some children. This bug is a nasty nano-virus designed by some bio-cracker reject from the Crypto Cops, no doubt. He shuts off his virtual vacation sequence and punches in the code for GeneFix, a small biotech company that specializes in troubleshooting genetically produced games.

Within hours, the company downloads a fix—an enhanced "super trait" that can be injected into the bio-foundry to render the "bug" powerless and correct the behavioral problem! Gotta love those bio-hackers. (Bio-hackers are the good guys; bio-crackers are the bad guys.)

A GeneFix Internet agent has also tracked down the probable culprit—MaxIntell, a competing Bio-Toy producer—and has filed a protest with the Internet security network. Rodriguez makes sure the fix is posted so all customers can download the genetic algorithm to "heal" the erratic behavior of the affected life form. That problem solved, Rodriguez punches an option on his virtual vacation package that reminds him of a toy his grandfather enjoyed—an old-fashioned steam locomotive. With a touch of nostalgia, he purchases the option, complete with trees, farmland, and river scenery.

Heck, he might even take the whole family to see the real Grand Canyon.

BioKids is back on-line.

The Human Body Shop

Cloning—the creation of an identical entity or organ from a single biological cell—merits special attention as a biotech industry, as a process, and as a challenge to Pre-Genomic Era thinking.

By 2010, cloning will be well established, with a major market being the "human body shop" for organ replacements. This is the real promise of cloning: being able to synthesize from our cellular material the perfect organ that will never be rejected since it would be an exact genetic match of the original. What would we spend to gain another 50 years with a cloned organ? Everything we have. The bio-industrial complex is listening.

The cloning industry will be developed so that we'll all pay a fee for a "body shop" of customized genetic material that can be replicated to prolong our lives. I predict that insurance companies will demand that we have organ-replacement policies. These would include cloning organs if a genetic scan shows that we are at-risk, for example, of kidney failure by age 75.

An entirely new industry will emerge based on cloning and related breakthroughs. By 2015, those companies that can provide functionality and services to assist this technology will see a level of profitability that can only be dreamed about in today's economy. Companies would be wise to invest today in preparation for such awesome 21st-century opportunities.

■ ■ ■

The following is a true account of the first creation of a human being to service and extend the life and health of another human.

The Foundation of Cloning

In 1988, Anissa Ayala, a high school student from California, was diagnosed with leukemia. Without a bone-marrow operation, she would die. After two or three years of searching unsuccessfully for a compatible donor, Anissa's parents made a decision destined to go down in the annals of science.

Anissa's parents decided to have another child to become the donor their daughter so desperately needed to survive.

Not knowing if the child's bone marrow would even be compatible, they proceeded anyway. Tests during pregnancy confirmed a positive match with Anissa. The bone marrow transplant was done 14 months later. The operation was a success, and Anissa's leukemia disappeared.

Don't humans have the right to protect life by using the latest technology? This and other medical, social, and ethical issues will shake our society as we grapple with how best to use the power of biotech.

Biocapitalism

That cloning of humans as inevitable can be deduced from the sentiment surrounding the 1997 cloning of the lamb, Dolly. At first, people were appalled, and California immediately passed a law against the cloning of humans. President Clinton signed a law banning the use of federal funds to further human cloning experiments.

Within a year, public sentiment had shifted. Researchers from the University of Massachusetts and Advanced Cell Technology, Inc., cloned a genetically engineered cow on January 20, 1998. The goal of creating transgenic cows is to mass-produce drugs for humans in cows' milk—a technology called "pharming." Additionally, animals will be bred to provide organs on-demand for countless patients who need them.

Infertility clinics that said they'd never clone have begun to experiment with human eggs. Also, the government is supporting new research on the cloning of monkeys, encouraging scientists to perfect techniques that can be transferred to humans.

There's even one bio-religious organization, RAEL, that has set up a company called Valiant Venture Ltd., in the Bahamas for the purpose of providing cloning services to wealthy families. The service, called CLONAID, would provide assistance to parents willing to have a child cloned from one of them. The price tag is $200,000, with the cloning expertise coming from partnering with laboratories in different parts of the world. For $50,000, the company will provide the safe storage of cells from a living child to create its clone sometime in the future should the child die. At some point, such cloning companies could well be a growth industry.

Genomic Medicine, Part II: Year 2015
Ken Investigates Organ Cloning

"And what about the cloning procedure we talked about?" Ken asks Jeffrey, his doctor at the Longevity Clinic.

"I determined that your genomic profile is a good fit for the Transgenic Cloning procedure," Jeffrey states.

"Great. When do we start? How does it work? What will it buy me in years?"

"Hold on. I think I can give you some estimates based on a genomic graphics display. Look at this." Jeffrey moves his hands in the air, and a virtual video screen comes on in front of them. Graphs go up indicating how much long Ken is likely to live with the procedure. "It's just a guess, Ken."

Jeffrey continues, "If we start the cloning process in a few weeks, we can have a kidney ready for you by Christmas. The kidney we grow will need some bio-implants, but it will be ready in time. We project that you can extend your life another 30 to 50 years beyond your current estimate of 150."

"About the transgenics part, once you've got my DNA, why do we need to use a baboon as a carrier?" Ken is nervous about involving an animal.

"Our ability to grow a healthy and stable kidney from your DNA is dependent on using a baboon as a host. We have FDA approval, and all the data show that it will be a good match."

"And once my kidney is harvested from the baboon?"

"The baboon goes on to live a normal life released into the wild."

"Is there any wild DNA or transgenic sharing of cells across the organ barrier? You know, am I going to start craving bananas once I get my baboon kidney? How about any stray bacteria or baboon diseases?"

"Everybody has this concern, Ken. Just remember: This is your DNA, incubated with the best human tissue and bio-engineering. The host entity just happens to a baboon. There are minor concerns about mixing baboon and human DNA, but I wouldn't worry about it. Tests show that there is less than a one percent chance of getting any transgenic diseases from the host."

"How about abnormal hair growth or an appetite for—"

"Oh, please. Look, Ken, I understand your concerns. The best thing is for you to see the Longevity Counselor to work through them. Will you?"

"What if I start walking on all fours? Should I be watching Tarzan movies?"

"You might be a nut case—don't prove me right. Relax. Take a swim. Play with the grandchildren. Don't worry." (To be continued...)

Transplanting Life

By 2010, we will be using our biotech savvy to go beyond ourselves and our personal desire for better organs, longer lives, and enhanced performance. Not only will we be able to grow organs on-demand, but also brains of organic neural networks by manipulating genetic materials.

The next step in this pathway will be to insert brains capable of performing humanlike thinking processes into mobile robots, linking the brains to synthetic intelligence as well as networked information systems. This will usher in the era of androids—productive, human-appearing robots that are mobile, smart, and autonomous. Artificial eyes, noses, and ears as well as limbs and physical characteristics will be grown for android deployment.

Biotech's emergence will exist with the parallel development of artificial intelligence, synthetic A-Life entities and smaller, faster, and more powerful computers that will redefine the whole classification of intelligence on our planet. Carbon-based life forms such as humans will be joined by thriving colonies of synthetic and bio-engineered life forms both on this planet and off world in space.

Genomic Medicine, Part III: Year 2028 Re-Animation Orientation

"Okay, Ken, time to wake up for your Re-Animation Orientation," says Jeffrey, his doctor, as he opens up the stasis capsule where Ken has been sleeping in a simulated Re-Animation test. This is designed to help train Ken about what to expect.

Re-Animation has not been a successful procedure yet. It is unclear if there is actually a Mind Transfer that occurs. Better orientation of the subjects is thought to be the way to achieve better results. Only volunteers, mostly terminally ill patients, have become test subjects. The next batch is brave explorers out to chart new dimensions of human existence. Ken is one them.

"You mean brain-drain don't you?" Ken jokes.

"Look, you're the one who wanted to be apart of the first experiments on downloading people's consciousness back in 2010!"

"That was before I was spending my life savings on telemerse-reversal therapy! Well, it is appealing to consider that I could live forever in a synthetic android body with my current brain," Ken defended.

"Consciousness, but definitely not your brain. That's just the casing for your mind," Jeffrey went on.

"Whatever my mind is."

"Now, the important thing here is for you to train yourself to wake up when stimulated so we can identify that it is you. This is important. Don't kid around. If we don't get the signal and you don't get Re-Animated, then we will assume you are dead to the download and try again."

"Listen, doc, I want this to work, so I will do everything I can. But what if the Bio-Transfer doesn't work. Will you continue to try to Re-Animate me?" asked Ken a bit nervously.

"The Cloning and Re-Animating Ethics Ruling made by the FDA states we get three chances to Re-Animate you. So if the Bio-Transfer or if some software or wetware glitch shows up, we will keep trying up to three times."

"After that, we have to return you to Mindware Stasis where you will be stored in memory until we can figure out how to bring you back."

"Great," laughed Ken. "Back on the shelf in memory. What an existence."

"Don't worry. You won't have any memory of the failure. You will be in digital bliss waiting to be liberated."

"You mean, what I don't know won't hurt me?"

"Be positive. Be positive," Jeffrey urged.

(Continued in the next chapter...)

Opportunities abound for those businesses that move forward to provide the slew of on-demand industrial and home applications resulting from this technological brew that is the convergence of biotech with other Power Tools. Imagine these future business scenarios:

- Leasing a bio-engineered brain to help redesign a manufacturing facility to enhance production. We could buy services from this bio-enhanced entity as we need it for creating new products or services over the Internet for our customers.

- That which is on our desks today—the PC—embedded in our heads. Tiny biochips composed of organic substances will make this possible. Real-time networking with Internet-based services, such as those described above, will be viewed as a competitive advantage.

- Relying on a combination of AI, human intelligence, and bio-enhanced intelligence to provide customer service, technical support, and more.

- Protecting the security of genomic databases so that people's DNA doesn't get stolen and sold to the highest bidder—especially highly engineered DNA of special value.

178

Shadow Lords As DNA Thieves: Year 2010

"Where did you acquire this outstanding package, Digger?" asks the excited customer, Sun, after downloading a gene-sequenced DNA sample. The sample was like a molecular hologram. It dazzled and danced under the bio-probe in the virtual lab set up on the Net. The data streamed across the screen.

"Interested. Good. Let's say that the Shadow Lords guarantees the highest quality DNA for the money," Digger, the Shadow Lord, hissed through her multiple lip earrings with diamond microchips glistening over the Net-TV link.

"But is it possible? This is the ImmunoBoost from ZeppaBio. This is *our company's* personal enhancement drug?"

"Yes, we bought it on the market very quietly, before your competition, the Bio-Kieretsu known as the Gates Group, could re-engineer it and make billions," says Digger, proud of her deal. They would both pay. She had a vision of off-shore digital money dancing through her brain implants.

After selling off their wireless holdings decades ago, The Gates Group went in big for biotech. They were ruthless, almost rivaling the Shadow Lords, but very good customers until now.

"The price, any price—I mean, what do you want? How much money?" The stuttering Mr. Sun was losing it fast.

"We want a controlling interest in Global BioData and all their DNA data warehouses—nothing less, nothing more," commands Digger.

"This is blackmail!" screams Sun, his temper rising.

"No, this is extortion. I will Vid-mail a copy of a confidential report indicating you stole the ImmunoBoost from your own Genomic data warehouse if you do not cooperate." Digger's satisfied smile showed how much she liked having complete control over her adversary. And, after all, he was from the weaker half of the species. He probably wasn't even enhanced. No matter. He would deal or be finished. His own people would terminate him, and she could make a deal with someone else or Gates. *No worry,* she thinks.

"My sushi is getting warm, Mr. Sun. Deal or not?"

Genomic Knowledge Management

Companies that want to harness the marketplace potential offered by biotech should start by recognizing a fundamental fact: The thousands of terabytes of genomic knowledge—DNA details—that we are attempting to control and manage will be the most valuable data warehouse in the history of civilization. Learning to identify how to use all this genomic knowledge will occupy much of the next century and beyond.

Companies not specifically drawing from this information to offer biotech products will find a niche in the middleware industry. They will use futuristic networked tools and marketing techniques to enable companies to deliver services that enhance and support the biotech revolution.

A leading-edge company that understands this is InforMax (**www. informaxinc.com**). Their software enables gene-discovery research to be undertaken and networked. They are providing the Power Tools that help companies manage bioinformatics, the knowledge that is critical to building a profitable biotech venture.

Their focus highlights a tremendous business opportunity in the knowledge management of genetic information. There is a need to rethink the infrastructure—the integration of systems, networks, software, and people—required to build out the next-generation biotech enterprise. Companies such as InforMax are leading the way.

Personal Impact

Around 2007, we will know how long we might live, what our talents could be, and what crimes we might be capable of committing. Genetically speaking, we'll know our destiny.

When our genome is accurately mapped out, a world of choices—some difficult to confront—may be presented to us. Corrective gene therapy, surgery, genetic enhancement, and other interventions at the genomic level will be available for our consideration.

Some of these choices may not be choices. Government-mandated legislation to correct some violent antisocial behaviors may be required. We may get to vote on some of these issues at the ballot box. In dealing with genetically based behaviors, it will become seductive to eliminate certain antisocial tendencies to create more order, progress, and peace in society. If we spot polygenic traits—more than one gene trait—in scanning tests that reveal a high probability of violent behavior, should we require this person to undergo gene replacement therapy? Or, if spotted in testing done routinely before birth, should these potentially violence-causing genes be turned off?

Some of the choices we are given about genetically altering ourselves may not be choices for another reason: Society will squeeze us out of opportunities if we are perceived as genetically inferior. In the 1997 movie, *Gattaca*, a future society is depicted as ultra aware to the point of obsession with people's DNA being the ticket to advancement. Will our genetic heritage be the determining factor in providing secure economic opportunity? Will our genome determine our ability to succeed? Like it or not, the answer is yes.

Knowledge about ourselves and others at the level of the genome—the Holy Grail of information—will be the driving force to forever alter the direction of civilization.

Living in a Perfect World

Should we strive to create a perfect human and a perfect world? Perfection is at best a subjective idea. Perhaps different subcultures will arise that celebrate different life forms, abilities, and cultures shaped by their bio-enhancements. We will struggle long and hard with defining what perfection is. And it will differ from culture to culture, person to person.

Biotech will give us the tools to remake our species and our world, but there are deep questions that must be addressed in exploiting the commercial opportunities inherent in the emerging biotech revolution. Companies that comprehend this delicate set of social issues can play a powerful leadership role in helping to put in place safeguards, as well as conduct breakthrough research to help humanity prosper. These companies will play a vital role in helping us transition to the Post-Genomic Era.

■ ■ ■

future Health

THE TOP TEN HEALTH-CARE TRENDS FOR THE 21ST CENTURY

1. Most hospitals, clinics, trauma centers, physicians, and patients will be connected to one large network enabling access to critical medical information.

2. Consumer health information, accessible over a variety of Net channels, will become the most in-demand content worldwide.

3. The medical industry will face an ethical and social dilemma over the disclosure of patient information.

4. Health-care professionals, available via remote Internet connections, will provide services to millions of people who were previously under-served.

5. Medicalbots, nonhuman intelligence agents, will dispense medical care to patients and doctors worldwide to save money and share expertise.

6. Advanced nano-biology and genetic technology will eliminate many diseases, accelerate healing, and increase longevity.

7. Bio-engineered food will help promote health and longevity.

8. A new generation of smart drugs, implants, and medical devices will enhance our health and performance.

9. Virtual-reality medical simulations will become the dominant mode of medical training.

10. Cyber-health care that is customized for us—designed to monitor, diagnose, educate, and intervene regardless of location or time—will be common.

Telemedicine On-Demand: Year 2003

It's one in the morning, and Ann's five-year-old daughter, Tyler, wakes up crying. She has a fever and is complaining about her ears. Ann logs on to her Home Health Watch Internet site and places a wireless thermometer over her ear, enabling her to send real-time clinical information to her online nurse practitioner. The Tele-Nurse analyzes the bio-data automatically with a direct access link to the 24-hour virtual lab. She prescribes a drug that Ann can get delivered from her local pharmacy in ten minutes. Since Tyler hates pills, the drug is an inhalant—one sniff per dose in her favorite scent, cherry. Information on-demand. Help when we need it. Welcome to the future of health care.

The health-care industry in the United States—next in size only to the defense industry—will represent a burgeoning $2.2 trillion dollar business in 2003. A whopping 14 percent of the U.S. Gross Domestic Product is spent on health care. Throughout the world, regardless of what nation or type of system, high costs and inefficiency plague people in need of treatment and health guidance. Some patients pay usurious fees for the best care, while others sit waiting for hours, weeks, even years for basic medical attention. Many more people in developing countries have no consistent access to health care at all. This can change if leaders cautiously build tomorrow's health-care system using the Power Tools of leading-edge technology.

There is little wonder that health expenses are out of control. First of all, no health information systems architecture exists today. It is as if the information age has missed the health-care industry, and unless this is fixed, health care will be on the critical list. Data points throughout the health-care system—collection of patient information, storing medical images such as x-rays, physicians' entries in patient records, billing—need to be brought together seamlessly. The impact of disparate information systems on health-care delivery is something we have all experienced to some degree. At least $300 billion could be saved just from switching from a paper-based system to a digital system for administration. This is one of numerous applications of new technology with the dual impact of cutting costs and improving service. It's still resisted, though, out of an ingrained, almost superstitious, attachment to paper documents and other "old ways."

Having advised the health-care industry over my career, I am concerned by the lack of vision with our leaders about unifying resources to deliver better services. But vision or no vision, they will have to change. Technology will force their hand. Consumers, free enterprise, and government will scurry toward the same goal: an efficient, cost-effective, and quality health-care system.

It is impossible to miss the potential. Breakthroughs in nanotech, robotics, biotechnology, and other tools of the telemedicine revolution *can* enhance quality, promote efficiency, and improve access for millions. Anyone who can see this potential, anyone who can understand the application of Power Tools to health care, can identify tremendous business opportunities today.

If we do not get health-care expenditures under control, by 2006 the U.S. will face a price tag of $4 trillion—much of it due to its 78 million aging baby boomers. There are few industries that need as much "healing" as medicine and health care, and massive doses of leading-edge technology are the best therapy. The following is a preview of what's in store.

Future Telemedicine

What we call "telemedicine" today will be simply "medicine" tomorrow. The use of technology to deliver health care anytime, anywhere—the broad definition of telemedicine—will be the way things are done in the 21st century.

At first developed to serve our astronauts, then later valued mostly for supplementing care to people in remote and rural areas, telemedicine is today being integrated into urban health-care systems by forward-looking provider networks. A pioneer in this field is Boston-based Partners HealthCare (**www.partners.com**), which is testing videoconferencing, the Internet, and new digital imaging technologies in a bid to gain market share, cut costs, and improve quality of care to a large urban patient base.

One Partners program, emergency stroke management, involves connecting remote community emergency rooms to a central "hub" for specialist help in the utilization of anticoagulant agents. Certain anticoagulants have strict criteria for use, and ER doctors are often reluctant to use them without a second opinion. Videoconferencing capabilities are being tapped for this particular project. Other urban telemedicine programs revolve around distance learning, home health care, and disease management.

Virtual Patient Monitoring

Home health care will become more efficient as remote patient monitoring over the Net is available. The homes of chronically ill patients—those the hospitals now call "revolving door patients" because of their repeated hospital visits—will be equipped with intelligence-enhanced "nurse-bots" for 24-hour duty. These medical assistants will be able to take vital signs and transmit them via small hand-held video teleconferencing devices to a central database. Their on-site actions will prevent the need for many trips to the emergency room. Physicians in another part of town, or another part of the world, will be instantly alerted if there's a problem and use their mobile phone LCD monitor to view the patient and make emergency recommendations.

Other patients—perhaps those with asthma, diabetes, and other less-severe chronic problems—will rely on home health monitors that are simple to use, non-invasive, and relatively inexpensive. The Medical College of Georgia first launched trials with such monitors in 1994. These devices will easily monitor liver functions, ovulation cycles, levels of cholesterol, and more with results transmitted to a central health bank. Daily or weekly videoconferences with a nurse or doctor will become routine.

Tele-Med Training: Year 2002

The famous heart surgeon, Dr. Karinchy, in her operating room at Stanford University Medical Center, is guiding an intricate triple bypass operation thousands of miles away in a Singapore Hospital. Medical students from around the world from 50 medical schools are watching the procedure via videoconference over the Net as part of their resident training.

"Now with this technique, which I am only perfecting as of now, I have found a way to make more refined incisions by using a fiber-optic tipped scalpel that has on-board intelligence," Dr. Karinchy describes.

"Does that mean that this process is more precise?" asked one of her students, Sanji, who is beamed in from India.

"Hi, Sanji, good to have you here today. Greater precision is one part of this new procedure, but speed is also a result of the smart targeting of the scalpel."

Over 30 different languages and cultures are represented with simultaneous real-time translation customizing the exchange between Dr. Karinchy and her top-notch team. After a grueling five-hour operation, Dr. Karinchy answers questions from the local and remote locations. Her answers and the questions are captured and shared over superfast networks and e-mailed to all present.

"Remember that this course is worth six credits if you download the homework and e-mail it back before April 3.

Visual simulations are required, so please don't submit your work without them. Dr. Karinchy offline."

Some of the residents later download the operation over the Net and simulate the teachers' actions in order to learn her technique. Other students interact with other teachers and students over a groupware Net link where they can make notes and diagrams while they play back the operation in slow motion.

The patients' vital signs, displayed as information streaming across their screens, lets them monitor the operations' progress. All of this information and the procedure can be redesigned, simulated differently, or stored for playing out different scenarios. The visualization of the surgical procedures enables the students to accelerate their education.

Net-Med Training

Even in the early days of telemedicine, it was clear to its pioneers that physician-to-physician communication was perhaps a more critical benefit than patient-to-physician contact. Real-time interactive tele-mentoring and medical training is far more efficient than books or journals. The education of medical students and the continuing education of physicians can be delivered very cost-effectively either by distributing lessons in real-time or filing them digitally over the Net for later review and study.

The Mayo Clinic began experimenting with real-time specialist-to-specialist tele-mentoring in 1993 by connecting surgeons in the Rochester, Minnesota, hospital with those in their satellite facilities in Arizona and Florida. They did this with an expensive satellite link among the facilities, but now with relatively low-cost access to a global Internet, this kind of professional tele-connection will soon become a common occurrence. Why wouldn't we want collaboration among the best experts if we're undergoing a life-threatening procedure?

Networked Health: Year 2005

Larry's had a long day and feels tired despite having taken an anti-fatigue pill called "Aware" to get through the last Internet videoconference on the company's newest product. A happy hour beer-fest at the CyberLounge is tempting, but just after leaving the building, a sharp chest pain stops him cold. The pain finally subsides, and he quickly slips his

Personal Health Record card into a slot on his cell phone, uttering the word, "Emergency."

Immediately, Larry is routed via the Internet to his health plan's Clinical Emergency Center for a diagnosis. This involves answering a series of yes-or-no questions about the symptoms and vital signs asked by a CyberDoc computer. Larry places a finger on the screen where his biosignature converts his EKG signals and sends them instantly to the Emerg-Med Team via a virtual Net center many time zones away.

The CyberDoc decides that Larry's condition may be acute cardiac ischemia and dispatches a Clinic-Mobile to his exact location. En route to the nearest emergency care unit, a battery of tests, including another EKG, are performed and transmitted via a wireless device to a lab for interpretation.

By the time the local Emerg-Med team reaches Larry, the doctor on duty has the results, along with a second opinion by a cardiac specialist 2,000 miles away. Larry's Personal Health Card has also provided his medical history and genetic predisposition to the on-duty doctor.

The doc has authorized several categories of treatment for the condition—a partially clogged artery. The receptionist takes Larry to a video monitor, where he can see and talk to both physicians who have studied his condition. On the split screen, the duty doctor shows Larry holographic 3-D color images of the vessel blockage via a microscopic camera inserted into his bloodstream.

The doctor recommends injecting an army of nanoscrubbers to clean out the arteries. Larry's asked to rest while the physician takes a virtual tour of his bloodstream to code in the correct markers for making the non-invasive procedure a success. Once deployed and completed with their mission, the nanoscrubbers dissolve harmlessly.

The actual operation takes only eight minutes, and Larry's discharged shortly afterwards. Before leaving, he's given a customized holographic health disk with an analysis of what dietary or lifestyle changes are needed for him to avoid another such incident.

A wristband will unobtrusively monitor Larry's condition for the next couple days, but he feels fine as he strolls out of the neighborhood care unit. In fact, he still has time to make happy hour. He just has to watch what he orders. His updated personal health record may warn him from ordering beverages that are not on his diet. Larry may hear this message: "Light Nutri-beer suggested—and only two servings."

Consider how we will be able to deliver individual health-care solutions anywhere, at any time of day when all physicians, hospitals, HMOs, and clinics are connected to the same online site; we'll call it "Global Health-Net." Savvy companies will anticipate that and get ahead of the competition by matching specific patient needs with information resources available via the Net.

Doctors' Helpers

The "Global Health-Net" will also have a prime, live-saving role in future disasters. Physicians and other front-line medical personnel will be equipped with lightweight mobile computing devices linked to the Net that can be hooked to their wrist, waist, or hard-hat. They will also have embedded artificial intelligence to enable practitioners to make more informed and faster decisions. A prototype of this kind of communications/computing device, nicknamed the "Dick Tracy Watch," was developed in the early 1990s for the U.S. Army.

With an accompanying small "black box" of diagnostic instruments, medics will help an earthquake victim, for instance. They could quickly take the victim's vital signs, do an x-ray of potentially damaged body parts, and transmit the tests for analysis to a telemedicine center specializing in disaster medicine. In turn, specialists at the center will transmit the solutions needed to the medics or doctors in the field to provide a virtual assist.

The future physician won't use a pen for taking field notes. Natural voice recognition will quickly translate spoken instructions into text that is instantaneously sent to the appropriate database and the patient's health history. This will leave the physician's hands free for patching up a wound.

Smart Card Saves Life: Year 2003

Milo is driving through a rainstorm in rural Spain on vacation near the sea shore when his car skids, hits a tree, and knocks him unconscious.

Luckily, Pablo, the local physician, is able to access Milo's personal code number from the back of the smart card in Milo's wallet by using his Physicians' Emergency Protocol (PEP). He quickly accesses the Net by saying "Code Blue, Code Blue" and an emergency access code. Milo's health history is downloaded. He finds that Milo is allergic to penicillin and has a history of hypertension. He adjusts his treatment protocol accordingly. Milo's life has just been saved.

Milo's personal doctor and his Home Docbots are also alerted in case their consultation, or intervention, is needed.

Health History on a Chip

Critical life-saving information delivered when we need it, where we need it, will soon be common with small, robust storage devices—the next generation of the "smart card." Such advances in health informatics, facilitated by the convergence of health care, computers, and networks, will have a comprehensive impact on consumer health.

Each of us will soon carry a personal health record "smart card" that contains all the relevant data about our health history on a tiny chip. In multimedia form, it will include our entire health record, including the drugs we've taken, operations we've had, medicines we're allergic to, and diseases or conditions we've suffered.

In addition, our genomic profile will be catalogued on our digital file. This information, critically important to our health, may be even more essential over time as new drugs and interventions born from unlocking the human genome will steadily become available after 2002. This smart card, hooked into the Net, can quickly alert us to new research on a mutant genetic trait we've inherited, or to a new "smart drug" to help cure memory lapses we've recorded.

Our health card acts as a tiny computer, another gateway to the Net, searching out information for our specific needs, and alerting the hospital or specialist when we need their services. It watches our health statistics and "knows" what we need when.

Health Ethics Alert

The ethical considerations of this scenario can be disturbing, which is one reason why there is currently such widespread reluctance to adopt some of this technology in its formative stages. Only the military in the U.S. and certain other nations have boldly gone forward in an effort to put medical records on a "smart card."

There will be so much personal health information available on such a device that it will be hard to believe that our rights to privacy will be fully protected. There will be abuses; there are now with a paper-based system—and paper is typically much easier to copy, deface, lose, and destroy than electronic records.

If one area cries out for change, it is the protection of health databases from unauthorized parties. And who are they? Do governments have the right to identify people with genes that are precursors for violent behavior? How about employers wanting to screen us before hiring to determine our cardiovascular potential? Does the public have a right to know a potential President's health and genomic history? This information will be virtually somewhere in our connected society. How and when we use this health data will determine employment directions, social policies, political elections, and relationships such as marriage, dating, and parenting.

I cannot overemphasize the need for laws and policies to protect the privacy rights of individuals in the future. The exploitation of personal health information is one of the greatest threats to democracy and personal freedoms that we face. I urge those companies that don't have privacy policies to form them now.

Selling Privacy

Smart companies will build new businesses around this privacy concern. Protecting and managing consumers' health information will be a very profitable business model for the future. Numerous businesses will emerge that will stand between consumers and industry to protect personal rights to privacy. If we as a society do not heed the warnings here, these events may occur: First, irate consumers will pass laws to restrict the collection of their personal data. Next, consumers will decide to charge companies for the rights to have access to their personal data.

With the emergence of genomics, information about people's DNA, there is nothing more personal than our health data. How protection of it is handled by the private sector will affect law, politics, and commerce for decades to come.

Leapfrog Technology

Instant access to patient data is made possible by the emerging telecom infrastructure built for high-speed wireless transmissions of voice, data, and video in *real-time*—superfast transmissions when and where they're needed. A telemedicine explosion will be triggered by the demands of emerging nations for the quality health care this infrastructure enables. This will create a short-term $100 billion opportunity in upgrading the electronic pipelines they need to be connected to the world's medical expertise. This will be a vital step in creating peace, prosperity, and enhanced quality of life worldwide.

Many nations with inadequate telephone and communications infrastructures will be able to leapfrog technologies by installing satellite-based wireless networks, satellite transmission systems, and the latest Internet-configured computer-TVs. Very simply, the proliferation of these technologies will make them affordable. Singapore's Telecommunications Authority leapfrogged by wiring the island with fiber optics, and instantly opened up a new world of telemedicine and electronic commerce. High-quality video and high-speed data transmissions, made possible by dedicated bandwidths and signal compression, will connect even the most rural sites to sophisticated clinical centers set up to do long-distance diagnoses and consultations.

Robo-Surgery

High-speed network communications will allow physicians around the world to do more than consult routinely with each other. Another outcome is that surgeons could use robotic techniques to operate on patients remotely. One scenario that is possible with current technology has the surgeon remotely guiding a robotic arm in real time, with the device filtering out any of the surgeon's minor hand tremors. The benefit of such surgery is twofold: The best surgeons will perform the operations they do best with the assistance of remote robots, and unique and "perfect" operations could be viewed by medical students in different locations as part of their training.

Robotic and robotically assisted surgeries can, in fact, be "perfect" because they can be programmed. Imagine a surgeon at Boston General Hospital's telemedicine center using a virtual-reality environment to "walk through" a complicated organ transplant procedure that will take place the following day in Los Angeles. The surgeon can program his robotic assistant in Los Angeles to carry out the step-by-step operation while he watches in real-time on his video monitor. His colleagues at the University of Southern California are also monitoring the program and are ready to step in physically, if need be, should a problem arise. Bringing in doctors from Harvard and Tokyo University via teleconferencing could add new insight, as needed, for a delicate experimental procedure.

Voxel Digital Holography (**www.voxel.com**) routinely uses data collected by Computed Tomography (CT) and Magnetic Resonance (MR) scanners to produce true three-dimensional images. The life-size, transparent holograms, Voxgrams, literally extend out in space. Voxgrams enable a physician to interact in, around, and through an image as if it were a real specimen of anatomy, making "programming" an operation a feasible goal.

By using such tools, we will also go toward less invasive surgery. Laser Industries, Ltd., and Biosense, Inc., for example, are jointly developing a system for using a catheter-based navigation system to guide laser beams to heart muscles for the relief of angina and coronary artery disease. The system (**www.sharplan. com**) allows for the delivery of energy to selected sites on the inner side of the heart wall and may do away with the need for 300,000 coronary artery bypasses each year.

Patients will benefit handsomely when telemedicine solutions involving robots, virtual reality, and computer-generated doctors reach the mainstream.

Cyberdocs

In the United States, medicine over the Net will be pervasive by 2008, and virtual "face-to-face" doctor-patient relationships will exist without the barrier of time and space. Sometimes, however, the doctor may be a computer, or cyberdoc.

Just as we have accepted other human-machine influences from voice mail to computers, we will come to not just accept, but also to demand and trust, cyberdocs. It is likely that consumers may get more help from an interactive, intelligent computer than a stressed-out human physician. This makes sense especially if we have a life-threatening illness and cannot afford human error.

HEADLINE FROM THE FUTURE

DATA SHOW THAT CYBERDOCS ARE SAFER AND SMARTER THAN HUMANS

Humans may no longer monopolize medicine after we develop robotic surgeons that are more precise than their human creators, and cyberdocs that perform routine diagnostics with predictable precision. This will lead to cheaper care available to vastly more people in need. In fact, insurance companies may come to require that robodocs and cyberdocs be used because their precision and reliability are higher than that of humans. The use of robotics or cyberdocs will be a shock to many at first, but so was voice mail and shopping on the Net.

CyberDoc Will See You Now: Year 2008

Feeling ill? The on-duty doctor's just a cyber-call away in the plugged-in health-are world of the near future.

Quickly, we are linked to CyberDoc—a powerful computer with a soothing voice whose office door is open 24 hours a day via our Net-linked smart card, our health history on a chip.

CyberDoc's brain is an updated network of expert systems, agents, and neural networks linked to a data warehouse tied to the Internet. CyberDoc is a powerful telehealth associate that both diagnoses and treats patients, as well as teaches and coaches doctors.

We can contact CyberDoc at a local Telemedicine Kiosk, which has large videoconferencing screens, or simply dial in using our small wireless Personal Digital Assistant (PDA). Our smart card, along with a voice recognition security system, gives us access to all the medical information we need to stay healthy.

CyberDoc may decide to connect us to its human counter-part, Dr. Jacobs, who is vacationing at a beach in Rio. Dr. Jacobs can scan our condition on her mobile Digi-Phone screen and order additional tests, which can be instantly conducted at our telemed kiosk and transmitted to her. If something seems suspect, she can quickly get a second opinion from an on-duty medical specialist in Kuala Lumpur. Dr. Jacobs can be brought in if needed to review the results, but CyberDoc doesn't think this is necessary.

Everything gets billed to our Singapore-based health main-tenance organization (HMO), which the next day sends us a curt reminder that frequent-flyer points are awarded to con-sumers who go through personal health assistants with their medical complaints, rather than directly to expensive physicians. The HMO also offers a 15 percent discount on next year's rates if we purchase the Cray Company of Switzerland's new interactive broadcast channel for our home entertainment center. We decline—and they offer us a PDA co-marketed by Pepsi. We rethink the "sweet-ened" offer.

Health Empowerment

We will demand that our cyberdocs, robodocs, and real docs support a mass consumer emphasis on preventive medicine—a program of taking care of ourselves through lifestyle modification to prevent illness and preserve. It will spawn the creation of hundreds of new companies in the 21st century.

In 1998, over 20 million people searched the net for health and medical information. Hundreds, perhaps now even thousands, of Websites focus on health. By the year 2005, 100 million or more consumers will be online looking for ways to prevent illness and support their good health. We are hungry for information on which herbs to buy, how many vitamin supplements to take, and who makes the best energy drink.

Fitness will continue to grow as a subsegment of the "wellness" industry. One type of new service that health clubs of the future might offer are "Virtual Health Adventures" that add excitement to exercise. Through a blending of VR, holography, and interactive multimedia, we could be transported to exotic places or adventurous liaisons. One offering could be a realistic dinosaur hunt where we would burn calories and get our heart rate up to a healthy pace in a dramatic escape from a tromping tyrannosaurus. A real-time calorie-burning chart could show our progress.

Health insurers will offer virtual cash and prizes for people to slim down, stop smoking, or reduce stress. There will be a variety of incentives for us to stay healthy.

If dinosaur hunts are too dusty, we could sign up for a virtual whitewater raft trip down the treacherous Bolo, or a climb to the top of Mt. Everest. For something tamer and in the confines of our own homes, there's always software that can bring us tennis lessons in our bedroom with Wimbledon champion André Agassi, or a weight-lifting workout with Arnold Schwarzenegger. The possibilities are endless. We'll have to pay to play, but the end results will be worth it.

Net companies could match these adventure firms—or other types of service providers—with "bundled" packages for customers who are likely to buy and use these products to take more responsibility for their health.

HEADLINE FROM THE FUTURE

DIAGNOSTIC HEALTHBOTS MONITOR PATIENTS FOREVER VIGILANT; THEIR AIM IS PREVENTION

Health Detectives

Predictive Programs containing advanced Artificial Intelligence agents will be a key part of prevention programs. For example, they will analyze patient information and accurately compute the probability of a cardiac condition.

Injectable nano agents designed for us personally from our DNA sequence will automatically scout the bloodstream for cholesterol-producing agents and neutralize them—turning them into "friendlies" with no ill side effects.

Smart Drugs

"Smart drugs" will join the technologies that play a key role in wellness, as well as a desire for enhancement. Over the next ten years, "smart drugs" will include a new class of nutraceuticals—or mixtures of nutrients, vitamins, and synthesized chemicals. These techno-cocktails will enhance productivity, memory, physical performance, and even entertainment and pleasure. Their growing acceptance may even eliminate street drugs, replacing them with legal pharmaceuticals.

Smart drugs today represent an emerging billion-dollar market, mostly in Europe, and increasingly in Asia and the U.S. The potential of the industry is unlimited as biotech discovers and creates potent new energy boosters. Once these hybrid drugs are accepted, much as coffee is accepted as a stimulant today, they will shape the way we work, live, and play.

Part of this trend will inevitably include ways to "package ecstasy." Anti-anxiety and antidepressant drugs are just the beginning. The idea of packaged pleasure in a pill will challenge the assumptions we have about leisure, work, and entertainment. Pharma magic in the 21st century will necessitate a brand-new look at the influence of drugs on society. Will we need smart drugs to cope, manage, or even understand the future we are creating?

■■■ HEADLINE FROM THE FUTURE ■■■

HERSHEY INTRODUCES CANDY KISSES WITH SMART NUTRIENTS; KIDS LOVE THEM

A high percentage of people using Prozac—an estimated 15 to 25 percent—do so to enhance their performance. They use it as a smart drug. Wouldn't we all like to eliminate anxiety, work smarter, be more productive, and be more successful? The pharmaceutical companies hear us loud and clear. Better performance through biochemistry will be a multibillion industry in the stressful, competitive, and chaotic world of tomorrow.

Chemically improving ourselves will become the rage as 21st-century smart drugs help to realize new human potential. Slow performance will become abnormal and *de classe*. Some drugs derived from natural sources are today pointing in that direction (DMEA, Ondonstron, Nimoditie, Milacemide, Parcenten), but tomorrow's techno-brews will do the job more predictably.

A recent discovery offers an excellent scenario for illustrating how to market such smart drugs. Supposedly, a component of green tea called ECGC may stop cancer by interfering with the way the disease invades cells and breaks down healthy tissue. An entrepreneur could buy a supply of green tea, isolate the ECGC, and then combine it with other known anti-cancer substances. The new tablet could be made chewable and marketed as "Cancer Fighter," via the Internet, where it would be targeted to disease-specific groups.

Who wouldn't want to take this anti-cancer cocktail to ward off disease? The $7 billion-a-year vitamin market fueled by over 100 million Americans alone is a strong indication of the power of this movement. I would forecast over a billion smart drug devotees ingesting over $2 trillion in instant health and performance products by 2003.

Medicine in the 21st century will not just be shaped by the convergence of "hard technologies," but will be forever changed by a new class of drugs, substances, and nutrients that alter our health, performance, lifestyle, and behavior on-demand.

Yuri's Diet: Year 2007

Yuri is a young Israeli medical student living in Tel Aviv who is concerned about his weight. He needs to lose 25 pounds, exercise, and get healthier. Finally, he decides to take action. Using his wireless videophone, he calls his Internet agent, Nanette, a Digitized Engineered Personality (DEP) who is bright, alert, and playful—characteristics chosen by Yuri.

Today, he asks Nanette to assemble a customized weight-reduction package that takes into account his rigorous academic schedule. He also asks her to scan the Net for available data related to his personal health records and to check for any bonus premiums of cybercash credits offered by his employer, HMO, government, or insurance company.

Nanette is configured for Max Intelligence Level 517. She also serves with a passion. Within three minutes, Nanette compiles a complete report, which she downloads to Yuri's remote computer as an interactive holograph with music, graphics, and charts. It is also delivered in text to his smart card fax.

Among her findings is a cybercash credit program offered by McDonald's-Walmart Health Care, Inc. She registers him and will help him stay on track.

As a true DEP, Nanette is able to self-evolve, learn, and adapt based on the moods, behaviors, and actions of her creator. For example, she knows Yuri's moods and limitations —such as being in denial about the reasons for his weight— and is able to integrate his responses to her in order to come up with solutions for achieving her prime directive, helping Yuri trim down. To this end, Nanette will navigate through all parts of Yuri's life, and will, for example, actually lock the refrigerator after 5 P.M. if necessary. "I'm sorry, Yuri, snacking is not approved on your diet."

Food not on Yuri's diet is no longer approved for purchase at the supermarket checkout. Ditto with cigarettes, which Yuri has vowed to quit as part of his new lifestyle. Nanette sends him this message each day: Veggies okay. Easy on meat and diary. Low and no fat is the ticket. Exercise is key.

In addition, Nanette offers encouraging reinforcement by assisting with finding research projects and hunting down discounts at Yuri's favorite Italian clothing stores. She also builds a network of support with Yuri's friends and relatives by letting them know his progress and how they can help him achieve the end goal. Nanette advises Goloy, Yuri's mother, not to drop off any more chocolate chip cookies. She arranges regular tennis, running, and exercise partners and coaches to fit in with Yuri's schedule.

Yuri made it clear that Nanette should be relentless in helping him fight the battle of the bulge. Yuri's contract for these health changes cannot be canceled for six months, and he has to live with the consequences of Nanette's zealousness.

The kicker comes when Nanette, unsatisfied with Yuri's initial progress—his weight is still high as is his cholesterol—puts together a holographic "This is Your Life" health magazine that depicts his family history of weight-related health problems and early deaths. A lifeline for Yuri shows that unless he sticks to the program, he's due to keel over at the age of 56.

Shocked by such in-your-face data, Yuri joins the gym recommended by Nanette, and quits avoiding the prescribed medications. He stops sneaking snacks and swears off nicotine. Before the six months are up, Yuri's reached his goal, dropped his weight, and has to spend a bundle on slimmer, more fashionable clothes. He's also got another problem—a sudden flock of admirers. This time, however, he decides not to call on Nanette. "Bring on the real," he muses. Nanette "feels" rejection.

Future Implants

The makers of medical devices are also gearing up for the new millennium, with products to help people cope with physical problems and mental disorders. New surgically implanted devices, similar to the way a pacemaker works to keep the heart beating normally, are being developed to remedy the symptoms of epilepsy, Parkinson's, tremors, chronic pain, incontinence, and sleep apnea. Researchers in this field believe a common thread to the disorders lies in the misfiring of the body's nervous system. An up-and-coming company, Medtronic (**www.medtronic.com**), is pushing the envelope on this approach, but competition won't be far behind.

But implants may be where the action is in the future. Implants, injected microprocessors, bio-implants made from organic materials, and even DNA implants will be a thriving industry. Implants will be used to enhance memory for Alzheimer's patients, replace limbs, retrofit nerves, and replace organs such as kidneys or eyes. Implants will also be used to enhance human performance.

199

Potential Future Implants

- Brain implants for:
  —improving and enhancing memory
  —enhancing intelligence
  —new languages and skills
  —increasing perception awareness
- implants for legs and arms to strengthen or make them flexible
- implants to replace organs, muscles, and limbs
- implants for assisting fertility
- implants for replacing eyes, ears, or noses; or enhancing sight, sound, smell, and taste
- longevity implants to prolong health and eliminate disease (free-radical scavengers)

Genomic Medicine, the Conclusion: Year 2045 Android Selection

"I can choose any of these android bodies to download my mind into?" asks Ken.

"That's it. We have five models to choose from, and we can simulate through our Virtual Reality console what you will look and feel like," says Jeffrey.

"When all is over, does that make me an android or a cyborg?"

"Actually, when the transfer is complete, you will be classified as a Human Cyborg versus the Synthetic Humans that are all android or robots that have no human parts or human DNA."

"How long will I live?"

"With the normal maintenance and upgrades, we're projecting forever, or until you request termination."

"Forever sounds fine," Ken asserts. "What about the risks?"

"Oh, the usual. Accidents, insanity, war," Jeffrey continues, "Of course, we are not expecting to try a full transfer for about ten more years, but I think we can keep you tele-mersed and harvest enough synthetic organs for you until then. How are those new eyes, nose, stomach, memory implants, and hearing implants working?"

"They're fine, along with the bio-fab knees and new heart valves. Though sometimes when I cough, I still see reruns of *I Love Lucy* shows in my vision field."

"That's that new AT&T-AOL-INTEL M4 chip. I will download a patch to fix that pronto. Why didn't you tell me about this?"

"Well, to tell you the truth, I am a big fan of Lucy, and I don't really mind it," Ken laughs.

"Okay, you love Lucy, too. Now let's talk about the Cyber-Mind download."

"So I can actually do a test run of the different android bodies to see how I like them? Cool."

Jeffrey moves his hands to attach wireless electrodes to Ken's head, and Ken is transported into a virtual scene where he selects an athletic-looking android called Beta Adonis 3000 to embody. "Looks good. How does he perform?" Jeffrey, represented by a Virtual Jeffrey in the simulation, asks Ken.

Ken is running up a virtual mountainside with the speed of a cheetah, while barely breaking a sweat. His android eyes see better than 20/20, and his hearing is very sensitive to the simulated forest around him. He is operating at optimum levels, exceeding human performance by 185 percent.

"Great. I'll take it," says Ken, terminating the simulation. "Tell me what's under the hood."

"Only the best that science can build and your money can buy. An Intel/TI Supercollider Penta 500 Hardware Bio-Engine and Picoflex skin smooth as a human's."

"No, I mean under the hood down there."

"Oh, don't worry. You will be fully functional in all areas for optimal sexual pleasure and sensory satisfaction, or you get your money back."

"How about getting my mind back?"

"Sorry, Ken, that's an extra we just cannot guarantee at this time."

"Great," says Ken, shaking his head and wondering what's next.

Future Health-Care Trends

Applying the Four Power Tools to health care will put certain trends in motion. I believe that the following trends will be business-critical to the health-care system of the future. They represent challenges, but also competitive advantages for companies that want to build the next-generation health-care enterprise.

- **Holographic projection:** The use of life-size transparent holographic images of the human body anatomy projected into a room or onto a virtual space online for physicians to interact with as if it were a real patient.

- **Augmented reality:** Supplementing the real world by adding virtual objects so that goggle-wearing surgeons, for example, can "see through" a human body as they perform an autopsy.

- **Robotic surgeons:** Performing operations with their movements controlled by a specialist at a remote site or preprogrammed for a specific task and monitored by a physician. Early successful trials were by Robodoc, of Integrated Surgical Systems, in Sacramento, California (**www.robodoc.com**), which focused on hip replacements.

- **Wetware:** Emerges as computer-implanted technology allowing direct brain access to extend intelligence, skills, and memory. Embedded intelligence becomes as natural as breast implants.

- **Synthetic tissue growth:** The growing of tissues and organs for human transplantation.

- **Neurogeneration:** The repair and growth of spinal cords and complex organs.

- **Cloning banks:** Repositories of an individual's cells that can be grown into organs on-demand to replace diseased body parts and prolong life indefinitely.

- **Health data piracy:** Black market sales of people's' health data. This will undoubtedly be a big illegal business in the near future.

Re-engineering Health Care

In one way, we're back where we started in this chapter. I want to reiterate the desperate need for a unified health systems architecture, connecting consumers providers and suppliers into one integrated network that will optimize care, productivity, and communications. The Internet certainly could be a backbone for such an architecture. The connected health-care enterprise, public or private, will be where the greatest cost and quality efficiencies will originate in the future. Today the Tower of Babel of discrete systems that serve the health-care system breeds inefficiency and waste. Care is compromised, and costs continue to escalate. Systems must talk to systems, providers, and consumers.

CURRENT PROBLEMS OF THE HEALTH-CARE SYSTEM

- Lack of information standards and systems
- Lack of unified enterprise connectivity and communications
- Antiquated stand-alone computer systems
- Paper-dependent procedures, records, and files
- Labor-intensive, human-dependent practices
- Little access to medical information on-demand
- Lack of electronic training and education

- Little use of electronic channels for patient education, monitoring, and care-to-patient communications
- No centralized electronic procurement of resources, services, and supplies
- No standardized consumer health information
- No standardized personal health record

BENEFITS OF A 21ST-CENTURY NETWORK HEALTH SYSTEMS ARCHITECTURE

- Lower costs for providing better care
- Greater security of records
- Authorized access to complete patient information on demand
- Real-time knowledge management, sharing, and exchange
- Human resource savings
- More efficient communications among patients, providers, and suppliers
- Elimination of paper, waste, and redundancy
- Real-time consumer network access to customized health information, health promotion, and prevention services

203

Designing a New Health Architecture

A new health architecture would bring together many different technologies to help people better communicate, share knowledge, and provide health care. The goal is to automate the complex administrative, clinical, and service components into one holistic network. Assuming in the U.S. that we could save $300 to $500 million from the deployment of a "Global Health-Net" model as proposed here, we could apply it to the improvement of health-care delivery quality.

APPLICATIONS OF A 21ST-CENTURY NETWORK HEALTH SYSTEMS ARCHITECTURE

- Net delivered education and training
- Wireless unified messaging
- Multimedia interactive patient files design and access
- Workflow telecommunications between care providers
- Groupware

- Clinical electronic file transfer

- On-demand knowledge access across the medical enterprise

- Research and development findings available over the Net

- Real-time lab data access on the Net

- Videoconferencing and telemedicine procedures and education

- Net-based patient billing

- Net-based scheduling

- Patient and physician communications over the Net

- Net-available patient health education and disease prevention courses

Health Trendsetters

I have watched the evolution, or rather the devolution, of health care over 20 years: No force will enable and empower change as deeply or as fast as technology. Here are some of the key trends that forward-thinking companies have set in motion to take health care into a new age empowered by technology:

- Ordering medication online will drive prices down and create a new competitive online market reaching millions (**www.Drugstore.com**).

- Physician quality management, for patients who want to evaluate and determine specialty information about doctors, will drive competition as well as improve physician quality assurance (**www.Digimed.com**).

- Health-care provider knowledge bases, such as **www.physicansonline.com**, will enable customers to access provider information and make better decisions.

- Electronic network procedures will eliminate the paper-based and labor-intensive procedures that create waste and inefficiency (**www.healtheon. com; www.kinetra.com; www.proxymed.com**).

A fundamental shift in the health-care system is coming, and it is driven largely by changes in the Internet and e-business, the networking efficiencies of the new economy. This shift will present a cornucopia of new business opportunities for companies that can provide agile and tech-enabled solutions to health-care delivery problems. It is an exciting time to be in this market. Many new paths will open up in the next millennium for companies that want to teach this dinosaur to dance.

■ ■ ■

CHAPTER ELEVEN

Nanotech—
The Ultimate Alchemy

The Top Ten Nanotech Trends for the 21st Century

1. Nanotech enterprises will provide the ultimate convergence of computers, networks, and biotech, and create products never before even imagined.

2. Nano-devices—invisible, intelligent, and powerful—will be used in every industry redefining the limits of what's possible.

3. Nanotech food compilers will create on-demand, low-cost, quality meals by assembling atoms into food.

4. Smaller than the head of a pin, surgical nanobots will operate from within the human body.

5. Nano-biology will prolong life, prevent illness, and increase people's health.

6. Nano-enhanced humans will have physical, intellectual, and sensing powers superior to other humans.

7. Nanotech will provide a cheap and available source of energy.

8. Nano-factories will build on-demand products in an inexpensive, flexible, and rapid process.

9. Nanotech will revolutionize the global economy, providing Power Tools that will produce high-tech products with low-cost and low-tech resources.

10. Nanotech will create new choices that will alter human evolution, raise dramatic ethical issues, and challenge social norms.

Maddy wakes up startled. She stares at the wintry snow scene in the Swiss Alps that engulfs her bedroom and jumps out of bed. Something is wrong. She is supposed to be enjoying a balmy breeze and a glorious sunrise on a Maui beach. "Maui Program, please," she orders.

Now she is streaming across a rich purple and red planet in some surreal galaxy in a space simulation she didn't order. "What's this? Travel Orb off!" she orders in frustration, and her Real World authentic bedroom scene returns. "I've got to get this system fixed," she says out loud.

Maddy makes a Thought-Note for her personal online Lifestyle Agent to look into the snafu. She thinks the command "Fix now," and it is sent intuitively to her agent, who facilitates the fix with the Knowledge Vendor online. The entire transaction takes less than 30 seconds for the Vendor to get the message and have a Servicebot download a diagnostic to find out what's wrong and fix it. "Needed an upgrade. Don't we all?" says Maddy as her Lifestyle Agent reports the fix.

Maddy is president of the DreamWare clothing line at Applied Nanofab, a leading fashion company. She will soon offer the line worldwide via the Internet only. Self-replicating nano-bots help her design, manufacture, and distribute her fashions. Nanotech operates much of the daily reality behind the scenes, just as computer chips did in the late 20th century. She can design a new line in ten minutes, or nano-minutes, she likes to say, setting the next fashion trend in motion. *Woman's Wear Daily Interactive* features her wardrobe each year.

"Nanotech is the underlying intelligence of this century, the next step for computers and networks," Maddy explains to her granddaughter, Jade, who has just beeped in from school to say hello. Jade's head pops up on the Vid-Window displayed on Maddy's blanket stretched across the bed where Maddy is relaxing.

"Nano what? Grandma?" chirps Jade, who has just turned five.

"Nanotech is the tool we use to make things like food, clothing, and energy," Maddy goes on to describe.

Jade seems satisfied for the moment and turns to her Playstation X, where a new program she designed last night on Dolphins is starting with Jade as the central character. "Love you, Grandma!"

Maddy signs off and heads for the kitchen.
(To be continued ...)

The promise of nanotech seems fantastic, even absurd, today. Cheap energy, the self-assembly of food, rearranging atoms like parking cars to build any-thing—indeed, nanotech sounds like science fiction. But the Nobel Prize win-ners, billions being spent on research, and myriad breakthroughs in the field indicate that nanotech, very small-scale engineering, is a serious endeavor and one that will realign global economies. There is a race now among nations and companies for developing nanotech Power Tools to better compete in the next century. Industries will rise and fall, markets will emerge and go away in the face of the changes brought by the power of nanotech.

Recall the ancient alchemists' attempts to turn base metals into gold, then consider the fact that nanotech's transformations will be even more dramatic and profitable in the 21st century. Nanotech—grounded in materials sciences, chemistry, computers, and physics—will be the culmination of digital conver-gence. Even if many of the breakthroughs that today's proponents predict do not happen on schedule, or at all, this supreme Power Tool will profoundly impact the new millennium.

The technological creation of an ultra-tiny invisible world with tiny "assemblers" and machines is about to alter our perceptions of reality and pro-pel futuristic businesses into unprecedented opportunities.

Molecular Manufacturing

Nanotechnology is an emerging science that builds objects atom by atom, molecule by molecule. It's the ascending futuristic technology with which we'll be able to manipulate the smallest building blocks of matter. This, in turn, will enable us to build the largest objects we can imagine, from skyscrapers to space habitats. Even organic life forms will be design strategies for nanotech if we so desire.

Nanotechnology is as spectacular an ascension to the next level of tech-nology as ancient alchemy is to modern-day chemistry and physics. In its ulti-mate application, it provides a mechanism for literally creating anything of any complexity, scale, or materials. But that is still only one explanation of nano-tech. Nanotech is also a gateway for creating new molecular devices, materials never before imagined or available. It cannot be stressed enough how signifi-cant this is.

Our Nano-Destiny

Nanotech is not a minor technical development, nor an obscure offshoot of a current technical discipline. This is as fundamental as the usage of the first tools by early humans and as monumental to progress. If we don't use this Power Tool for all it's worth, we may not achieve much of what we need to sustain life on this planet.

By 2025, we will have almost tripled Earth's population. The availability of essential services such as health care and education, as well as the access to resources such as food and shelter, cannot keep pace with that growth at current production levels. Only advanced technology holds the promise of delivering what we will need.

To put the awesome Power Tool of nanotech in our hands, leaders of all industries must recognize the credibility of today's research and plan accordingly. Nanotech will not be a single, sudden transformational event. The impact of nanotech will be rather a series of interrelated technologies and processes all woven together. A series of thresholds will be passed. The first was simply having a clear vision that nanotech is possible. The next threshold will be the creation of nano-tools that we will use to rearrange the atoms and molecules to form objects such as food, energy, steel, and water. Nanotech is the ultimate chemistry kit.

Nano Visionaries

Nobel Prize–winning physicist Richard Feynman first talked about the creation of smaller-than-microscopic machines in a 1959 talk called, "There's Plenty of Room at the Bottom." It gave a prescient vision of nanotechnology, although the term wasn't yet used. In the talk, Feynman forecast the ability to "…arrange the atoms the way we want; the very atoms, all the way down!"

The first person to lay down a conceptual model of nanotech was Dr. K. Eric Drexler, head of the Foresight Institute. A genuine nanotech pioneer, he saw what nanotech could be long before the science was there to prove or disprove his theories. He had bold vision to think way outside current science when he proposed nanotech.

We may see the day when macroscopic "assemblers" are able to build molecular machines, and self-replicating Artificial Life forms can be configured to clean the oceans, be caretakers of our bodies, or explore the solar system. A study of nanotech by the Rand Corporation helped legitimize the concept, saying that research into molecular manufacturing could result in some near-term benefits. What an understatement.

The Institute For Global Futures has been studying the evolution of nano-tech. Our findings are that nanotech is a vitally new and important technology that will determine the rise and fall of companies and nations. Nanotech will be as strategically important as oil was, or the invention of the computer. This will take as much as 20 years to come to fruition, but when nanotech becomes a mature industry, even if the innovations are a fraction of what today's futurists are predicting, nanotech will change our world (**www.technofutures.com**).

The convergent streams of quantum mechanics, computers, biotech, and telecommunications are driving the emerging nanotech revolution. The para-digm shift from the steam-and-steel Industrial Revolution to the Information Age to the Biotech Era will culminate with nanotech (**www.foresight.org; www. links2go.com/topic/Nanotechnology**).

Reverse Engineering Life

Another way to view what the impact of nanotech may be is to look at how nature works. All living cells are, in essence, "living nanofactories." They create life forms on-demand based on specific design blueprints. Assembly instructions, a kind of "how-to manual" represented by the sequencing of protein pairs in a double helix configuration referred to as DNA, informs the ribosomes and other components in the nuclei of living cells to "rearrange" molecular materials to form into new cells. These instructions then result in the formation of tissues, organs, and ultimately, an entire organism.

Nanotech may prove to be a very similar process. The difference is that, in nanotech's assembly of atoms, any object—organic or inorganic—or any combination of materials—natural or synthetic—can be synthesized "from scratch." We would compete with DNA for efficiency in the fabrication of life. Building anything becomes possible.

From Vision to Reality

Here are some of the signs that Feynman's 1959 vision of submicroscopic construction is taking shape.

- Toyota created a nanoscale automobile that could stand on the head of a match, and even got the engine running. The power source was electrical.

- A nanoscale test-tube was developed to conduct experiments on the molecular level. This breakthrough gives us the ability at the nanoscale to explore, invent, and eventually build a host of new products.

- StuffDust' by San Francisco-based minus9, Inc., marks objects and materials with serial numbers that are invisible to the naked eye, but easily read with an optical microscope. StuffDust' is composed of micron-scale particles, each of which is smaller than a human hair and carries a serial number. It is being marketed as an efficient and secure way to mark computers, currency, explosives, toxic waste, and more. Once deployed, it will create a new way to thwart thieves, as well as improve inventory controls and manufacturing.

■ There are micro machines that take existing technologies and miniaturize them, such as what takes place in the sub-micron electrolithographic production of semiconductors with hundreds of embedded transistors for use in smaller, more powerful computers.

■ The world's first implantable micro-machine, insulin-dispensing device was developed in 1998.

■ Miniature cochlea ear implants are giving hearing back to thousands of people.

In about 10 to 15 years, products of nanotech will be all around, impacting our lives immensely.

The Forever Car: 2008

Ted put in his order for a nanofactory-produced Forever Car, but he didn't realize that all the extras would increase its price tag. What makes it a Forever Car is the materials— self-replicating, self-diagnostic, self-fixing systems constantly tuning themselves.

Still, he figured that it was cheaper than a Mercedes circa 1999. The nanofactory builds the Forever Car in ten days from a nano-genetic blueprint designed by an online computer agent. Molecular modules "grow" the engine, chassis, and body. Even the tires are organically synthesized.

Did Ted really need the "smart" road map? Or the additional 50-year warranty? No matter, the car is ready, and Ted can't wait to get behind the wheel for a test run. As he slips into the driver's seat, the engine purrs into action.

"Are you comfortable, Ted?" asks the car. The Forever Car's personality and intelligence are designed to fit Ted's specifications. Ted's online car dealer, who uses advanced A-Life programs to achieve a perfect match, captures these traits. "Where would you like to go?"

A list of preprogrammed destinations pops up on the dashboard, and Ted punches the one for his favorite lunch spot. The car automatically sets the course. Ted knows that it will take a couple weeks before he and the car get used to one another. Once they do, the car will be able to handle his Internet downloads and monitor important calls via its wireless invisible hood antenna. It will also correct Ted's sloppy driving habits.

In many ways, the Forever Car is "alive" because it has millions of "smart chips" or embedded intelligence throughout. Its nano-enhanced engine and other parts work together as an integrated system, and include nano-scale "scrubbers" to keep everything clean.

If the engine sputters, an army of nano-mechanics corrects the problem. Ted trusts his Forever Car to repair itself on-demand, install online upgrades when needed, and transport him safely to and from his destinations.

Nanotech Wizardry

Nanotech will become a multitrillion dollar industry by 2020, and will still be in its embryonic stages. What will happen when we can create steak from sawdust, pizza from trash, or auto engines from old tires? Once understood and harnessed, nanotech will enable us to create anything that presently exists, as well as unimaginable new things.

Nanotech will be the pinnacle of humanity's next stage of evolution: the purposeful design of human beings and the environment. We could help resolve much of what ails humanity—poverty, ill health, and scarcity of resources—through nanotech if we as a society look comprehensively at its benefits.

Micro-machines will be able to repair our body's cells or organs. Tiny nano-labs will create energy by rearranging common molecules. Already on the drawing board are plans to make diamondoids—material as strong as diamonds —for such uses as repairing bones and teeth so they never break or deteriorate. There will be a vast morphing of reality with this nanotech Tinker Toy set.

Sub-micron-sized "supersmart" chips, an early application of nanotech in the already miniaturized computer world, could be profound. Such chips would give a quantum leap in competitive advantage to companies wanting to increase the intelligence of industrial and consumer products. Nanochips could be built on-demand, with digital empty spaces to be filled with new applications when needed later. Outside the computer industry, such nanochips could be used in home appliances, automobiles, pharmaceutical products, medical devices, space probes, and industrial machinery.

BIOCHIPS IN PAPER TELL YOU— "DON'T THROW ME OUT!"

Among other things, these chips would make possible intelligent nano-scale devices that deploy drugs in the human body to exactly where they're needed. These "Incredible Journey" nano-cruisers that we'll see by 2015 will attack viruses and neutralize the triggering devices for cancer or AIDS. Eventually, entire interactive medical libraries will be accessible by supercomputers the size of a matchbook. Specific materials or images we require may be projected on a wall or viewed by a holographic generator that pops from "inner space." Like nano-magic, this customized health data will show up when we need it, then disappear.

Intuitive Products

In a commodity-driven marketplace of nanotech machines—from dishwashers to energy compilers—customized features will determine the winners. How well products "know" our needs will determine their adoption. Nanotech can accelerate this intimate merchandising process through the "intuitive bonding" of humans and technology, which will rely on gesture recognition and other biometric capabilities to make objects aware of humans and our intentions. (Also see the chapter on computers.)

212

SMART METALS SHAPE ON-VOICE COMMAND

As we extend intelligence into new sensors and microchips, embedding them into objects around us, these objects will start to wake up and learn to communicate with human beings. Our clothes may be able to warn us of danger, or our pants may contract or expand with our waistline. The deep stage of intuitive bonding involves a seamless linkage between humans and objects where thought is a catalyst for action. For example, the news will appear on a display screen when it occurs to us that we want to see it. Nanotech manufacturing at the atomic scale will enable many of these scenarios to come to life.

Feeling hungry, Maddy goes to her new nanofood compiler and considers breakfast. She directs her thoughts about the menu to the compiler and out jumps a 3-D hologram displaying a Life Source Super Drink, which comes with coffee and nutra-rolls. She says, "Yes." The meal is "built" at the atomic level with elements that produce a tasty but low-fat, good-cholesterol meal.

Afterwards, a HouseCare Robo cleans up the kitchen. These are nano-assemblers, like synthetic super bacteria that break down garbage into biodegradable recycled molecules, or harmless atoms that are stored in the house's nanofoundry. Later these atoms will be converted for molecular manufacturing of clothes, cleaning supplies, and other objects as needed. They also continually clean the rugs, freshen the air, and sanitize the bathrooms. This works for Maddy since she hates to clean.

In her customized Net morning report, "Go for it, Maddy," news, stock market data, her stock portfolio, and ski reports are flashed onto a large flat wall while she eats. She checks her company's manufacturing timetable at the same time, sending out some e-mails.

Glancing at the weather report, Maddy notices that a nanotech-based weather system was producing rain for desert regions. It was also creating powdery snow for some ski slopes that just opened in the "warm belt" regions of the U.S. The thriving ski industry generates nano-snowflakes to produce a blanket of white for holiday skiers in the New Hills of Florida and many other southern locations. In other news, a fleet of tiny robotic spaceships fueled with solar energy is homing in on an asteroid in search of life near the outer edge of the Milky Way.

There's also a group of pickets gathered outside the 18th annual Bio-Robotics Convention to protest the proposed use of nanofactories for constructing "perfect" humanlike androids. Since the introduction of robots made with DNA and grown to look human, a huge ethical debate has raged. "Will these people get a life?" bemoans Maddy.

Maddy switches off the screen by thought control. It disappears. She checks the status of her granddaughter's overnight stay with friends through her "NannyCheck" sensor, which shows Jade is at the specified location, Mingo's house. She is monitoring Jade's location data while her daughter Casey is on vacation in Tahiti. It's a service tied to the GPS satellites and can access real-time images of her granddaughter up to five inches of her face. Jade has a virtual sensor with her digital signature on it to help the GPS system get a fix on her location for Maddy.

"Cute kid. Catch picture, send via Net mail to Casey," she orders as she downloads the picture and attaches a voice message for instant delivery to Tahiti. Maddy imagines the signal bouncing off satellites as the mail travels halfway around the world before she can say, "End program."

(To be continued...)

The Nanotech Enterprise

Many nano enterprises will have nothing to do with the actual manipulation or creation of nano-scale products. Their business will be the Knowledge Value that will enable companies and consumers to use nanotech tools, processes, and products. Just as today's biotech industry has evolved into an industry with unlimited potential to mine knowledge, so will nanotech. Nanotech data warehouses on the Net will provide personalized Nano-Knowledge for individuals and companies who must be on the absolute leading edge in order to compete or even survive in the extreme future.

If I were looking at the near future for a profitable long-term business investment, I'd consider as excellent opportunities the information service industries that will support the deployment of nanotech. Companies are beginning to realize the potential impact of nanotech knowledge management and becoming online information brokers of nanotech data and processes.

Foresight's posting of the latest nanotech research on its Website (www.foresight.com) demonstrates the emergence of "middleware players" that use Knowledge Value services to teach, inform, and empower people to use new technologies. Similarly, our Institute For Global Futures creates reports and conferences examining the business opportunities of nanotech and other emerging technologies.

Got Nano? Year 2018

Ricky has one heck of a headache. Her Nano-Tek is acting up again. Nano-Tek is a term referring to nano-device enhancements. This one's a nanoscale device smaller than a pin's head that was part telephone, TV, computer, and Net gateway. Ricky's Nano-Tek, embedded just below her right temple, is state-of-the-art—that means the best available today before 9 A.M. New York time. Voice, eye, and thought commands give her 24-hour access to anyone and any information in the galaxy.

This Nano-Tek is an Azimov 3000, one awesome package of networked supercomputers, blue lasers, and neural optics—the best stuff this side of the Mars colony. At least that's where she had downloaded her Nano-Tek because of restrictions to such enhancement products here on Earth.

An off-world Nano-brew, she chuckles. "Gotta relax and download a nano-patch. Do it NOW," she commands, and wireless data travels at the speed of thought energizing her Nano-Tek with the right fix, flushing her mind and body with a rush of Nutro-Sooth, a hybrid nanobiologic. "Calm down," hums Ricky to herself. She must be in the right mood to negotiate this big deal.

No matter. Ricky knows she got the best Nano-Tek money could buy, complete with a free ten-year package for downloading upgrades over the Net. This was a really good deal even though the purchase price was high.

Ricky absorbs two Feel-Good pills for the pain. They are virtual pills accessed via her Website and streamed into her nervous system. It takes eight seconds for the pain to leave. These are a new type of nanobios made up of pain-suppressant agents that are personalized and programmed to analyze and cure her headache in real-time. The digital delivery of pharms is common.

Bowing low to show respect, Ricky sits down to negotiate a large space mining joint venture with Yakamoza Corp. As she is served green tea, her right eye projects background information on the three negotiators—two corporate lawyers and an engineer. They all play golf—badly. One lawyer likes to gamble too much, and the other collects vintage cars. She could possibly use the information to help make the deal. With a blink, she closes the files.

Ricky's universal translator goes online as soon as she is addressed in formal Japanese. "It is an honor to meet you, Ricky-san," says the engineer.

Ricky's embedded agent, Sandy (named after her mom), captures her host's voiceprint by wireless biometrics, then offers Ricky further personality analysis, but she declines the interruption. Instead, she answers in perfect Japanese: "Arigato. No, it is I who am honored by you, Dokio-san, for meeting with me. How was your golf game at Pebble Beach yesterday?"

Caught off-guard, Dokio-san stammers a bit, but seems pleasantly surprised. He expects nothing less than strong Nano from his American friend. Dokio's Nano scan of Ricky was not as thorough. Disturbed by not having the advantage, Dokio makes a mental note to have his Nano upgraded today with the latest A-Life Net gear. Faster, stronger Nano is mission-critical in this economy. He dials up a Nano download sampler to review later.

Now, for the deal. Ricky has the edge and she works it. "Lunch before golf?" her hosts offer with a newfound respect. *The Best Nano gets the best deal,* thinks Ricky. Her agent, Sandy, quietly hums an agreement.

Nano Markets

Enterprises that benefit the most from nanotech will support innovators who understand that the technology's impact is pervasive. Japan, realizing that the potential of nanotech, has launched a $200 million, ten-year nanotech initiative and major research centers in other countries are getting aboard the nano-express. NASA (**www.nasa.gov**) envisions a day when an armada of tiny space ships that are light, cheap, and smart will explore the galaxy's unknown regions, sending back valuable information to Earth.

The revolution is under way. According to our Institute For Global Futures research, more than 100 companies generated over $7 billion in revenues in 1999, mostly through nanofabrication and industrial nanoproducts and processes. By 2010, business activities falling into five domains will generate annual revenues of $100 billion. The Institute is a participant in The National Science and Technology Council's Interagency Working Group on Nano Science, Engineering, and Technology. We are creating a plan for U.S. nanotech research and development for the next decade (**www.technofutures.com**).

Five Domains of Nanotech

1.   **Nano tools:** Nano tools enable scientists, researchers, and companies not only to visualize atomic structures and create nano-simulations to observe

interactions, but also to manipulate individual atoms purposefully and to design molecules for commercial applications. Products in this category include Scanning Probe Microscopy Equipment (Nanoscopy) and Molecular Modeling Software. Eventually nano-compilers, gears, and engines for molecular manufacturing will be developed.

2.   **MEMS—micromachines:** This form of nanotech uses technologies aimed at making things progressively smaller, working from the "top down" to the nanoscale. This category includes the following areas: Micromachines, MEMS (Microelectric Mechanical Systems), and Nanolithography. MEMS are already working in tandem with microchips in sensing devices in such things as airbags and carbon monoxide detecting kits. As MEMS become smaller and more ubiquitous, their use will explode into what I believe will be a $100 billion industry by 2010. Smart sensing gadgets will be everywhere, in all types of products such as toys, clothing, computers, and TVs. This arena is not always considered part of nanotech, but I believe MEMS will reach their potential when nanotech tools can be used to develop very small devices and materials.

3.   **Super materials:** Super materials constructed at the atomic level have unique properties that make them superior to conventional materials. These "nanophase" materials are used to manufacture special bondings, coatings, capsules, catalysts, and plastics with current commercial applications in microelectronics, automotive components, business machines, and personal care products. Imagine shape-shifting metals. These super materials have memory and embedded intelligence and will, in the near future, be networked to communicate with external systems such as the Internet.

This sector also encompasses a range of novel nanoscale materials—organic, synthetic, and hybrids. Among them are sub-microscopic carbon tubes containing atoms that can be snapped together like a Lego set to create stable, new constructions. These super materials include fullerenes, zeolites, organic crystals, high-temperature superconductors, starburst dendrimers, piezoelectric materials, and shape-changing alloys. These unusually assembled structures have unique behavioral properties with increasing commercial applications.

4.   **Microscale molecular fabrication:** The combination of "top down" fabrication processes, as are used in computer chip manufacturing, MEMs and other microscale devices, will make molecular fabrication possible. Again, it's like putting together a Lego set of atoms and then molecules and eventually

objects. The ability to deposit molecules on a surface smaller than the end of a needle allows for the creation of complex machines, such as motors, pumps, valves, and so on, at micro precision scale with extraordinary operational characteristics. Soon we can start to see the building of microscale molecular engines and factories to manufacture numerous products.

Molecular fabrication involves the development and use of complex molecular machines (assemblers) capable of reproducing themselves in large numbers and then gathering and positioning other atoms and molecules in desired constructions—for example, lunch boxes that create lunches. Almost any product may be manufactured to exact specifications and perfect quality and with no waste. Current theoretical, and quite possibly imminent, molecular manufacturing has profound implications for medicine, robotics, transportation, life sciences, energy, construction, electronics, defense, and food production.

5. **Organic nano-engineering:** This process has far-reaching potential to impact the human race. Organic, molecular nano-engineering, much like its predecessor, bio-engineering, is the process of creating and manipulating biological, molecular, or DNA elements to make such things as:

■ computer biochips with organic materials to replace silicon;

■ viruses and proteins as molecular machines or nanofactories to build commercial products;

■ synthetic DNA, nanogeonomics, to use for creating cloned life forms, robotics, human organs, and hybrid synthetic/organic compounds;

■ nano-informatics, the use of advanced computers to "grow" nano-engineered products from informational models; and

■ new drug development through nanobiology and nanopharmacolgy.

The Greater Mission

The long-term vision for these nanotech business activities is meeting every human need. Nanotech food, housing, health, and clothing assemblers residing in neighborhood kiosks will dispense inexpensive, even free, goods to people on-demand. Corner Kitchen Kiosks will become advertising-sponsored giveaways to grow customer loyalty and increase brand awareness. How different will our society be when we can cheaply replicate almost anything we choose to?

Based on planetary-scale nanotech developments, many "have-nots" can become "haves" by the year 2008. Nano manufacturing, agriculture, and engi-

218

neering will deliver everything from basic foodstuffs to prefab buildings, automobiles, energy, new drugs, and a host of other products for enhancing our quality of life at price points that will be affordable. Nanotech will level the playing field, reducing the advantages of big companies over small nano-entrepreneurs wielding the supreme Power Tool of the 21st century.

Much of the failure of social engineering in the 20th century was due to our lack of access to sophisticated tools and resources. We wanted the world to be well fed, well educated, and have proper clothing and shelter, but we could never effectively mobilize enough resources to accomplish that. Nanotech has the potential to transform this proposition, making available a bounty of resources to remodel the planet.

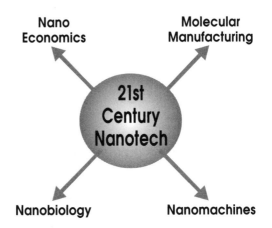

What DNA Wants, DNA Gets

Nanotech may also enable us to remodel ourselves as a species. Perhaps it's the stealth way that DNA gets human beings to jump to a new level of evolution. Although this may seem like a radical idea, I believe that as we experiment with genetic material through biotech—and as we learn to combine the tools of nanotech assembling, creation, and manipulation—we will be forging a new direction for the human species.

Is this DNA's plot to perpetuate the human race? Is humanity blundering upon the tools of creation? Or is this part of the purposeful advance of our civilization? Only time will tell, but one thing is certain: Just as we will learn to clone human organs, nanotech will give us vast new tools to design life itself. We will learn, perhaps, that we must become stewards of more than just the planet. We must become stewards of *humanity*.

Think about how different our world would be if the microchip were invented in the 1880s. How about if we skipped the invention of the radio and went directly to TV—would that have accelerated economic and social evolution? We will have the power to leapfrog existing technologies, products, and innovations with the advent of the nanotech Power Tools. Just as the silicon microchip that powers computers today will be obsolete in giving way to chips made from optics, DNA, or electrons liberated from the quantum, nanotech will unleash vast new innovations.

I predict that by 2015, cybernetic enhancements at the nanoscale level will eliminate many diseases; tiny machines will roto-rooter cholesterol from our veins; and "nanites" will give people eternally youthful complexions, reverse organ breakdowns, provide intelligent enhancement, and improve agility.

Nano-Life, Part III: Year 2035

Satisfied by a wonderful breakfast assembled by her nano-food compiler, Maddy signals for her Forever Car, already programmed to whisk her to the office of her orthodontist where she's having three teeth rebuilt from the roots up by an injection of "nanites" developed for such a task. There's no pain. In fact, the trip is quite pleasant since her doctor is hooked into the V-Travel Network where she takes an exotic adventure to the ski slopes of St. Moritz during the 30-minute procedure. *I've just got to work on those jumps,* thinks Maddy.

She had nano-surgery the year before to repair a knee injury she got back in the '90s, and they rebuilt the muscles from her cloned DNA. Nanites, containing the exact DNA for maximum regeneration, gave Maddy a knee better than the one she was born with. It has been enhanced to give her the extra performance boost she needs for skiing.

After work, Maddy stops at a comedy club to meet some friends. Places where there's real human contact are suddenly popular, giving rise to thriving business opportunities such as distressed-looking French cafes and chic beauty parlors. Most of the friends are there in Real World, a few in E-World (virtual, off the Net).

She muses that this upswing in nostalgia will soon be a thing of the past. The on-stage actor instantly turns into a

Robin Williams lookalike, startling Maddy. "He must be using some type of holo-nanotech Cipher-mask," she says to her friends. She hurries outside into the sunlight, a little nervous about the fast-changing technology that's such an integral part of her existence. Maddy can feel the soothing nanites reconstructing, healing, and nurturing her body. It feels good.

Nano Realpolitik

The realm of nanotech has potential dangers as well. While airborne "nanites" could monitor our streets and homes for safety, they could also strip us of much of the privacy we cherish today. Will lack of privacy be the price of eliminating crime? Will a life free from disease be worth having if the price is being "terminated" by age 300 to allow others to live in a nano-managed world? Are we ready to ask and answer these questions?

Also, who will be in charge of the new "engines of creation" that will give some people everything while denying others? The 21st century may become a confused world of conflicting agendas. Just as today, we will see authoritarian governments, vigorously "protecting" their corporate and individual citizens, in less-than-harmonious co-existence with nations devoted to free speech, free trade, and democracy. The real politics of this new technology will create competitive alliances and alter power structures worldwide. It is hard to accurately predict the outcome, but the transition into a nanotech-dominated global economy may be gut-wrenching for many.

Media Report: Year 2018
Nanotech Disaster Strikes East Leone

The Pharmetec Corporation reported today that they had called for an immediate evacuation of all employees from the East Leone Nanotech Research Center due to an explosion. Authorities from the United Nations Nano-Biology Rapid Deployment Command confirmed reports that the Nanites had assimilated over 20,000 miles of East Leone, dissolving all terrain, rivers, and forests. These Nanites were designed to devour and neutralize toxic waste for environmental cleanup. Somehow the Nanites got out of control and broke free from the incubation tanks. Authorities have warned that all persons in the vicinity should immediately leave or be at risk for being dissolved. An airborne nano-fix will take 24 hours to render the Nanites harmless.

The End of the Game

It may be difficult to imagine nanotech scenarios today because much of this technology exists only in the visions of scientists. In the 15 years or more that it takes us to reach these choices, challenges, and opportunities, we should do strategic planning with those visions in mind, though. That's how we will engineer a prosperous global market economy.

For businesses looking to start or sustain a competitive advantage today and into the 21st century, nanotech will provide revolutionary new options. This is the big one. Don't miss it. Prepare today for the coming changes and choices from nanotech, the ultimate alchemy.

■ ■ ■

CHAPTER TWELVE

Entertainment and the Digital Future

The Top Ten Entertainment Trends for the 21st Century

1. New digital technologies will reshape the economics, production, distribution, and marketing of the entertainment industry.

2. Traditional media enterprises must learn to adapt new Internet and computer technologies to maintain competitiveness.

3. The convergence of the Net with TVs, telephones, kiosks, autos, and wireless devices will create many new media channels.

4. On-demand interactive entertainment content that is personalized for our preferences will be a standard feature.

5. Advanced virtual reality bundled with digital agents and holographic entertainment worlds will transform our experience of entertainment.

6. Movie theaters will receive digital broadcasts and satellite downloads of movies, video conferencing, and other interactive programming.

7. Faster, smarter, and more powerful multimedia communications devices will enhance our capacity for producing and distributing entertainment.

8. Digital TV will provide new programs where we will experience real-time participation with the media content, personalities, and shows.

9. Edutainment, the merger of entertainment and education, will offer a new genre of programming that will be greatly in demand.

10. Nontraditional entertainment producers, empowered by Power Tools, will change the industry, offering new products, channels, and innovations.

Danny went to film school, but he doesn't direct, produce, write, or act. He creates the best digital actors for the media industry from his digital warehouse of personality fragments of "the greats." He was going to buy the digital rights to classic stars such as Bruce Willis and Cary Grant, but instead, he sampled their personalities and created look-and-act-alikes. He can create digital impersonations whenever required. These are digital actors that simulate the behavior, voice, and personalities of real actors.

Last week Danny got a call from a director with one of the big studios that his Real World actor couldn't finish his film —some type of cold. *Probably a contract problem,* thought Danny. They needed a digital double.

Lily, the director, was frantic.

"No problem. We do the best Digi-Doubles this side of Hollywood," says Danny proudly. "You choose what you want based on the story, and we create the best digital actor for your film."

"It's a cop movie, and we need our hero to be macho in a complex, vulnerable sort of way, you understand?" she asks.

"Torn-up but tough. I got it. I am entering a search now, I received your visuals of your guy. Is this Jackie Rebel?" a surprised Danny asks.

"Yes. I need a real-time Digi-Double with these personality and physical attributes I am downloading to you *now*. He's go to be ready to act in 24 hours."

"Take it easy. I got the best A-Life Digi-Doubles. My stuff is military strength, and we make you look good. See my Digi-Double Net page, and choose the behaviors you want. There's an extra fee for a 24-hour turnaround. We Net-deliver to you when you're ready, Lily."

"How much?"

"Our usual of one percent of the actor's contract and 3 percent of his royalty stream for all markets, all media."

"That's about $2 million. I can live with that. Done. I'll have the lawyers e-mail the signed agreements in Real-Time. Let's do it." Lily signs off.

Digital actors created inside of computers. Virtual-reality mystery programs. Interactive games. Cross-platform media marketing from Net-connected street signs that "know" us. Personalized programming for an audience of one beamed to our cars. Media appliances that we can use to produce interactive entertainment. The Net will dominate entertainment, driving a new type of media unifying TV, telephones, and computers into one gateway. It will link everything to us wherever we are. We will not just *experience* entertainment in the next century—*it will become part of our lives.*

An arsenal of digital technologies will reshape the entertainment business. These new multimedia Power Tools, accessible to anyone, will end the era of entertainment created solely by an elite group of TV networks and movie studios. In the digitally driven future, many new faces will produce and distribute entertainment over Net-enabled channels that will find synergy with traditional channels such as TV and movie theaters.

New Media, New Choices

By 2005, much of the new media will be interactive, with many choices available, such as virtual-reality documentaries, interactive mysteries, groupware science fiction, or self-directed adventures. Sample sessions could include the following:

- Designing our own personalized show from preprogrammed media components.

- Watching others interact in real-time in the program of our choice.

- Participating in one- or two-way interactivity with other audience members and actors.

- Buying, selling, and trading products, services and program ideas.

- Interacting with targeted groups of people, large and small.

- Becoming an actor in a show or creating an avatar that follows our direction.

- Real-time collaboration among artists, actors, and entrepreneurial businesses.

Many of these activities exist in some form already. For example, to create the 1997 summer blockbuster *Batman and Robin,* Warner Digital Studios used artists at over 100 remote Silicon Graphics workstations (**www.sgi.com**) to create the 3-D rendering, painting, compositing, and other special effects applications.

They were able to work in real-time using asynchronous transfer mode (ATM) technology, which can deliver data, voice, and video across networks and which gives on-demand access to the Internet.

Until recently, technology has been an expensive line item in producing media, but soon we will be able to do more by spending less. Even in the movie *Titanic*, which had a titanic budget, cost-saving technology created digital actors. Crowd scenes were digitally generated with thousands of synthetic actors, each programmed to perform a specific behavior. The ocean scenes where the Titanic was streaming along in the Atlantic were digitally engineered. The ship itself was partially created from models and then digitally "pasted" together on a computer first, and then for the screen.

Digital Movie Delivery

Part I of *Star Wars, the Phantom Menace,* debuted the first totally computer-generated digital actors. This technology points to a time when we may use digital actors to film an entire production. In fact, perhaps we will build the sets as well, dropping our digital actors into synthetic entertainment worlds to totally create every aspect of the movie. It is cartoons reborn.

As the producers, we could then just download the movie to a satellite distribution center that will deliver the film to 500 theaters worldwide in minutes. George Lucas of *Star Wars* fame has a vision of digital satellite delivery of movies that will save millions in not having to produce the actual film. Film-less digital distribution of digital productions will be a bestselling feature of the future (**www.lucasarts.com**).

The Hollywood we know today will be part of the nostalgic past. A few studios will push the envelope on budgets and technology in an attempt to dazzle audiences with even greater effects, images, and graphics. By early in the next century, however, we will see aspiring filmmakers compete inexpensively using a desktop computer and digital actors, then broadcasting their shows directly to consumers over the Net and digital TV.

The Digital Entertainment Network (**www.den.com**) is one of dozens of new Net-based media networks that is producing media for the Net in a TV or movie style. They are allowing independent producers and directors to shoot short works and distribute them through their site. Soon this content will be on the Net, but we will be able to access it over the TV or telephone lines. This is the beginning of cross-platform distribution of media that will open up many new opportunities.

For what it costs to shoot home movies today, we will be able to produce quality media and broadcast it to a hungry global audience of billions. Internet multicasting over digital TV will redefine the media that today dominates news, entertainment, and public affairs programming worldwide. Nontraditional media moguls, like the day traders in the stock market that buy and sell stock over the Net, will be producing and distributing entertainment. This will place competitive pressure on large companies to keep their entertainment franchises. The audience wins one way or the other.

Calling All Digital Actors

Imagine the thrill of rubbing shoulders with a digitally "cloned" Humphrey Bogart, wearing his fedora and trench coat from *Casablanca* and greeting us with the words, "Here's looking at you, kid." Digitally engineered entities, designed for entertainment in commercials, TV, and movies, will come to rival human actors.

We can meet Bogie right now at the studios of Sherer Design Associates (SDA) in Rancho Mirage, California (**www.sda.com**). SDA got an early start on creating digital facsimiles of humans, including a 13-year-old ballerina named Michelle, a modern-day cowboy, and Abraham Lincoln recreated from archival photographs. Perhaps we can scan ourselves and create a movie using our own images. Some studio of the future will no doubt help us create a theatrical karaoke!

HEADLINE FROM THE FUTURE

MAKE-A-MOVIE WITH "YOU'RE THE DIRECTOR!" CHANNEL
YOU CHOOSE ACTORS AND PLOTS

In Japan, a young female virtual entity, Kyo Data, has achieved a level of stardom close to that of human actors. She has a large following of fans who don't care that she's not a real person. They are attracted to the entertainment value she delivers. Researchers at MIT, Stanford, and New York University have developed virtual characters like her who can "perform" from scripts and even interact with human thespians.

As mentioned earlier, the Intel-Creative Artist Agency multimedia lab (**www.caa.com**) has "captured" Danny DeVito to demonstrate how a virtual character could display emotions on-demand for movies. In a virtual screen test, DeVito explained how digital actors could display different emotions such as sadness, anger, or happiness for the director who could then shape these virtual experiences into stories. How long before we don't need directors either, and the entire process of creating media is automated? Bizarre but true. These experiments give us an indication of where entertainment is going.

Some entertainment companies are already casting virtual characters who can be embedded into movies, television, and commercials. Hollywood agents are scrambling to figure out how to represent these virtual performers.

Casts of virtual characters with "lives and destinies" that we can interact with, program, and even co-exist with are on the near horizon. How will this change lifestyles and society when entertainment is provided by virtual Mel Gibsons and Demi Moores? Will we even care as long as we are entertained? Probably not.

We Are the Show

In the future, if we'd like to see ourselves in a production, there will be scanning systems to graphically replicate our face and body, which can then be inserted into an interactive drama or action adventure game. This will be a very compelling feature for entertainment. We can assume the personality of an actor in a scripted show, or design our own character or an entire show. Perhaps we'd like to star in a techno-thriller about catching the murderer or retrieving the serum to save the world!

Once scanned into the show, we can choose plot points, other actors, and where we want to travel to solve the mystery. Perhaps we'd like to go to Rome. We will be able to "see" ourselves inside of these stories. We interact with other human actors or synthetics.

The Vatican Mystery Show: Year 2007

Show Background Briefing

The Vatican Mystery Show is an interactive customized program about a detective who is hot on the trail of a thief who has stolen a priceless manuscript from the Vatican in Rome. The manuscript is really a map that leads to a treasure of unknown origin. Interpol, the international police, has asked the detective to help them catch the thieves and recover the manuscript.

The job of the detective, your role, is to go to Rome, interview the suspects, meet with the police, and collect clues to solve the case. The job of the thief, Sky, is to keep the police and you guessing who it is while you find the treasure. There are a variety of characters to play either simultaneously or serially, based on preference. There are many random plot turns and unpredictable events, even new characters "generated" from the interactive fabric of the game show. There may also be other humans that contract to play different roles in the show.

Plot points can be automatically generated by the Story Engine or customized to achieve maximum enjoyment. See story settings for more. Team playing is also available; check the Media Mode button. Voice Help is always available from the Story Guide. The show can be stopped and saved at any time for interacting with at a later time.

Media Mode Choices: Select One

Please select one or more Media Modes to engage the program after your Pay-Per-Interact Account has registered. Media Mode Selections available for this show include:

Virtual Reality-First Person, Virtual Reality-Observer, Observer, Director, Team Playing. Customized settings are available. No designer characters from other copyrighted shows may be dropped into this show. Designer characters that are avatars, extensions of yourself or others, or Free Agents with their own agenda, may be introduced in Random Action if you choose.

Story Settings: Select One

Story Settings can be changed on-demand if you choose. Each Setting comes complete with a Story Orientation and Interactive Help at any time, callable by voice command. The Goal is to have fun and solve the mystery. The reward for winning is described in the Show Sponsors's Net-TV channel guide. Now select Story Setting and get going.

- Reveal all secrets
- Allow discovery
- Show script
- Rewrite story
- Random action
- Surprise

Thank you for playing the Vatican Mystery Show produced by Big Time Producers, Inc.

There's No Business Like Show Business

Digital entertainment entrepreneurs in the 21st century will be able to instantly lease toolkits over the Internet to create movies or Net shows that could once only be done by a big studio or media group. Inexpensive and powerful media tools will come complete with digital actors and sets, predesigned and ready for production and distribution. Just as important, they'll be able to distribute their product on the Net—aimed at a specific audience already established through data mining and Knowledge Value Engineering.

Shows will be produced for small audiences that previously could never be served due to costs, distribution, or access issues. As microprocessors get smaller, cheaper, and superpowerful, we'll all be able to have a "Studio on a Desktop" for creating or participating in the latest music, movies, or magic. As a corollary, we'll be able to create, direct, and produce our targeted entertainment media from practically anywhere—while sitting on a deck overlooking the sea, or if we choose, on the streets of New York City.

We will also alter entertainment produced by others to suit us. While *Jurassic Park Part V's* super 3-D effects in the new Cinema Emporium of 2003 may still draw big crowds, there will be a trend away from passive entertainment and toward interactive immersion, telepresent "shows" that are adaptable. We will have choices about how we want to interact with the medium and will happily pay as we go. Not everyone will choose the same media-enhancements. The online or off-line audience will configure and design their own shows. We will vote on redesigning media while we are watching or participating.

HEADLINE FROM THE FUTURE

CONSUMERS LOVE TO RUN FROM T-REX DIGITAL TV SHOW — *RETURN TO JURASSIC PARK PART V* NOW COMES WITH TREADMILL

Media Goes to the Net

An early example of adapting new applications to entertainment is the partnering of Attitude Network (**www.attitude.net**) with Hollywood powerhouse Universal Studios On-line (**www.universalstudios.com**). The offshoot is an interactive site for kids that will feature a wide array of family-oriented titles from copyrighted properties such as *Hercules: The Legendary Journeys, Crash*

Bandicott, Xena: Warrior Princess, The Land Before Time, Rocky and Bullwinkle, Woody Woodpecker, Beethoven, and *Chilly Willy.* The site will enable kids to interact with Universal's characters, play games, and chat with other young fans.

As part of its $350 million commitment to original animation, Nickelodeon has created an all-new family of animated stars with its new character laboratory, Oh Yeah! Cartoons! (**www.viacom.com**) Using the latest in computer technology, kids are starring with animal characters in a series of original half-hour cartoons for TV.

Tuning in to Us

Digital TV will provide thousands of channels of opportunity for developing and distributing this new abundance of entertainment. The convergence of digital TV and the Net will accelerate creative business opportunities and offer many new channels and types of interactive, multiplatform programs never before possible.

How about TV shows that interact with tele-toys or communicate over the Net to wearable media on clothing that comes alive with a character from a show? Or a videoconferencing virtual window that pops up over my shoe to offer me an entertaining tour of a new product? This will completely transform advertising by offering many new electronic portals.

How will we decide where to tune in when there are unlimited entertainment choices? In addition to having a personalized menu of viewing preferences prepared by an entertainment agent, there will be digital tools such as "Virtual Cable" already offered by American Interactive Media (**www.virtualcable.com**). It's the first Internet source where viewers can sample in real-time the programming of dozens of cable networks.

Virtual Cable's full-motion video streaming gives each cable network's programming, accompanied by portions of its Website, program schedule, and marketing information. These applications and others to come will give channel surfers a way to navigate the interactive media of the future.

At some point, though, the media will find us. Intelligent agents will tell media producers about our desires, which help them with their creative process, financing, and distribution, and help us by saving us time.

The Art of the Net-Deal

A big driver of on-demand entertainment is the coming of age of interactive business transactions. If our personal Internet agent finds five million people interested in mystery stories about Sherlock Holmes, then advance "tickets" could be sold to assure the successful financing of the project. An e-cash virtual bank account that can process this transaction will be essential. Instant e-cash streaming across the world will green-light the new media projects faster than we can say, "That's a wrap."

Once our audience is assured, our Net agent can help seek out sponsors who are interested in reaching that particular subscriber base. Even value-added sales, corporate ad sponsorship, licensing, and product merchandising for various markets can be generated well before the entertainment product is created. Investment bankers could also market a corporate E-Bond over the Net to raise cash, a concept used successfully for rock star David Bowie in the '90s. He sold Bowie Bonds; these were contracts on his potential record sales. Bowie leveraged his intellectual assets before he actually sold any music.

The New Producers: 2006

Miles Travling is an author whose first interactive online book, *Worlds Beyond,* was a smashing success. He's now ready to pitch his idea for a series of multimedia-enhanced Net products titled *Fiery Adventures.* Charlene, his personal agent, arranges a meeting with the heads of several major publishing companies. The site? A virtual yacht for a sunset dinner cruise. No one will physically be there; they will be virtually represented.

The publishers' bot-agents accept the invitation. As a special treat—and to help sell the package—Miles has enlisted Virtual Happenings not only to customize a simulated yacht, but also to arrange a cruise by an island where a spectacular volcanic eruption will occur at the precise moment when he finishes his *World's Beyond* pitch. His virtual guests will be able to see and feel the beauty of the spectacle as if they were there.

Charlene gives her nod of approval, along with a personalized profile of each of his guests. At the appointed time, Charlene connects everyone together at the online site engineered by Virtual Happenings. Miles welcomes them, and off they sail as the sun sets and the glow of a full moon lights the surrealistic scene. Noting that the guests all like jazz, Charlene has ordered a Deluxe Jazz Trio featuring a virtual Herbie Hancock on piano. The adventure is a roaring success, and several publishers express interest in Miles's new project. Charlene notes their interest and sets up an online auction for the next day where the best bid wins the creative property.

> To celebrate, Miles books a real Hawaiian vacation to relax before starting the project. Actually, his authorbot, Shakespeare, will write the first draft based on the concept developed by Miles. Ah, the good life.

Advertising will be redefined, too. Smart sponsors will learn how to bundle their products with media shows that authentically reach their selected consumer base with laserlike precision. Or, these shows might be more dynamic by popping up randomly in areas where surveys reveal consumers of their products frequently visit.

And after the show airs, product spin-offs and customized reruns—where a viewer can join the cast and take a part—will generate additional income. Imagine this future ad campaign: Be First to Own the Play-at-Home Version of *Lethal Weapon 10.*

Everyone's a Comedian

In the future, we won't even have to have performance anxiety when the "big break" comes to be a media star. We can be coached virtually by those we admire most. Want to learn how to perform standup comedy? Try *The Billy Crystal Show* for beginning comedians on the Web-TV Comedy Channel, and be coached by the virtual comic genius. Can anyone become a good comedian with this super coach? Maybe not, but we'll all have the chance to try, and have some laughs in the process.

We could compose a song for our favorite group and then perform it for our friends. We could create the, lyrics and music and have the band represented by avatars—virtual representatives of the real members—in a tele-immersion environment that we could enter at any time. Although they're not the real band members, these avatars are Artificial Life forms who can self-evolve, helping to construct new songs and verses in real-time to satisfy our musical tastes.

We won't have to worry if we can't reach those high harmonies during the Beach Boys VR Jam, either. We'll simply go to a Knowledge Value music vendor who will synthesize our voice in a higher key–in real-time. The Knowledge Vendors of tomorrow will be the equivalent of the Rolling Stones and Stephen Kings of today. More important, the digital media sharing their talent will provide economic and creative opportunity for those of us who want to participate in the entertainment industry.

KARAOKE AGENTS HELP YOU SING
LIKE MARIAH CAREY

One forward-looking multimedia company, Creative Technologies, has already held the world's first online international MIDI music composition contest, and there will be many similar competitions by other companies in the future. From Argentina to Zimbabwe, amateur and professional musicians from 57 countries around the world submitted more than 1,100 original musical compositions. The six-month competition was held on the Creative Inspire Website (**www.creativeinspire.com**). Creative Inspire is one of the first Internet applications that gives users everything they need to listen, watch, and experience multimedia entertainment on the Internet.

Music, Music Everywhere

Perhaps the shape of things to come is reflected in the MP3 music craze. The MP3 standard has taken the music industry by surprise. It enables people to send and receive quality music over the Net. They can store it on their computers or download the tunes to small devices for playback. This fuss is because there are thousands of Websites to access this music in MP3 today. Much of it violates the existing copyright laws, but this hasn't stopped people from exploiting the producers and artists. Regardless, there will be numerous digital formats; this is just one of the latest that enable the Net to be distribution platform for acquiring music. Many more exciting schemes will combine video, audio, and data so that people can produce full-length multimedia and distribute this over the Net.

Networked Playing

In gaming, Activision, Inc. (**www.activision.com**) was one of the first to take real-time action strategy to new heights with the product NetStorm. Developed specifically for Internet play by Titanic Entertainment (**www.titanic. com**) it combines original gameplay, environments, and units for various level skills. NetStorm also matches up online players with similar experience and power. Networked entertainment over the Net is a vitally important part of the digital future. Manufactures are realizing this rush to the Net by offering multiplayer games and environments for hungry players of all ages.

Perhaps the most imaginative and soon-to-be-imitated technology emerging is the next generation Playstation from Sony. This potentially

Artificial-Intelligence game console combined with superfast and rich graphics will also be networked for online playing.

Already a leader in music, movies, and games, Sony is taking the next big step into competing for the ownership of the home market. The Playstation II will have the graphics capability of today's supercomputer and cost less than $400. This game console will be easier to use, faster, and perform with richer graphics then any computer on the market, says Sony. This is truly an amazing development that is ample evidence of much of what this book is all about. This will change the gaming entertainment business; it will also place competitive pressures on every other computer and game producer to try to beat Sony. Radical market-shifting technology is reshaping this world.

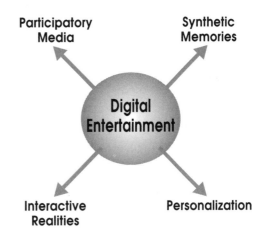

Future Entertainment Products

Here is an overview of the various media that will be available in the 21st century. Interactivity, personalization, and fun will be critical success ingredients:

■ **Designer multimedia:** Anyone can be a producer, director, or actor. If we belong to a user group fascinated with 14th-century Spain, we can create stories for that population based on our Net research and configured with the help of a personal Net talent agent. A promo can be produced and shown to the user group and orders taken for the final product. Commercial groups compete to sponsor this entertainment as a way to increase their market share.

■ **Smart books:** These digital books with embedded intelligence learn about our needs and values and create stories based on our preferences. If we're fascinated by time travel, our smart book will search the Net for information or the best vendor to create a story that outdoes H. G. Wells's classic, *The Time*

Machine. Embedded intelligent agents can negotiate in the background for a knowledge vendor to deliver a program within our price range. Intuitive computer programs will design stories based on our interests or learning needs. We'll get a preview of four or five choices, along with a sampling of music and a cast that will bring the story to life. Options might include a virtual-reality interface we can tether to plot points and experience a journey through time. Educational agents will analyze our learning needs and design programs to help us achieve maximum efficiencies. We will also be able to get instant feedback on our educational growth. Parents will be able to design customized learning themes and skill areas for their children.

■ **Immersion cinema:** While theaters will still offer passive entertainment, interactive enhancements will dominate. Total immersion cinema, where we are put into the movie, will be very popular. This will be available at traditional cinemas, kiosks for a private experience, or theme parks designed around the immersion media experience. We'll be able to smell the smoke from the campfire scene or tether to a character with special gloves to experience his sensations during a car chase through the hilly streets of San Francisco. The force-feedback systems that let us "Real-Feel" objects and people will be in hot demand, and two-ounce virtual-reality headsets will put us in *Jurassic Park Part V*, being chased by T-Rex. A standards code will restrict interactions in films projecting horror, violence, and sex, but a thriving underground of "art" theaters will flourish. Entertainment pharmaceuticals that provide pleasure enhancers making experiences authentic will be standard reinforcement for Saturday night. Experience *Titanic*—feel the freezing water without getting wet!

HEADLINE FROM THE FUTURE

VIRTUAL REALITY THEATER PROVIDES REAL-FEEL

■ **Games:** New interactive and online games will offer real-world challenges, teach skills, and be Big Fun. Most games will have numerous media modes of varying interactivity. They will propel us into other times, experiences, and fantasies. Every aspect of new technology, from force-feedback to virtual reality, will be streamed into the gaming experience. Gaming will take many forms, too, from home-based games over cable or phones, to virtual remote-device gaming from handheld devices. The ultimate games, though, will be "smart games" that we can design on demand and play with other enthusiasts anywhere on the planet via the Net. They will learn from us and adapt to help us win. The demand for online interactive games is growing and will become a huge market by the year 2002. I predict that subcultures of pro-gamers will emerge based on their desire, and proficiency in playing them.

The Gaming Society: Year 2004

Members of a gaming society called Akalden compete against other societies throughout the Net in specific skills such as auto racing, ecology lab, interactive literature, science and inventions, and virtual war. These contests are staged on virtual landscapes. The players, using VR equipment, are embedded as the drivers of robotic tanks that do battle with the challenging society over the rugged surface of the planet Mars. Some of these pro-gaming teams are sponsored by multinational corporations, which help promote the events to the global Internet audience. Some entrepreneurs put together pro-gamers with specialty coaches that will help them enhance their skills. Some of these gaming societies develop their own ideologies, and many are revered as techno-spiritual achievers—even heroes. Ad sponsors finance them.

■ **Mega-arcades:** By 2004, young people will gather at urban gaming mini-malls for "challenge matches" paid for with e-cash or smart cards. These silicon-based, sensor-embedded play arenas will contain a labyrinth of virtual games and rides to attract the entire family. Players can reserve time on their favorite games in advance via the Internet and practice on their wireless PCs en route. Multi-user online tournaments will be very popular as contestants win credits and prizes. GameWorks, Disney, Sega Corp., and Universal Studios are already planning these mega-arcades. Entire gaming societies will emerge, much like the Olympics or Goodwill Games, with cash prizes and prestige.

■ **Cyber worlds:** A variety of interactive virtual characters will invade the earth. "Virtual Safari" creates an environment where players hunt down animals to shoot by using a virtual camera; they build an album that can be shared over the Internet. In the near future, enhanced products of this sort will sing and play with us in realistic virtual environments. Cyber worlds designed to teach us a foreign language or master a skill will be in demand. The next step is kids creating their own creatures and designing the characters they want to live and react with in these cyber worlds.

■ **Wearable media:** Devices, appliances, and chips will be woven into our clothing to enhance our media receptivity or media production capabilities. We will change channels, download e-mail files, and surf the Web with our clothes. Wearable media will give us wireless links to numerous electronic channels provide anywhere, anytime.

Robo Entertainment

The ability of robots and androids to capture and replicate human experience and then incorporate that into art, music, sport, or drama will be a fascinating new form of entertainment in the 21st century. Imagine groups of robots putting on a Beethoven concert. Androids, which have more humanlike aspects, could create their own music, sell it via the Internet, and be interviewed about their latest hit on *The Tonight Show*. Imagine David Letterman's "Ten Top Stupid Things That Robots Do" being criticized as "unsympathetic" toward synthetic life forms.

Fast-forward eight to ten years. Androids, cyborgs, and robots will entertain us and rival the talents of humans. We will laugh at robot comedy.

Cooking with Cyborgs

Synthetic entities of the future will do everything from flipping Big Macs to performing surgery to entertaining us on sitcoms. Artificial characters in entertainment will make us laugh and cry. We will forget that they aren't human. It is when these synthetic life forms start to watch and grade *us* that we'll know things have really changed.

We will soon come to accept entertainment delivered by androids who are believable, smart, and creative. Part human/android orchestras will bring music to our communities. Synthetics will create their own entertainment. We are creating a reality that will be populated by a variety of different kinds of synthetic intelligence. Virtual agents, androids, and cybernetically enhanced humans who share a common destiny to increase the quality and productivity of our lives will mediate this reality.

Cyber-Addiction or Silicon Nirvana?

As the blurring of virtual reality and authentic reality becomes the norm, there's a danger that we could become lost or disoriented in these new experiences. Although VR will be entertaining, educational, and exciting, it could result in a generation of cyber couch potatoes, particularly when our brains are "wet-wired" to the Net, and we can access media anytime, anywhere. I predict

238

that many people will come to prefer tele-worlds to real environments because it's where their unfulfilled fantasies can be realized. This is the potential dark side of the entertainment revolution. Machines will seduce us with silicon nirvana. We will come to value synthetic experience over the "real." It's inevitable that new entertainment technologies may destabilize some individuals.

Welcome to Virtual Disney: Year 2005

The "character agents" at Virtual Disney World are self-evolving, adaptive, and programmed to customize visits for guests. They've found out that Ken's daughter, Charlotte, will be six and that she loves Mickey Mouse and his friends.

Charlotte is sent an invitation inviting her to Virtual Disney World to dine with Mickey, meet Minnie and Pluto, and get a personal tour of the park's sub-world, where she can have tea with the Mad Hatter, who "knows" all about her. Or, she could become Minnie and go on an adventure with Mickey and Pluto.

She might even learn math in the same experience since she needs some help with it. And, she can enjoy the entire experience without leaving the comfort of her living room. There's a fee, of course, payable via Ken's cyber-cash account.

Designing Reality

Instead of passively watching a soap opera or cowboy movie, we can weave the entertainment for tonight into our lifestyle. We can direct our involvement in the media capturing our experience, our life, and our reality. This future scenario describes the awesome power of tech-enabled entertainment to merge with and shape our lives.

The seductive nature of entertainment technology and the economics of advertising will produce an endless array of the greatest shows on Earth. Anyone scouting for a digital enterprise of the 21st century should look very closely at the opportunities in entertainment, and how to use convergent technologies such as the Internet, digital TV, and smart agents to unlock the full potential of this marketplace.

■ ■ ■

CHAPTER THIRTEEN

Space— The Next Frontier

The Top Ten Space Trends for the 21st Century

1. Many innovations will be developed by space enterprises that will accelerate the establishment of a global space market.

2. New energy sources developed to navigate space will accelerate the exploration of our galaxy enabling us to explore deep space.

3. Miniaturized cost-effective spacecraft will explore the stars long before humans are capable of venturing out into deep space.

4. Space mining will yield new resources, elements, and materials that will enhance the quality of life on our planet.

5. Robonauts, robot astronauts, will stretch our imaginations with fantastic information from their space adventures and be our new heroes.

6. Humans will learn to leave their home planet of Earth, terraform far-away planets, and colonize space.

7. Extremely valuable space assets, from materials and drugs to minerals and innovations, will create a space race among global companies.

8. First contact with alien life through the identification of life-supporting planets may come closer to becoming a possibility.

9. Space discoveries will have a profound impact on the advancement of human science, medicine, education, entertainment, and culture.

10. The exploration of space will spark a new "big-picture" understanding of human evolution and human destiny as we reach out into the galaxy.

When Columbus—perhaps the greatest of all the early explorers—first saw the New World, he and his men stared in wonder at what they had accomplished. It was as if the world stood still for a moment to honor their victory. Columbus's discovery was about much more than finding a new trade route for precious spices or uncovering hidden gold. Columbus defeated the belief that there was no New World. He redefined what was possible. He beat back the narrow-minded ideas that ruled his time. Setting out to reach the New World, a journey of incalculable proportion in 1492, opened up possibilities as never before—for commerce and every other aspect of human endeavor.

Human beings have always been explorers searching for New Worlds to discover. We continually crash through the limitations of our beliefs and stake our claims higher and further than before. Humans are more than curious. We are driven to celebrate the new and explore the unknown. Columbus would rejoice to see humanity reaching out to the stars. He would understand and marvel at how far we have come since the Santa Maria set sail in search of destiny. Columbus would understand our hunger for unlocking the ultimate mysteries of life that may be found in space.

Destiny Calls

Space exploration will yield knowledge that will change humankind. No one alive today can accurately predict or imagine the impact of this quest on science, business, society, or human development. Space exploration will be as arduous and rewarding a journey for human beings as climbing the evolutionary ladder to become homo sapiens.

I believe that our destiny as a civilization is rooted in the development of the leading-edge technologies that will be essential to exploring, colonizing, and deriving knowledge about the universe. This is the greatest challenge our civilization will ever face: developing the capacity to leave our home world and venture into the unknown universe. The exploration of space will revolutionize belief systems, fuel innovations in science, and expand our understanding of life. The exploration of space and the discovery of its secrets will be the nexus point for humanity to realize its collective destiny.

NASA's first brave steps will seem primitive against the panorama of space accomplishments that will emerge in the 21st century. We are just taking baby steps as we reach out to Mars and other planets in our solar system. Our adventure will accelerate as companies and nations deploy a network of probes, ships, robots, and space habitats. The eventual outcome will be off-world colonization.

The exploration of the galaxy, first by robotic drones like those used on missions to Mars, later by sophisticated A-Life androids designed for deep space missions, and finally by humans "enhanced" for space travel, will open up new vistas that will affect every Earthly endeavor. From medicine and manufacturing to food production and energy, technology developed to take us to the stars will have enormous impact on commerce here on Earth.

Robonaut J. Glenn Report: Year 2018

This is Robonaut J. Glenn reporting in to Space Station Bradbury. I am an Azimov 3000 T Robonaut designed with an on-board supercomputer as my brain-source. I am named for the human astronaut John Glenn. I carry 5 percent of his DNA and have a complete download of his experiences. My spacecraft is fusion-driven with solar cell backup thrusters. I have nano-propulsion Generation Aqua systems that assimilate anti-matter for energy.

This is report number 25 since I left Earth's orbit in 2007. System operations in steady state, A-Okay, as you humans like to say. Report commences.

Passing the outer rim of the Milky Way, I encountered a cosmic anomaly. None of my computers could find a comparable event, so we set up a new file including video, audio commentary, and infrared and blue radio spectrum analysis. You should be receiving the full file approximately 180 days after this radio transmission.

What was strange was that a star system just beyond the horizon of the Milky Way was going supernova, and the explosion had reached my ship. All time seemed to freeze. I could see everything stop. I could not move, as if I were caught in a strange supernova backlash. Then the star, which seemed bigger than Earth's sun, exploded.

This celestial anomaly lasted for what seemed only a few minutes. Suddenly we came out of this frozen state, and the ship was hurled many light years off course. I am recalculating our position and attempting to correct my course headings. I must say, though, that where we ended up just south of the axis horizon of the rim of the Milky Way has revealed a star system that doesn't appear on any charts. I suspect it was hidden. With the supernova now gone and my new position, I will investigate further. Report complete. (To be continued...)

A Cosmic Gold Rush

Space exploration has always been a potent symbol of humanity's quest for uncovering the mysteries of life itself. Beyond that, colonization of other worlds will spawn a "made in space" multibillion-dollar commercial bonanza for the benefit of those on Earth, as well as those who choose to live off-world.

A cosmic gold rush in the 21st century will offer opportunities for discovery and adventure unmatched on our home world. Recently we reached a new threshold when private space investments and sales generated more revenues than the public space market. A private sector space race is heating up, and we will carry our ambitions and competitive fever to colonies on other planets. Just as Columbus sailed across a vast ocean in his quest to prove the existence of faraway lands and riches, humanity will go in search of rewards well beyond the Milky Way galaxy. In doing so, we will play out many of the space dramas captured in our entertainment over the past 100 years.

Growing Up with Star Trek

Many of us baby boomers grew up with the *Star Trek* TV series and later with the movies of the same name. *Star Trek* defined many of the aspirations of a generation. The stories were a metaphor for achieving an exploration of the future; it just happened to be in space. Produced by Gene Roddenberry, part genius, part science fiction buff, *Star Trek* captured our imagination and offered us a hopeful and adventuresome vision of "exploring strange new worlds." Inspired by an optimistic vision of the future—the basis of the series' success—Trekkies defied age, sex, or nationality. If we let the Trekkie spirit take hold as we gaze at celestial events through the Hubble telescope, we will see the glorious opportunities awaiting us in space.

HEADLINE FROM THE FUTURE

SPACE PROBE MADONNA CARRIES A-LIFE COMPUTER FOR EXPLORING GALAXY

Einstein's Universe

If he were alive today, Jules Verne, the 19th-century science fiction writer, would applaud this spirit. He would be proud to be a citizen of the 21st century, in which he could finally realize his visions of planetary travel. Verne would not be surprised to learn that a significant sampling of humankind in the latter part of the 21st century will live off-world on asteroids, other planets, and orbiting space colonies.

There are plenty of oracles such as Verne today, spinning visions of our future in space. It's time we paid them heed. The linkage between visionary and scientist is often only a matter of time. Today's scientists often build their theories on yesterday's visions of what's possible.

Arthur C. Clarke, the brilliant science fiction writer, had theorized the possibility of establishing a network of communication satellites at a geostationary orbit above the earth. He even calculated the positioning of the satellites to optimize their performance. His ideas, at first dismissed as foolhardy, proved to be accurate. Today a network of satellites covers the earth, providing a blanket of communication services to global citizens everywhere.

Albert Einstein, perhaps the most innovative scientist of our era, had a very difficult time getting the establishment of his day to accept his ideas. His thinking was so out-of-the-box that he required a staff of assistants to help him translate his breakthrough thinking into the theoretical language of physics so that others could follow him. Even today, some of his theories that are fundamental to space travel, such as his Unified Field Theory, is only understood by fewer than 100 people. But, if it were not for Einstein, many of the scientific building blocks that have led to atomic energy; our understanding of time, energy and space; the possibility of space travel itself; and the nature of the universe might not exist today.

Many other scientists originally dismissed his contributions as heresy. Often it is the rebel whose ideas transform our world. Space travel will be the fulfillment of many of these early visionaries' dreams and speculations on the future.

Exploration on Overdrive

Space exploration will serve as an incentive, much like the Cold War did, to be innovative and daring. Many of the technologies we enjoy today, from the laser to computers to the Internet, were created first for military purposes. Although someday, war may be extinct, challenges like those that drove defense-related innovation in the past are necessary to spark new technologies. The new space race will be a catalyst of immense proportions for developing innovations.

Since the Space Age began on October 4, 1957, with Sputnik, we've had spectacular successes—and numbing failures—with advancing technologies and associated costs becoming critical factors in setting priorities for future space missions. The entire agenda about what the objectives are for exploring space will be rewritten over the next decade. This will accelerate space exploration, bringing answers to vital questions as well as numerous commercial opportunities. The real space race hasn't begun.

The Madonna Probe: Year 2010

Expectations and imaginations were high that the Madonna Probe, a deep space robo-ship, would bring back evidence of life from the outer reaches of our solar system. All the Net-papers and media groups were anxiously anticipating its return to Earth.

Deployed in 2005, the Madonna Probe had wandered across endless light years of space—searching, watching, and collecting data on the universe. The probe's ability to "call home" stopped after the first nine months due to a malfunction that apparently couldn't fix itself.

NASA named the Madonna Deep Space Probe for the pop singer Madonna. She was a big sci-fi fan and wanted to contribute to the space craze affecting early 21st-century society. Madonna even wrote a bestselling song, "Space Women," which went superplatinum.

Five other deep space probes had disappeared mysteriously —or just never returned to our solar system. Scientists at the Nebularn Foundation, which was firmly committed to space commerce and exploration, were perplexed over the missing probes and looked hopefully to a successful Madonna round-trip.

Nebularn, a private global consortium, had already set up remote satellite pharmaceutical factories, industrial and nano-development facilities in orbit around Earth and the moon.

Now their hopes for uncovering deep space mysteries were with Madonna, a new breed Class 5 probe equipped with a new-generation computer called Reality2 A-Life. This on-board computer had a self-learning personality chip that made the robo-ship very smart, adaptive, and committed to fulfilling its mission—just like a human.

Would Madonna detect alien life forms? Discover fantastic new substances? Madonna had the synthetic brain to identify, analyze, and "decide" what to do in the event of such close encounters. This was a big step forward from sending into

246

space the dumb drones at the turn of the century. Madonna, having been launched with great fanfare, was expected to return triumphantly. Scientists at Nebularn were holding their breath. (To be continued...)

Hello, Saturn

In 2004, when Cassini reaches Saturn for a four-year probe of the ringed planet, it will already be an obsolete vehicle. The instrument-laden, plutonium-powered spacecraft is the last of its kind. Cassini's mission will still be scientifically valuable, but by the time it starts to transmit data, NASA (**www.nasa. gov**) will be launching an armada of lighter, smaller spaceships that are relatively cheap, powerful, and loaded with new sophisticated micro-sensors for exploring the galaxy.

Including its orbiter and probe, Cassini is the largest, heaviest, and most complex interplanetary spacecraft ever built. Once in Saturn's orbit, it will carry out 12 experiments to unlock the secrets of the planet and its hurricanelike storms and dense gaseous mass. A probe of the haze-covered moon Titan, with a nitrogen-based atmosphere and a surface that may hold an ethane sea, is expected to provide clues to how primitive life evolved on Earth.

NASA, with lofty goals but a dwindling budget, is now future-focused on launching smaller, faster, cheaper spacecraft like the Mars Pathfinder and Mars Global Explorer. The Jet Propulsion Laboratory's Center for Space Microelectronics Technology (**www.jpl.nasa.gov**) is working on "cameras on a chip" and other innovative concepts for making everything aboard a craft smaller and more efficient. By 2004, NASA foresees launching as many as 12 to 20 micro spacecraft a year that are packed with tiny sensors and solar powered by featherlike wings.

Future Fuels

Many scientists have considered the implications of new types of propulsion systems, such as solar and anti-matter, that will defeat time and space barriers. There are many different types of propulsion technologies that will take us to the stars and beyond by enhancing our ability to travel long distances efficiently and safely. And these systems vary according to their payload: humans require much more energy then robonauts. The following theories are being discussed as future propulsion systems:

- **Anti-matter:** Anti-matter engines may unleash the most powerful energy source in the universe.

- **Laser propulsion:** Harnessing the strength of super lasers could lead to an energy force for propelling a spacecraft's engine.

- **Fusion:** A new generation of nuclear fusion utilizing superconducting technology may provide clean and powerful propulsion.

- **Electromagnetic:** Capturing the power of clean noncritical mass from electromagnetic fields could offer many efficiencies in traveling long distances.

- **Bioenergetic:** The development of advanced organic and genetically engineered biological systems could optimize systems for deep space travel.

- **Quantum:** These systems would capitalize on unlocking the potential of quantum mechanics, releasing a new generation of superpowerful yet efficient energy sources.

- **Solar:** The abundant solar energy available in the universe is a practical and renewable resource for generating the power needs for spacecraft.

- **Electric:** An electric propulsion system would be practical and clean, yet provide perhaps a very adaptable energy source for powering spacecraft of the future.

- **Nanotech:** These spacecraft would have self-generating, self-replicating capabilities to use whatever atoms, materials, or gases were available as building blocks to "assemble" energy on-demand, from whatever the environment is, wherever the craft is.

The bioenergetic and nanotech models, which use genetic and biological materials to "grow" organic systems and anti-matter systems, will be the most advanced. There may be many different systems developed for different kinds of space travel. The most efficient systems may entail a hybrid of solutions to propel our future starships.

The Space Biz

I believe that private industry will step forward and help create the quantum leaps necessary in technology development to produce and launch inexpensive, miniaturized spacecraft. This is the next evolution of the space industry, the privatization of space. NASA sees the handwriting on the wall and has taken initiatives to capitalize on this technology transfer.

The U.S. Space Program has pioneered some useful products, not only for celestial ventures, but also for applications on Earth. To this end, NASA has developed Commercial Space Center partnerships that are working on projects such as the following:

- **BioServe Space Technologies,** University of Colorado: Research in five areas—bioprocessing/bioproduct development, physiological modeling, biomolecular electronics, and enabling device capability.

- **The Center for Commercial Applications of Combustion in Space,** Colorado School of Mines: Research in the areas of combustors, fire safety, ceramic powders, semiconductors packages, and combustion synthesis.

- **The Center for the Commercial Development of Space Power and Advanced Electronics-Solidification Design,** Auburn University: Space research on thermophysical properties of casting alloys. Container-less measurements, taken aboard the shuttle and space station, will provide better values for use in computer models that will improve the manufacturing of cast metal parts.

- **The Center for Macromolecular Crystallography,** University of Alabama: Specializes in determining the 3-D structure of protein crystals using a process known as x-ray crystallography. By bombarding space-grown protein crystals with x-rays, diffraction patterns are produced, which allow the structure of the protein to be determined. The crystals are grown in space because the near absence of gravity allows near-perfect crystalline structures to form.

- **The Consortium for Materials Development in Space,** University of Alabama: Developing materials that can be used to build structures in space; utilizing the microgravity environment to advance understanding of liquid metal sintering for improved commercial structures, and vapor-grown single crystals for electronic and acoustical optical applications.

- **The Marshall Space Flight Center's Space Product Development Office** in Huntsville, Alabama, a NASA field center: Developing materials in photonics and electronics, including the space processing of fluoride glass fibers for communications systems and processing in space of nonlinear optical film materials.

- **The Langley Research Center** in Hampton, Virginia: Commercial research in improved polymer materials in collaboration with Paragon Vision Sciences, an Arizona firm that is a major distributor of contact lens products. (Paragon is interested in developing a rigidized contact lens that will be more durable and machinable than soft lenses, but will be more comfortable to the wearer than traditional hard contact lenses.)

- **The Microgravity Automation Technology Center**, a part of the Environmental Research Institute of Michigan: Improving the efficiency of microgravity-based product development research. Terrestrially, this area is known as the laboratory automation industry. One technology under development involves the use of digital imaging microscopy over very long distances.

- **The Space Vacuum Epitaxy Center** in Houston, Texas: New techniques to use the ultravacuum of space for processing ultrapure, thin-film materials for improving electronics and computers.

- **The Wisconsin Center for Space Automation and Robotics** at the University of Wisconsin-Madison: Commercial technologies for future long-duration space missions and terrestrial applications with a focus on the use of microgravity to enhance production of plant materials for pharmaceutical and agricultural purposes.

The New Space Race

These joint efforts are all part of a space race that's heating up. Unlike the old one, this space race is not between governments, but between global high-tech companies realizing that materials, resources, and innovations related to space exploration will soon become valuable strategic assets. But, we can't use what we don't have. Space companies must go into space to acquire the assets that will drive their next millennium business. This is not an option. The opportunities from the leverage of space assets such as new materials and new minerals will reshape economies, realign nations, and forge new alliances.

NASA will continue to play an important role in partnering with the private sector, but it is vital that industry buy into space ventures with leadership, innovation, and capital. And buy-in they will. Space will be a multibillion-dollar marketplace as we move into the 21st century.

One of the puzzles that industry must solve before cashing in, however, is reducing the cost of leaving this planet. The cost of putting a small communications satellite into orbit today is mind-boggling. Adding a 12-ounce can of soda to supplies bound for an orbiting space station costs $10,000 because of its weight.

In the near future, costs should drop dramatically with new, small, lightweight materials and efficient propulsion systems. Private-sector advances in nanotechnology, microengines, and quantum computers will add to the efficiencies of space technology.

Robonaut J. Glenn Report: Year 2022

This is the report by Robonaut J. Glenn. All systems A-Okay, Bradbury Space Station. Operation parameters have been altered as have navigation controls. Report commences.

The strange anomaly that I reported in 2018 has yielded a key discovery that you humans will enjoy. It appears that a Class M planet similar to Earth has been located in what I am calling the Hidden Valley star system.

Further analysis is being conducted now to determine the planet's atmosphere, gravity, and terrain. Since the identification of Class M Earthlike planets is my highest mission priority, I have changed my navigational controls to come closer to the star system. My intention is to launch a probe to determine a closer analysis. Report Complete. (To be continued...)

Space Entrepreneurs

SpaceHab (**www.spacehab.com**) is a model for 21st-century space enterprise. Producing pressurized containers for NASA cheaper than anything the agency could manufacture has put SpaceHab into orbit. The revolution in space may be driven more by profit than by a desire to explore strange new worlds. To wit, a Southern California company called Celestis (**www.celestis.com**) has started the first space-age mortuary business, sending two dozen ash capsules of remains into orbit by hitching a ride on a Pegasus XL rocket that was carrying a commercial satellite. In a couple years, the rocket will reenter the atmosphere and disintegrate, forming a vapor trail. The ashen remains—including those of Timothy Leary and *Star Trek* creator Gene Roddenberry—will flash like a "shooting star" in the firmament. All for the price of $4,800 per passenger.

▬▬ HEADLINE FROM THE FUTURE ▬

NEW METALS FOUND ON AZURE ASTEROID TRANSFORM MANUFACTURING

A study by KMPG Peat Marwick and a space venture capital company, Space Vest, indicated that space business is generating $85 billion annually.

Over $121 billion is forecast by 2000. The private-sector space business is now generating more revenues than the public market dominated by NASA. Although this is serious money, the estimate is probably low considering all the activity and interest driven by telecommunications and the Mars Explorer success. And these revenues may be generated not just by the large aerospace firms such as Lockheed or Boeing, but also by smaller, leaner entrepreneurs like SpaceHab.

More than 400 satellite launches over the next three to five years will drive space commerce. The need for NASA-friendly products and services to support the space industry is on an uptrend; so are profits. And much of what NASA does today, business will do on its own tomorrow. Space commerce is where entrepreneurs want to place their bets for growing their businesses in the future.

This may involve relocation. We should think about working and living in space as a career choice by the mid-21st century. At first, we will colonize the moon and then go on to Mars and establish bases within ten years. Choosing to live in space colonies established throughout our solar system will no doubt be as accepted 20 years from now as moving to another country is today. People living and working in space—on planets, celestial bodies such as moons and asteroids, and space stations—will be an attractive lifestyle, with opportunities for prosperity as well as adventure, in the mid-21st century.

Space Tourism

One company, Seattle-based Zegrahm Expeditions (**www.spacevoyages.com**) is already taking reservations for what it bills as the world's first tourist space shot on December 1, 2001. Itinerary: A low-orbit "astronaut altitude" cruise around the earth at 62 miles above sea level. The Zegrahm Space Voyages trip costs $98,000 for the 2 ½-hour flight. The company has joined forces with Vela Technology Development Inc., to construct a two-stage shuttlelike craft for the venture.

The moon, where astronauts have stepped and which sparks poetry in romantics, may be the perfect base for starting our celestial adventures. A robotic mission to the moon took place in January 1998 after a ten-year void of spacecraft visiting Earth's nearest neighbor. It won't take that long for the next trip. The moon is already being eyed as a spot for early space tourism. Back in the 1960s, Pan American Airways—as a publicity stunt—took reservations for the first moon flight. Perhaps early in the next century, the tickets will be honored.

Moon Colonies

Plans to colonize the moon were a featured topic at the 1997 International Astronomical Union's general assembly, a gathering of the world's leading astronomers. The astronomers, frustrated by human-made noise drowning out their efforts to tune in to the universe from radio telescopes on Earth, look toward the moon as an answer. They believe a super radio telescope can be placed there to provide crystal clear reception from deep space. They unveiled an ambitious plan to establish bases on the moon from where they can monitor radio signals from the heavens in the not-too-distant future.

The Artemis Society (**www.asi.org**) is a group of space enthusiasts who are raising money to colonize the moon. Members want to build a lunar base using SpaceHab modules that could be pieced together over time to "grow" a livable habitat—with a terrific view.

Space Health

As we use space exploration to satisfy our need to know the unknown, we can expect to solve some fundamental problems on the earth at the same time. Micro- and zero-gravity environments offer solutions to a multitude of health problems, for example. The possibilities for the health industry are abundant.

Space shuttle missions have already demonstrated some of the effects of micro-gravity on organic material. One example is illustrated by experiments in which orbiting scientists fused two types of white blood cells, creating a hybrid cell that produces antibodies against viral diseases. When performed in micro-gravity, this procedure produces hybrid cells with remarkably higher efficiency than in Earth laboratories. Orbiting scientific laboratories and pharmaceutical factories built on asteroids and planets will be common because cheaper and smarter drugs can be made in space. Drugs to combat cancers, viruses, and other illnesses, some yet to emerge, will be developed off world in zero gravity med-space labs.

People with medical problems that can be alleviated by living in low-gravity environments might also opt to inhabit orbiting space stations or settle on the moon. In those environments, cardiac patients would have less pressure on their hearts; there would be no pollen for asthma sufferers; mobility would be easier for the physically disabled. Companies in the health and well-being market will design off-world habitats for colonies of medically challenged people who will benefit from the move.

Some individuals may even choose to migrate into space as a way to travel forward in time, using the spacecraft as a time machine to cheat their own mortality. Extending their life span by traveling in space may be an appropriate choice for individuals threatened with health problems for which there's no help. Will insurance companies pay for the travel and relocation to a new, healthier world? If the price is right, perhaps.

Off-World Living

Some of these habitats will be extraterrestrial, such as planets or asteroids that may actually be more pleasing than Earth. Lush, exotic Tahitian-style beaches or Aspen-type ski slopes may be very appealing even if we don't have medical conditions.

To live off-planet, we will have the choice to be genetically altered to better endure the rigors of space and new environments. This will be a growth area for the biotech industry and an array of informational support services to recruit settlers.

Some off-worlds may be just boring, dim planets or space stations in remote parts of the galaxy. Mining operations in faraway worlds may not be that different from those mining operations we have today on Earth, but they most likely will be the habitat of robots rather than humans.

Robotic colonies established throughout our solar system over the next half-century will enable us to pursue cosmic commerce on a vast scale. Imagine the year 2030 when we have over 1,000 robotic extraterrestrial missions deployed throughout our solar system, all networked, sharing real-time information, and working on a variety of different manufacturing, design, resource mining, and communication projects.

Terraforming Planets

The full potential of leading-edge technology will result in our ability to terraform other planets. Terraforming is the ability to manipulate an inhospitable planet or asteroid to create a livable habitat for humans. We will learn to design a planet environment using advanced nanotech to create the air, soil, terrain, and weather. Entire atmospheres will be designed and deployed to sustain human habitats in preparation for colonization. Other terraforming may involve auto-terraforming, where we send robotic missions off to terraform distant planets making them ready for us.

Terraforming game plans are on the drawing boards today. We will deploy terraforming missions, both human-led and robotic-led, that will enable us to colonize other planets and celestial bodies within the solar system by 2030.

254

We will be able to create entire planetary systems someday. Synthetic planet-domes housing millions will be the next stage after we succeed in sustaining small colonies of people on orbiting space stations. Learning to grow food, harvest nutrients, and create atmospheres to support life will be commonplace in the latter part of the 21st century and early 22nd century.

There are already theories being discussed about terraforming Mars. Since Mars has a similar yearly cycle to Earth, as well as a comparable atmosphere and terrain, there are many possibilities for this scenario. Mars also is relatively close to Earth, and, most important, has water. It is frozen in ice caps, but available. Perhaps we will soon have the technology to begin this process of melting the ice, introducing a habitable atmosphere, and reengineering the terrain to make Mars suitable for life.

Many of the technologies discussed in this book, from nanotech to advanced computers, will make terraforming a reality in the next millennium. As part of the scenario, solutions arising from petrochemical or nuclear destruction on our planet will someday be applied to creating more ecologically balanced systems in space. Maybe we will get a second chance to create a world without pollution.

Designer Worlds

Space habitats will be constructed off-world to attract those who want to pursue high-performance sports, medical research, engineering, and the creative arts. Imagine vacationing on a synthetically created world where we can dance under three moons and find fresh beginnings in a pristine wilderness untouched by pollution or crime.

Once the travel and hotel industry gets into this market there will be no stopping the Marriotts or Sheratons of this world from colonizing off-worlds. It's time to plan our vacation or retirement spheres today!

If we can find and travel to an existing planet that meets our needs, great. If not, there will be companies who will design a world for us. Customized specialty environments will be created to cater to the needs of business and lifestyle. Personalized terraforming will be a hot business in the future.

Billboards in Space

Space merchandising will be a hit in the 21st century. The slogan, "Made on Mars," could easily become a bestselling brand here on Earth, representing out-of-this-world quality and performance.

Consumers will seek out clothing, computer products, and medicines that come from extraterrestrial environments and which boast an extra set of high performance features. These will include, for example, shape-shifting alloys for skis that instantly adjust to our movements, powerful new antibodies, and clothing that shimmers with that hip new Mars-green glow.

Space itself, and the products created there, will cause a merchandising stampede by the mid-21st century. We will at first exploit space in a typically crass commercial fashion. Next, we will learn how to tastefully package space products and services to meet new sophisticated consumer demand. Sitcoms and romance novels will be filled with Martian themes and escapades that are no longer science fiction, but reality.

Much of what is developed in space will be sold on Earth and in other extraterrestrial colonies as galaxywide marketing networks are established.

When Madison Avenue discovers space, there is no telling how fashions, foods, and lifestyles will be affected. Imagine Armani space suits cloaking the supermodels that show off the latest fashions in Paris. Yes, free enterprise will come to space in a big way in the 21st century, giving rise to market-driven demands for celestial merchandising.

Wormholes

While the spin-offs from space travel will be staggering, the real dream of humanity—to explore the stars—will be the ultimate test. After the robot voyagers have come home, new technologies will make it possible for humans to take their turn at extraterrestrial adventure.

We will tire of the tele-robotic adventures witnessed through the eyes of drones and yearn to experience the real thing. Earth will be boring as we learn what's out there, and we will have the technology to go and find out what's there ourselves.

Once we've perfected cryogenic suspension—the ability to put humans safely into suspended animation for long periods—journeys into deep space will be inevitable. This is not a technology that is ready, and we may not choose to travel frozen long distances, but it may be possible by the mid-century. Of course, such a traveler's aging processes would be slowed considerably. When the astronaut returned to Earth a half-century might have passed—but only a fraction of that will have been experienced by our still youthful traveler.

Even traveling at the speed of light, a space voyager wouldn't reach the nearest star, Alpha Centauri, for 4.2 Earth years, making travel to celestial bodies hundreds of light years away seem impossible. But not necessarily. For the movie *Contact*, based on astronomer Carl Sagan's novel, heroine Ellie Arroway travels through a wormhole in search of extraterrestrial life.

Wormholes are theoretical gateways in outer space that can transport us instantaneously into another far-flung region of space, like an elevator through the universe—or a stairway to heaven. My six-year-old daughter, Mariah, was explaining wormholes to me recently. "Wormholes," she said authoritatively, "are doorways between worlds, Daddy." I knew that, really I did.

Although speculative, scientists believe that such wormholes could exist, stretching the laws of physics to an entirely new realm. Is it possible that with all of the breakthroughs we are discovering every day, that we will learn to design a way to travel safely to deep space? Time will tell, but unless we can reengineer the human body to withstand terrifically long and stressful space voyages, our robonauts will be taking the long trips alone.

Robonaut J. Glenn Report: Year 2025

Report by Robonaut J. Glenn. Systems malfunctioning. System failure imminent. Navigation system damaged by asteroid shower. Ship unable to self-repair or adapt fast enough. Fusion reactor about to go critical. This may be my last transmission, Space Station Bradbury. I am setting up to jettison the escape pod and will attempt navigation down into the Hidden Valley system. The nearest planet is covered by dense atmosphere but resembles a formative stage of Earth. Volcano eruptions, ice storms, rapid tectonic plate movement. My data are incomplete, but the initial analysis would suggest that either life exists as we define it, or that the planet would be suitable for terraforming. I will compile a further report if I can avert system breakdown. (To be continued...)

Next Space Missions

Bolder steps to reach the threshold of deep space exploration are coming soon. A number of exciting, early 21st-century missions involving different kinds of probes and robotics will yield more knowledge and discoveries than ever before. Here is a partial listing of some of the most promising planned explorations and their launch dates.

- **MAP**, 2000, sponsored by NASA, will research the universe's origin and evolution

- **INTEGRAL,** 2001, sponsored by ESA, to study neutron stars and black holes
- **GALEX,** 2001, Galaxy Evolution Explorer, sponsored by NASA, to collect data on star systems, galaxies
- **Corot,** 2002, sponsored by France, will look for planets in star systems
- **MUSES,** 2002, sponsored by Japan, to retrieve samples from an asteroid
- **VESPER,** 2002, sponsored by NASA, to study Venus
- **ROSETTA,** 2003, sponsored by the European Space Agency (ESA), to chart three comets' paths
- **Deep Space 4,** 2003, sponsored by NASA, to probe the Comet Tempel
- **Messenger,** 2004, sponsored by NASA, to map and explore Mercury
- **Mars Surveyor,** 2005, sponsored by NASA, to collect Martian soil samples
- **SIM,** 2005, sponsored by NASA, to identify star systems that may have similar planets to Earth that support life
- **Next Generation Space Telescope,** 2008, sponsored b NASA, to establish a clearer view of our solar system and other galaxies
- **Terrestrial Planet Finder,** 2010, sponsored by NASA, to search for planets orbiting star systems

The next set of launchings will be into deep space, and the outcome will be highly unpredictable and complex as we go into space with all of its unknowns. (For more on past and future NASA missions, see **www.ksc.nasa.gov/ shuttle/missions/missions.htm.**)

The Mysteries of Creation

Perhaps the mystery of creation hidden in the deep voids of space will be unlocked over the next 10 to 15 years. The Hubble telescope has given us a small glimpse of the fantastic off-world universe. A wider window on creation will take place as we deploy the Big Brother of Hubble within the next decade.

We have recently learned that thousands of planets orbiting suns that are stranger than anything we could have imagined. The calculated design, atmosphere, and makeup of these planets are forcing us to rethink the basis of astrophysics and metaphysics. It's an exciting time to be alive. Check out Hubble's "Greatest Hits" online at **www.stsci.edu/.**

Toward a Theory of Everything

Physics is an ongoing story about the fundamental relationship between life, matter, and energy. Physics seems more art than a science; theories change rapidly, and there is little consensus about what's real or not. Proofs of most of the theories are being rewritten often, and there are various camps of ideas, many of which don't fit with each other. For example, Quantum Mechanics and Einstein's Theory of Relativity cannot both co-exist and explain the same universe we live in. Einstein's theories explain the very large celestial systems, and Quantum Mechanics seeks to explain the very small quantum universe. A rationale link between the two does not exist.

Superstring and Metaverse are the latest theories to explain these different views of one reality, but the fact is, at the end of the 20th century we still don't have one unified theory to explain our universe, sub-atomic *and* celestial. The big theory of everything is an elusive goal. This says something about the primitive nature of science, since physics underlies all sciences from medicine to chemistry, even psychology and philosophy. We are still in the Dark Ages about understanding the world and ourselves. Perhaps this too will change as we learn to apply the new Power Tools and reach out into exploring the galaxy.

259

Robonaut J. Glenn Report: 2028

Report by Robonaut J. Glenn. Systems stabilized. I am back to normal functioning. My spacecraft's fusion core is damaged but functional. Navigation is within system parameters. Class M Earthlike planet in Hidden Valley complete. Indeed, life exists, but not intelligent life as I am programmed to determine. There is a host of bacteria, plant, and animal life forms. The plant life is aquatic and seems to have a symbiotic relationship with the terrestrial land animals, which appear like a mixture of some type of flying birds and fish. My probe data capability is only a first step, and there is a need for further research about this new discovery.

Although there appears no higher intelligence present on the planet, my probe has provided enough data for the following recommendations:

1. Prior to considering this planet as a candidate for terraforming, an ethical analysis should be conducted as is mandated by Alien Life Discovery Protocol #2KK499 by the United Nations Treaty on Terraforming.

2. Although no intelligent life has been found, it is possible that higher life forms do exist and have either not been detected by my probe or my analysis is insufficient.

3. It is further recommended that additional probes be sent with a more sophisticated data collection capability than I have deployed in order to properly review this situation.

4. I will settle on the nearest planet as a base to await further instructions.

End report. I will expect your radio transmission in seven years. Robonaut out.

Galactic Rules

Until recently, we considered our solar system pretty typical. We were wrong, off by light years. We don't even have language to explain the uniqueness of the different solar systems now being discovered, let alone grasp the wonder of cosmic rules at play.

New pictures of gaseous, liquid, and solid-state evolution in the dark regions of space defy our experience and our capacity to explain what is happening. We've now discovered sub-atomic "muons" that redefine our knowledge of astrophysics. The more we look the more we see, the less we understand.

Our ancestors viewed the earth as the center of their solar system. This may have been the height of narcissism or just ignorance. Nevertheless, some of this limited thinking persists today. The belief that life on Earth is unique and that there is no other civilization like ours seems absurd to me. It is just too remote a case given all the celestial real estate out there. We have found evidence this past year of primitive life forms, microorganisms that lived on Mars. This should give us hope by lending merit to the statistical argument that it is more likely than not that there are other planets that support life, perhaps even intelligent life.

Return of the Madonna Probe: Year 2025

As the Madonna probe races back through our solar system, it passes the supercool blue-green rings of Saturn, the glistening purple and aquamarine moons of Jupiter, and on to the rich red planet of Mars.

Ten agonizing months passed before contact was made. Something strange happened. One hundred teraflops of data came streaming out of Madonna into Nebularn's computer downlink of the probe. There was enough data to fill three football fields, or so it seemed. This data-burst was complete in six seconds.

The Nebularn scientists based in Houston had achieved a scanner lock on the probe when the inexplicable happened. Two streams of intense white-hot laser beams of energy shot out of Madonna. One beam was targeted back where Madonna had come from—deep space. It disappeared into the cold blackness of the cosmos. The other laser beam simultaneously shot an energy ball to Earth, landing in a remote deep-sea location under Antarctica. Both beams of intense energy lasted less than five seconds and abruptly stopped.

The Nebularn scientists were scrambling for answers where there were none. The news media went nuts looking for any relevant scoop or analysis of what happened. There was hardly a clue. A Nebularn rapid response team was deployed to the crash coordinates deep beneath the Antarctic Sea to determine what evidence the area might hold.

The Madonna probe exhibited behavior clearly outside its original programming. What had happened? The Nebularn scientists considered these possible scenarios: 1) Malfunction. The probe had simply broken down. 2) Reprogramming. Who or what could have reprogrammed the probe? 3) Unknown. Some other factors outside the possibility set. Alien interference?

The existing Madonna probe was finally recovered. The onboard computer entity was debriefed and the travel log analyzed. This data, along with the results of the deep-sea Antarctic expedition, would give the Nebularn team a glimpse of what happened. It would take more than ten years to unravel the real mystery of the Madonna probe.

Space Competition

The balance of power on Earth may be determined by what is discovered in space. An entirely new political and economic order may arise, leveraging the assets and resources found there. For example, a new shape-shifting metal that is indestructible would give an edge to any nation or company. New classes of space-born drugs that heal cancers or viruses would monopolize markets. Companies should prepare today to think and act in a space-oriented direction. Leveraging Knowledge Value information generated by space installations and missions will be essential for the digital enterprises of the next century.

Space-invading companies to check out include Lockheed Martin Missiles & Space (**www.lmms.lmco.com**), a leader in the design, production, and integration of spacecraft and missile systems for global commercial companies. Lockheed maintains world leadership in remote sensing, including satellites for defense and civilian meteorology, Earth observation, and commercial space imaging. The diverse space science portfolio of Missiles & Space ranges from the Hubble Space Telescope to International Space Station and Lunar Prospector. Other companies offering insights into space-age profits include Boeing (**www.boeing.com**); Orbital Sciences (**www.orbital.com**); Rocketdyne (**www.rocketdyne.com**); Teledesic Corp. (**www.teledesic.com**); and Earthwatch, Inc. (**www.earthwatch.com**).

Technology development, unfettered by the limitations of Earth's rules of physics, will provide a variety of revolutionary business strategies, products, and services in the future. These will be accompanied by business development, distributed manufacturing and marketing breakthroughs. Fierce competition for space technologies, industries, and markets will determine the fortunes of both large companies and small entrepreneurs in the 21st century.

Yet, no matter what we invent, discover, or mine on other planets, the most gripping moment in our space program will be when we encounter alien life.

First Contact

I am sitting at the Annual Contact Consortium meeting (**www.ccon.org**) co-sponsored by NASA and held outside San Francisco. Scientists from SETI (The Search for Extra Terrestrial Intelligence), NASA, and our Institute For Global Futures, among others, are giving presentations on the speculations about first contact with alien life. These are serious people who have developed models, theories, systems, and strategies dealing with every aspect of human and alien contact.

Experts in exobiology, computers, nanotech, and physics present scenarios as the audience of mostly scientists is in rapt attention. After two days of mapping out countless scenarios, it is clear to me that the preparation for first contact is of deep concern to a select group of scientists, and not just the realm of the recent alien abductee movement. (Many of them were out of town.)

Scientists now estimate that there are hundreds of planets comparable to Earth in composition of surface and atmosphere, capable of sustaining life as we know it. This is a very recent discovery of immense importance. Up until this point in time, the proximity of space—how long it took to travel from planet to planet—and the fact that we had no hard evidence of other Earthlike planets, made belief in alien life forms impossible.

The ramifications of discovering planets that may be similar to Earth pose dramatic questions that challenge our assumptions about intelligent life other than human in the galaxy. The possibilities are that: 1) Intelligent life exists similar to humans; 2) life forms exist that are more diverse or complex than we can comprehend; and 3) what we could consider nonhuman, even chemical or inorganic, may exist as "life" somewhere. We should be prepared for inexplicable life to show up.

The discovery of alien life, be it primitive or intelligent, in our galaxy will be a decisive turning point in the evolution of our species. Our contact with other life forms will completely reshape our views of reality and force a comprehensive rethinking about the diversity of life.

The Next Chapter

There will come a time when new technologies will dissolve the distinctions between reality and imagination. We will be willing to expect anything and consider the concept of "impossible" as anachronistic.

President John F. Kennedy, in perhaps his greatest hour, challenged America to reach out to space, inspiring us to take this path toward the future. If President Kennedy were alive today, he would be proud to see that the challenge he set before the nation and the world is being fulfilled.

Destiny calls. With an essential act of human self-determination, we are using leading-edge technologies to their fullest to explore and harvest the knowledge that will surely come from space exploration over the next millennium. We aim at the stars as we step into the 21st century.

■ ■ ■

CHAPTER FOURTEEN

High-Tech Innovation and Leadership

What are the top technologies that we must have to drive competitive advantage in the future? How can we use technology to differentiate our company in a commodity-based global market? What are the key technology strategies that will help us win and keep customers? Understanding how to manage change about technology may be one of the most important business-critical challenges facing leaders today, and the least understood. Technology strategy and change management is one of the central ways the enterprise will survive in the next century.

On one level, this book is a briefing document about the powerful technologies that may transform the future. On another level, *Technofutures is about how to manage change to be able to develop an integrated technology strategy and thrive in the 21st century.* Every business leader needs to be able to read these signs and meet this challenge to survive the tech-intensity of the 21st-century marketplace.

At the Institute For Global Futures, we have studied technology change and its impact on customers, business, and society. The following findings are forecasts for today and into the next millennium.

■ **Finding #1:** Why customers adopt most new products and services has more to do with how they relate to personal change than with the actual products or services.

■ Finding #2: How leaders manage the change process in the corporate culture, with customers, and in the marketplace (support for training and customer support and promotion) often determines the success of the entire company, not only just the product line or service.

■   **Finding #3:** There are four change management styles that can be used to diagnose how people: customers, employees, suppliers, and partners relate to technology change. This is most important when diagnosing leaders.

Four Change Leadership Styles

We devised a model that I have found useful to explain how people embrace or deny change. We have used it to diagnose leaders, teams, companies, competitors, and customers. It can be applied to nontechnology change as well.

When confronted with technology innovations, people manage change differently based on a variety of factors. This is not to say that every innovation should be blindly embraced, but with the daily emergence of complex technologies, it will become vital to an organization's growth that its leaders adopt an openness to innovation.

Four change management styles make up our model. They are the *Traditionalist,* the assertive resistor of change; the *Maintainer,* the covert resistor of change; the *Adapter,* who embraces change and is willing to learn new things; and the *Innovator,* the leader of change, a risk-taker.

Traditionalists

Traditionalists are assertive individuals who openly resist change. They tend to reinforce a philosophy of "If it ain't broke, don't fix it." They can elucidate numerous reasons why "things ought to stay the way they are;" often "time tested" is a big reason behind their resistance to the change. "This will never work and let me give you the ten reasons why" is the authoritative response to a creative proposal. Most organizations that have difficulty changing are dominated by Traditionalists. Their open resistance is the death knell of the enterprise. They can be extreme supporters of denial.

Maintainers

Maintainers tend to be silent, covert resistors of change. They say yes, but mean no. Maintainers are difficult to spot, often hiding behind Traditionalists or even being apologists for Traditionalists: "This is why it's just not a good idea," they rationalize. Maintainers tend to want to maintain the status quo even more than Traditionalists. They don't like to "make waves." In the past, this culture of "get along and go along" up the corporate ladder of success was the key to survival. Today, that is the end of the game and often spells the end of a career. When a new technology or innovation emerges, Maintainers are very cautious, slow to react, and resistant to learning why it has value. "Why do customers need information about their orders on the Net?" This is the statement of a true Maintainer.

In the past, Traditionalists and Maintainers have dominated entire industries. The U.S. auto industry in the 1960s couldn't see the need for smaller, more fuel-efficient cars even as oil prices where going through the roof. This led to foreign competitors, with compact cars seizing a commanding piece of the U.S. auto market. Appearing to be oblivious to the young computer revolution, Wang Computer Company stayed in the word processing business. IBM missed the competitive advantage of leading the personal computer business early on, never believing that PCs made any sense. United Parcel Service created their competition by not listening to customer requests for computerized billing and other customer-centric innovations.

Companies that were change ready built profits and grew market share. Companies such as IBM, General Motors, and UPS learned to change and have made stunning comebacks in the marketplace. Others such as Wang and Western Union never learned to manage the business-critical changes necessary to survive. They are gone never to be resurrected.

The Traditionalists and Maintainers of the world, either in our organizations or our customer mix, need help. These folks are often valuable, but have the wrong approach to the shifting realities of today's business environment. These are the CEO that invested heavily in that information technology project that was antiquated before it was complete. The call center manager that doesn't understand the value of the Net. The supply chain VP who still thinks its about warehouses and not information and logistics. As we move into the future with the convergence of new technologies changing everything in Net time, change management is business-critical. Either we understand that or we are history.

The change needed to succeed in the 21st century requires more investment in training and education for employees, and superior, personalized marketing and customer service. This is mostly about a mind-set that either is open to or denies change.

Adapters

The Adapter is the type of individual, organization, or customer that is open to change. Adapters have a willingness to learn new things—to learn whatever is necessary to grow the business, increase quality, and identify breakdowns to achieving success. They are key stakeholders in the change. Adapters don't necessarily enjoy dealing with change any more than Traditionalists or Maintainers, but they are more courageous about taking actions to manage change. They are willing to take responsibility for managing the change process and enrolling others to change. Leaders with this mind-set managed companies we studied that changed quickly and deeply. They are ready for the new millennium. They drank the Kool Aid, and it was *good.*

Innovators

The fourth change management style is easy to spot. Innovators are the folks who, after leading the charge about an innovative solution, have at least a few arrows in their back. Innovators are the early adopters of a new idea; they are the pioneers of change. Often dismissed as crazy or driven, they are the inspiration for companies, customers, and industries changing.

Steve Jobs, Charles Schwab, Michael Bloomberg, and Ted Turner are classic examples of Innovators who saw into the future and used this insight of emerging change to build successful companies. Their success may be described as having to do with more effectively managing change than their competitors. Many more Innovators struggle every day to get their leaders to understand how to manage the changes they see coming over the horizon. It would serve leaders well to listen to the visions and voices of those Innovators that are providing direction for managing the future. Not all may be today's leaders, but they are candidates for the company of the future—either ours or our competition's. Innovators will always find work. If we don't listen to them, they will leave and create opportunity elsewhere. There are too many examples of this to illustrate. Having eyes to see this as a leader is business-critical to success.

The Customer As Innovator

Part of the dynamic of managing change is how organizations deal with customers. We don't ever want to be out of synch with our customers. It's a recipe for disaster. We want to enable customers by delivering what they want precisely when they want it. Often in the past, Innovator-companies were too far ahead of customers. Innovative products that were a technological triumph would fail to be accepted in the marketplace. The opposite is more the case today. Customers are driving change. Customers want easier to use, faster, smarter, and more cost-effective technology solutions. Customers are more often the Innovators pulling their Traditionalist and Maintainer vendors along: "We need more electronic customer service." "We need faster time to market." "We need more information, and we need it *now*."

I forecast that the key competitive pressures on the marketplace will come from customers as Innovators who are establishing higher and faster benchmarks of performance for their suppliers and vendors. The solution is to better manage the change process internally and learn to dance the dance of providing fast-track innovation. Otherwise, customers will go to someone else.

Does this management of change really have anything to do with adopting new technology? Yes, but first it has to do with having an openness to see the changes and embrace the future possibilities. Eventually this translates into analyzing the potential impact and marshaling the resources to change people —corporate cultures first, then products and services. Managing change starts with people who have a mind-set that's open to change.

The Leader As Futurist

The entire idea of being a leader is shifting, given the rapid changes in technology, markets, and society. The need for leaders to develop a futurist perspective, to be able to be more aware of the business-critical trends that will shape tomorrow, is now essential. Every day, presidents of companies are losing their jobs for not moving forward fast enough. Companies are losing market share for not understanding change. Customers are hungry to exchange their loyalty—not for name brand or tradition—but for innovation. Innovation is the celebration of a successful effort in managing change, whether this translates into a new product or innovative customer service solution.

A better understanding and management of high-technology futures— be it the Internet or e-business, cloning or computers, genetic markers or smart drugs—starts with being open to innovation and managing change. Keep this old saying in mind: "Wherever we look, we find what we are looking for."

Many of the technologies and their scenarios in this book may have seemed strange to you. But then, who would have predicted that the Internet would have impacted business and markets so fast? Be open to seeing the innovations unfolding. There are many opportunities for business leaders who have the courage to keep an open mind in peering into the future.

The next millennium is now.

■ ■ ■

Index

"At present, indexes cannot be electronically made, for the decisions required are of a far higher order than computers are yet capable of."

THE CHICAGO MANUAL OF STYLE, 14TH ED.

immersion cinema, 236
immortality, 164–165
implants, 199, 202
Incyte, Inc., 159
Industrial Era, 8
Industrial Revolution, 209
industry, robots and, 102
informatics, nano-, 218
Information Age, 209
information ecology, 30–31
Information Era, 8
information vendors, 135
InforMax, 179–180
Innovators (in management), 268
"in silico," 76
Institute For Global Futures
    alien life and, 262
    Fujitsu and, 78
    global education market and, 141
    Internet commerce and, 126
    nanotech and, 209, 214, 216
    Ostman, Charles, 27
    sim-agents and, 89
    technological change and, 265
Integrated Surgical Systems, 201
Intel Corporation, 84, 148, 227
intelligence, 17, 55, 162, 202, 217
intelligence systems, business, 127–129
intelligent agents, 75. *See also* smart agents
    entertainment and, 231
    health care and, 183, 185–186, 195–196
    the Internet and, 55, 57–58, 87–90
    smart books, 235–236
    smart wallets, 129
Interactive Process Transactions, 24–26
interactivity
    A-Life and, 71
    e-business and, 124–126
    electronic education and, 149–150
    entertainment and, 223, 225–226, 230–233,
        236–237, 239
    health care and, 187
    holographs and, 201
    the Internet and, 51, 52–53, 57–58
    learning and, 139, 140, 145
    television and, 132–133
Interagency Working Group on Nano Science,
    Engineering, and Technology, 216
International Astronomical Union, 253
International Business Machines Corporation
    (IBM), 29, 38, 81, 83, 111, 267
International Conference on Evolvable
    Systems—from Biology to Hardware, 28
International Conference on Intelligent
    Materials (ICIM), 31

International Data Corporation, 141
International SigChi (Special Interest Group
    Computer Human Interface), 23
International Space Station, 262
the Internet, 47–69. *See also* e-business; electronic
    education; telemedicine; tele-med training
    Alexandrian Library, 48
    Artificial Life (A-Life) and, 71
    Blended Reality, 67–69
    censure and, 63–64
    class structure and, 69
    community and, 50
    cyber art and, 40
    digital convergence and, 119, 223
    economics and, 56
    entertainment and, 223, 225, 226, 230–233,
        234, 236–237
    "experience" and, 55, 62
    filters for, 56–57
    Global Health Net, 189
    "Hack In," 67
    health care and, 183, 187–189, 204
    intelligence and, 55
    interactivity and, 51, 52–53, 57–58
    knowledge and, 56
    Megaverse, 51–52, 54–55, 58–59, 66–67, 68
    navigation modes of, 53–54
    Next Net, 66, 69
    Project Oxygen, 56
    search engines and, 57
    speed and, 51, 55–56
    synthetic pleasure and, 63
    telepresence, 60–64
    trends of, 47
    virtual communities and, 58–59
    virtual reality (VR) and, 59–64, 67
    Webcasting, 64–67
Intranets, 21
intuitiveness, 17, 23–26, 97, 134, 212–214, 236
Intuitive Transaction Environment, 134
IS Robotics, 103
ITT Sheraton Corporation, 255

J

Jackson, Michael, 75
jellybeans (computer chips), 38–39
Jet Propulsion Laboratory Center for Space
    Microelectronics Technology, 247
Jobs, Steve, 268
Jordan, Michael, 168
Jurassic Park Part V, 230, 236

K

Kasparov, Garry, 81
Kennedy, John F., 263

King, Stephen, 233
Kitchen Kiosks, 218
KMPG Peat Marwick, 251
knowledge
  e-business and, 111–112, 116–117,
    135–136, 137
  the Internet and, 56, 66
  nanotech and, 214
Knowledge Brokers, 135–136
knowledge capital, 150–151
Knowledge Mining Agents, 87, 89
Knowledge Value, 66, 135–136
  computers and, 45
  electronic education and,
    143, 152–153
  entertainment and, 233
  nanotech and, 214
  space and, 261
Knowledge Value Engineers (KVE),
    135–136, 137–138, 147, 148, 230
Knowledge Value-Ware, 149–150
Knowledge Vendors, 233, 236
Korkin, Michael, 28
Kovacs, Gregory, 32
KVE (Knowledge Value Engineers),
    135–136, 137–138, 147, 148, 230
Kyo Data, 227

L

Laboratorie des Materiaux Moleculaires, 31
The Land Before Time, 231
land mines, robots and, 103
Lands' End, Inc., 124–125
The Langley Research Center, 249–250
Langton, Christopher, 83
language, 39, 51, 96, 127
Laser Industries, Ltd., 193
laser propulsion, 248
lasers, surgery and, 193
leadership, technology and, 265–270
leapfrog technology, 191–192
learning. *See* electronic education
The Learning Company, 144
Learning Products Group (Simon & Schuster),
    145
Leary, Timothy, 251
Lethal Weapon 10, 233
Letterman, David, 238
Life-Programming Agenda (LPA), 76
Lincoln, Abraham, 227
L.L. Bean, Inc., 134
Lockheed Martin, 252, 262
longevity, human. *See* human longevity
LPA (Life-Programming Agenda), 76
Lucas, George, 226

Lucent Technologies, 30, 55
Lunar Prospector, 262

m

Macintosh (computer), 20
Madison Avenue, space and, 256
Madonna, 75
The Magic Planet (software), 78
Magnetic Resonance (MR), 192
Maier, Hermann, 171
Maintainers (in management), 267–268
management styles, 266–268
manipulation of matter. *See* nanotech
    (Power Tool)
marketing, 87–89, 171–173, 255–256.
    See also biometric marketing
marketing, biometric, 131–133
Marriott International, Inc., 255
Mars, 255
Mars Global Explorer, 247, 252
The Marshall Space Flight Center's Space
    Product Development Office, 249
Mars Pathfinder, 247
Martin, George, 163
Massachusetts Institute of Technology (MIT),
    95, 227
  Media Lab, 23
materials, nanotech, 217
The Matrix, 67
matter, manipulation of. *See* nanotech
    (Power Tool)
Maxwell Plank Institute, 32
Mayo Clinic, 187
medicalbots, 183
Medical College of Georgia, 186
medical insurance, 162–163, 254
medicine
  biochip implants and, 32
  genetics and, 159, 162–163
  human genome and, 9, 12, 157–158,
    175–176, 176–177, 200–201
  implants and, 199
  robots and, 94, 102
Medtronic, Inc., 98, 199
mega-arcades, 237
Megaverse, 51–52, 54–55, 58–59, 66–67, 68
memory, 44–45, 217
MEMS (Microelectric Mechanical Systems), 218
merchandising, space and, 255–256
Merck & Co., Inc., 166
messaging, unified, 38–39
Metaverse theory, 259
Michelle (digital actor), 227
Mickey Mouse, 75
microchips, 9–10, 11, 82

About the Author

Dr. James Canton is one of the world's leading technology futurists. He is president of the Institute For Global Futures, an internationally recognized think tank that advises Fortune 1000 clients on the strategic impact of leading-edge technologies on customers, markets, and society. An in-demand keynote speaker, he delivers more than 100 presentations a year. He is also a guest host on CNN Financial News, where he reports on business and technology trends. Dr. Canton is editor-in-chief of the *Canton Technology Report*.

For more information about Dr. Canton, and to receive a FREE trial copy of his online report, see his Website at: **www.technofutures.com**.

To communicate with Dr. James Canton, contact:

Institute For Global Futures
2084 Union St.
San Francisco, CA 94123
(415) 563-0720 • (415) 563-0219 (fax)
E-mail: Jcanton@msn.com

■ ■ ■

■ ■ ■

We hope you enjoyed this Hay House book.

If you would like to receive a free catalog featuring additional
Hay House books and products, or if you would like information
about the Hay Foundation, please contact:

Hay House, Inc.
P.O. Box 5100
Carlsbad, CA 92018-5100

(760) 431-7695 or (800) 654-5126
(760) 431-6948 (fax) or (800) 650-5115 (fax)

Please visit the Hay House Website at:
www.hayhouse.com

■ ■ ■